AMERICAN HERITAGE

June, 1969 · Volume XX, Number 4

© 1969 by American Heritage Publishing Co., Inc. All rights reserved under Berne and Pan-American Copyright Conventions. Reproduction in whole or in part of any article without permission is prohibited. U.S. copyright is not claimed for color plates on pages 4–16, 26, 50–60, 72–79.

A DROP OF WATER UNDER THE PEOPLE'S MICROSCOPE.—POLITICAL ANIMALCULÆ.

When this cartoon appeared in 1871, the first of America's great municipal bosses, William Marcy Tweed—here "Boss Leech"—was in full retreat, publicly accused of using the construction of a new New York County courthouse (lower right) to funnel off some $13,000,000 in graft. Tweed's chief accomplices were the city controller, Richard "Slippery Dick" Connolly, shown at left as a snake; the city chamberlain, Peter Barr "Brains" Sweeny, drawn here at upper left center as a "dead beet"; and Abraham Oakey "The Elegant Oakey" Hall, of whom it was said that as mayor of New York City he had only one defect: a lack of ability. Cartoonist C. S. Reinhart, no subtle satirist he, pictured the Mayor as a mare in pince-nez, wounded by the arrows of newspaper revelations. The courthouse scandal finished the Tweed Ring and dealt a damaging (though not fatal) blow to the Tammany organization. Elsewhere, the political boss as an American institution was just getting started; over the next three quarters of a century most of the major cities of the nation —and even entire states—were boss-ruled for at least limited periods. Within the span of a single lifetime, all but one of the once-vigorous machines have died. As younger, better-educated, more independent mayors seek to cope with their legacy, it may be instructive to look back at the old-time bosses. We consider them in this issue from two perspectives: "The Age of the Bosses," beginning on page 26, gives an over-all view of their rise and fall; "I Am the Law" (page 32) focuses on the career of one of the last of their company, Frank Hague of Jersey City.

AMERICAN HERITAGE

The Magazine of History

SENIOR EDITOR
Bruce Catton
EDITOR
Oliver Jensen
MANAGING EDITOR
Robert Lincoln Reynolds
ART DIRECTOR
Murray Belsky
ARTICLES EDITOR
E. M. Halliday
ART EDITOR
Douglas Tunstell
ASSOCIATE EDITORS
Robert S. Gallagher   David G. Lowe
Barbara Klaw   John L. Phillips
COPY EDITOR
Brenda Niemand
EDITORIAL ASSISTANTS
Mary Dawn Earley   Rosemary L. Klein
Mary A. Hawkins   Joanne Shapiro
CONSULTING EDITOR
Joan Paterson Kerr
PUBLISHER
Darby Perry

ADVISORY BOARD
Allan Nevins, *Chairman*
Carl Carmer   Louis C. Jones
Gerald Carson   Alvin M. Josephy, Jr.
Marshall B. Davidson   Howard H. Peckham
John A. Garraty   Francis S. Ronalds
Eric F. Goldman   S. K. Stevens

American Heritage Publishing Co., Inc.

PRESIDENT
James Parton
CHAIRMAN, EDITORIAL COMMITTEE
Joseph J. Thorndike
MANAGING DIRECTOR, BOOK DIVISION
Richard M. Ketchum
SENIOR ART DIRECTOR
Irwin Glusker

AMERICAN HERITAGE is published every two months by American Heritage Publishing Co., Inc.; editorial and executive offices, 551 Fifth Avenue, New York, N.Y. 10017. Treasurer, George W. Breitkreuz; Secretary, John C. Taylor III. Correspondence about subscriptions should be sent to American Heritage Subscription Office, 383 West Center Street, Marion, Ohio 43302. Single copies: $4.25. Annual subscriptions: $16.50 in U.S. and Canada; $17.50 elsewhere. An annual Index is published each spring, priced at $1.00. AMERICAN HERITAGE will consider but assumes no responsibility for unsolicited materials. Title registered U.S. Patent Office. Second-class postage paid at New York, N.Y., and at additional mailing offices.

Sponsored by
American Association for State & Local History · Society of American Historians

CONTENTS   June, 1969 · Volume XX, Number 4

THE LONGEST WAIT *Text by John Lord/Photographs by Anthony Howarth*	4
FIRST TO FLY THE ATLANTIC *by Bernard A. Weisberger*	16
BEFORE THE COLORS FADE: THE RETURN OF THE EXILES *by Janet Stevenson*	22
THE POLITICAL MACHINE: I. RISE AND FALL: THE AGE OF THE BOSSES *by William V. Shannon*	26
II. A CASE HISTORY: "I AM THE LAW" *by Thomas J. Fleming*	32
THE KEEPER OF THE KEY *by Milton Sweeney Colwell*	49
THE BANNER YEARS *by David G. Lowe*	54
". . . AND THE MOUND-BUILDERS VANISHED FROM THE EARTH" *by Robert Silverberg*	60
FACES FROM THE PAST XXIII *by Richard M. Ketchum*	64
"THE SCENE OF SLAUGHTER WAS EXCEEDINGLY PICTURESQUE" *by Wesley Marx*	66
THE PRESIDENT'S PROGRESS *by James Thomas Flexner*	72
THE JAY PAPERS III: THE TRIALS OF CHIEF JUSTICE JAY *by Richard B. Morris*	80
HELP-WANTED AD FOR JUNE GRADUATES	112

COVER: She is, of course, Evelyn Nesbit Thaw, and this drawing of her by Charles Dana Gibson served as the frontispiece of her autobiography, *Prodigal Days*. Once, as a young girl, she was walking down a street in Pittsburgh when a lady stopped her and exclaimed: "What a lovely child! Those eyes will break many a heart someday!" The prediction came true, with a vengeance—Evelyn became a model for famous artists, a popular showgirl, and the apex of one of the most lurid triangles in American history. It is all recalled on page 65. *Back Cover*: These amusing little caricatures of actually existing birds and insects were done by one Madalene S. Pasley, apparently for her own amusement, nearly a century ago. They come to us by courtesy of the Old Print Shop in New York City.

THE LONGEST WAIT

The G.I.'s were far more numerous than any army that ever occupied Britain; none left so little visible trace, none so touching a legacy

Text by JOHN LORD
Photographs by ANTHONY HOWARTH

A cold coming awaited Melburn Henke in all respects but one. A leaden Irish sky, damp air that mortified the flesh, a mournful horizon of rusting cranes and dilapidated warehouses, channels of gray water and drab groups of longshoremen—these made up Henke's landscape. He was wearing a steel helmet with a shallow crown and a flat brim cocked somewhat rakishly over one eye; on his back a regulation pack sat trim and heavy, a bayonet as long as a sword strapped to it, and from his right shoulder hung an M-1 rifle no longer new. His expression was confident and, considering the climate, happy. Those old enough to recall it might have thought him every inch a doughboy en route for the Argonne or Belleau Wood. Certainly there was something of repetition about Pfc. Henke's appearance that wintry morning, for he was the first American soldier officially to set foot on the soil of Great Britain in World War II, and the term "G.I." was not yet in common use for his species.

It was January 26, 1942, and the United States was entering the eighth week of war with Germany and Japan. When he actually stepped ashore, as flash guns popped and a band played, Henke achieved immortality of a sort: the spot was later marked with a plaque. Henke himself described the experience as "one I won't easily forget" and marched smartly out of the limelight. No one could have seen in Private First Class Henke that dank morning the first physical indication that the United States of America was about to assume the leadership of the Western world.

Two million Americans, most of them very young, followed Henke into the European Theatre of Operations. They razed cities with high explosives and fire; they levelled hills and built temporary towns with their great machines; they killed the innocent in their assault; and with their allies they broke the armed power of Nazi Germany. But in Britain, the greatest change they effected was not in executing policies hatched by Roosevelt, Churchill, and Stalin, but simply by being there. The ordinary commerce of day-to-day living rubbed away illusions and antipathies, introduced new attitudes and modified old ones; and familiarity bred not contempt but a deep and lasting understanding. Britain already bore many marks of former armies, beginning with the forts the Romans garrisoned; none had been so numerous or so massively equipped as the divisions that now poured in. None left so little visible trace, none so touching a legacy.

Twenty-five years after D-Day the memorials have to be sought out. When found they are no more than bronze tablets listing statistics, stone columns, or foun-

The harbor at Dartmouth, England, whence thousands of G.I.'s sailed on the night of June 5, 1944, never to return

5

tains filled with rocks from Arkansas or Maine. A few English pastures that are too meager to be farmed are still crossed with runways that once shook under the wheels of Flying Fortresses and Mustangs, concrete that once men kissed, tumbling deliriously from their planes, out of joy at having survived one more mission. There were afternoons when those airstrips, so small in this jet age, ran pink as ground crews hosed out from shattered turrets what was left of gunners caught by machine guns or the jagged shards of flak. Now, gray and anonymous, softened in summer by buttercups or the proud lavender of rosebay willow herb, they speak of nothing.

On the edges of beech woods or in clearings among the pines there are still oblongs of brick and concrete where the quonset huts, black and echoing, were home or hospital, workshop, bar, church, or prison for a community of men. They carry no echoes now. The pubs are still there, as they were after Cromwell's troopers had clattered by, a few with insignia torn from a uniformed shoulder and pinned to a beam, or with scribbled alien signatures fading on the ceiling. The names are still the same—the Queen's Head, the St. George & Dragon, the Star and Garter, the Royal Steamer, the Eagle and Child—but the signs above their bars that warned of careless talk or exhorted everybody to dig for victory have been replaced by arch verses refusing credit, or announcements of bingo nights at what was once the village hall. Beside a hawthorn hedge here and there deep ruts still record the tracks of tanks or howitzers moving into their parks; but they might have been made by long-forgotten harvest carts. Of the tarpaulined dumps of shells and bombs that lined mile after mile of English lanes; of the acres of cannon, wheel to wheel, their muzzles pointing dumbly to the sky and aligned as if with millimeter gauges; of the pyramids of rations looming in open fields, the drums of gas and oil, the coffins prudently stacked by the hundreds in hangars; of all the impedimenta of a civilized and mechanized army there remains hardly a trace.

And yet, what was left behind was more enduring. For in the memory of a generation of Britons and Americans there are responses that spring to instant life at the mention of a name—Rainbow Corner, Spam, Glen Miller, Omaha—and being reborn they bring the legacy back to consciousness. It is, in a sense, a folk legacy, unwritten and mostly unarticulated, in which the collective memory has glossed over what was brutal. But it is all there, an invisible memorial to what was then called without any sense of bathos The Great Crusade.

The men who followed Private Henke when it all began did not think of themselves as knights in shining armor, however. They were too bewildered. When Europe had first gone to war, the standing army of the United States could not muster two hundred thousand men; for more than two years it had slowly grown, and now it was about to mushroom into millions. Its organization was not designed to promote the welfare of the individual, and its schedules did not allocate much time to self-contemplation anyway. Life in the army was concentrated on the immediate—on what was for the next meal, on who got weekend passes when, on the name of the smallest part of the Browning automatic rifle, on how to avoid crawling through the stinking puddle in front of your nose, and above all, on who was lucky at mail call. Men seized eagerly on such trivia to anchor their logic in a crazy world. That world opened for John B. Thomas of Gallatin, Tennessee, as it would for thousands of others, one midnight in the staging area at Indiantown Gap, Pennsylvania, when he was given a rifle clotted with black grease and told to clean it. He had never in his life

"The pubs are still there, as they were after Cromwell's troopers had clattered by— a few with insignia torn from a uniformed shoulder and pinned to a beam, or with scribbled alien signatures fading on the ceiling."

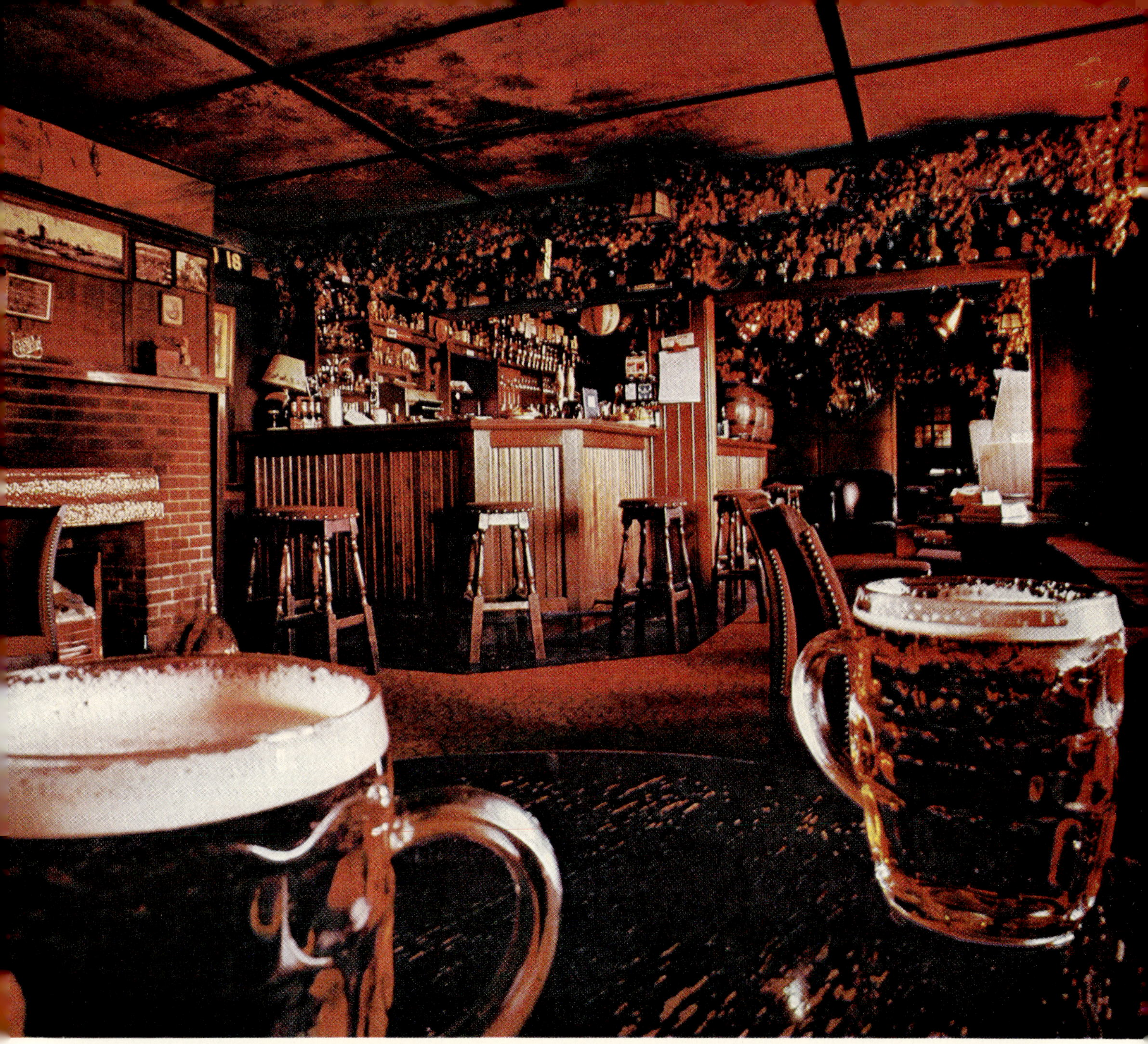
18

U.S. CAVALRY
Sgt HUARD
407 Sqdn
OTTAWA
(FRENCH) CANADA
WILLIAMS
South Dakota USA
PEGGY GREGORY V.A.D. B.R.C.S.
Stan Marsh

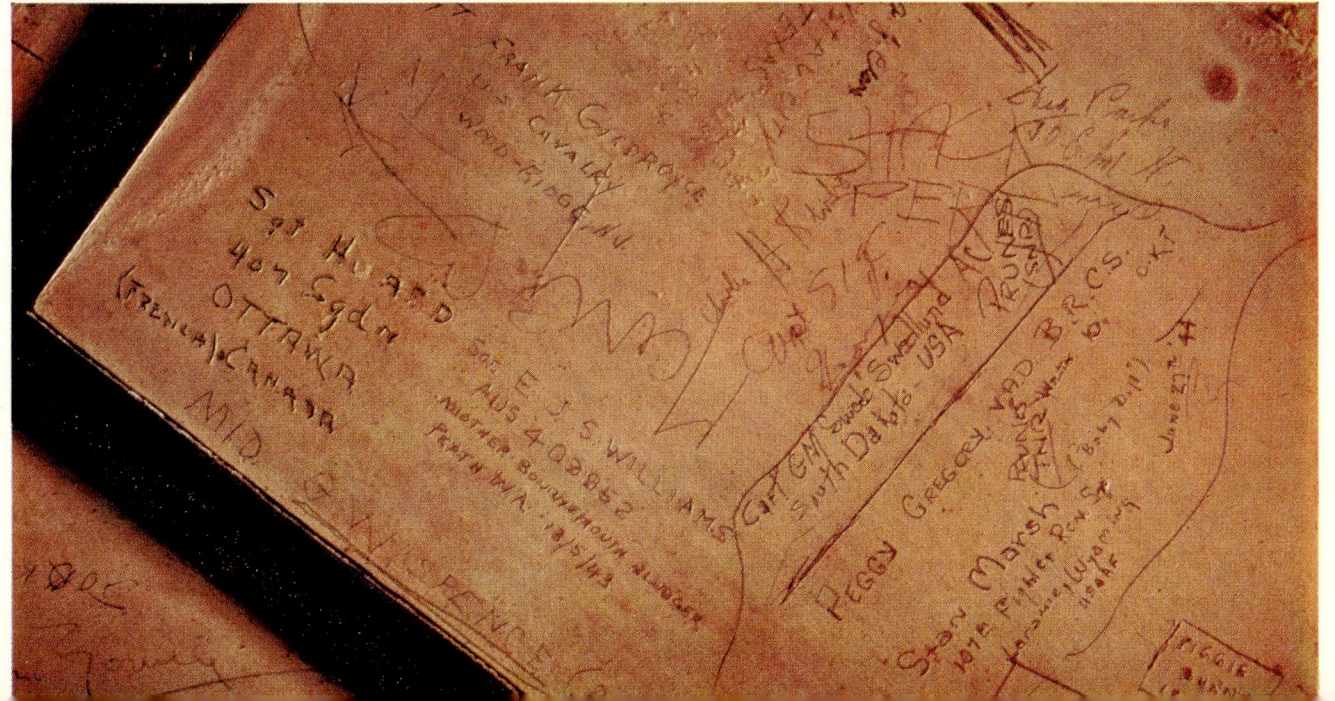

seen such a repulsive object, and it never occurred to him that the last hands to touch it must have been those of a doughboy of his father's generation. Busy all night with old newspapers and interrupted several times to accumulate dozens of articles of equipment, including gasproof underclothing, by dawn Private Thomas was ready, as ordered, to move out with his comrades. A month later they did so, having learned the first lesson of war—that the waiting around greatly exceeds the fighting.

The British had been waiting for a long time, though they would have been taxed to explain for what, exactly. They had seen defeats and had triumphed in a few battles, but as yet they saw no end to the war. They had fought in France, in Norway, in the Mediterranean, and in Africa; in the clear, sweet summer of 1940 they had won an unimaginable victory over the Luftwaffe. They had stood without arms to await an invasion that miraculously never came. They had suffered, rallied, and endured. And yet they were still being bombed, their finest army was surging back and forth across the African desert without being able to reach a conclusion, and the whole spreading continent of Europe was still the fiefdom of Germany. Being stubborn and romantic, they expected to win the war; but in 1942 none of them could see just how to start the last battle. It was then that the answer came, in the shape of John B. Thomas, all innocence, not yet a soldier by any standard but full of enthusiasm, willing and able. To the grim British he seemed an unlikely sort of savior.

The first big contingent of American troops, 10,368 officers and men, arrived in the *Queen Elizabeth* at Gourock, Scotland, on June 9, 1942. The troops' last parade before embarking had been a "short-arm" inspection, and their first on disembarking would be the same; but the indignity did not diminish their pleasure at arriving on dry land, which they accomplished through lines of Scots waving and cheering in welcome. Though convivial, it was a confrontation of total strangers. To the British the Americans seemed fresh and full of energy, bright as new paint, the bodily expression of what Sir Edward Grey had noted about their country a generation before, comparing it with "a gigantic boiler. Once the fire is lighted under it there is no limit to the power it can generate." They also looked soft.

To the Americans, the British looked pitiful. They had known that Britain was at war, but there had been little reality in the fact until now. They had been aware of far-off battles; they had lost ships themselves even before war was declared. But nothing of this had hit with the shocking impact of what they now saw. Their reaction was natural: they gave away what they had.

Before his induction, George W. Marshall had been a delivery boy in Los Angeles. Now an acting corporal, he was under orders to deliver twenty-seven G.I.'s to some place he had never heard of. He figured the train ride would be brief since the country, according to the army orientation lectures, was hardly bigger than Minnesota. The ride took nine days. They were in a baggage car with no lights, no liquor, and nothing but K rations to eat; and after spending their first night immobile in a tunnel taking shelter from an air raid, they began to feel oppressed. Then they saw the kids, standing silently on a station platform watching the trains go by, looking with solemn awe at the young, healthy strangers smiling back at them. There were some cherries in Marshall's freight car, packed much the way California grapes might be back home. The cherries were disbursed. But at other stations there were more kids and some adults. Cigarettes, soap, razor blades were handed out. When they were gone there were still more stations. One man broke out his gasproof clothing and disposed of it; then finally others began dropping out their duffel bags just as they were. When the train reached Waterloo station in London, there was a lot more room in the baggage car. Marshall decided to take a stroll. Outside the station it was pitch black and the streets were empty. He could see searchlights playing and he heard the quick *whump-whump-whump* of antiaircraft guns and the faint, warbling drone of aircraft engines. There was a sudden descending whistling noise, and a man running toward Marshall yelled at him what sounded like "It it, matey!" When Marshall stood still in surprise the man charged into him and knocked him flat. In the same instant a bomb crashed into some houses a little way up the block.

By now the Londoners had a routine for air raids. Some slept in the subways. Some with their own little houses had brick shelters at the end of the back yard, equipped and decorated according to taste, the more luxurious with bunks and with stoves for making tea. Some put their faith in interior shelters built like steel tables, under which they would crawl when the bombs began to fall too close. Still others merely huddled into their broom closet underneath the stairs until the worst

". . . the quonset huts, black and echoing, were home or hospital, workshop or church. . . .

A few English pastures . . . are still crossed with runways that once men kissed, tumblin

*deliriously from their planes, out of joy
at having survived one more mission."*

"Mothers of teen-age families remember without rancor how as lissome girls they clung closer in dark parks or on the banks of placid streams and whispered, knowing already the answer, 'Will you really take me to the States?'"

was over. Private Joseph Veto of Manchester, New York, found himself in this predicament one winter night in a house in Argyll Street, London. His knees were touching his chin and he was trembling with fear, though he said it was the cold. He heard a far bigger noise than the rumble of the bombs; it was a tearing, anguished noise as though the sky was tumbling down. A plane was falling. It hit a house farther along the street, its dead pilot landing on the owner's bed. His skin was crisp, like roast pork.

London offered other diversions than the bombing, which in any case was past its worst. One handsome young American lieutenant could often be seen standing on Shaftesbury Avenue, far enough removed from Rainbow Corner to avoid the heaviest competition, staring in a puzzled fashion at a shilling in his open palm. When he saw an attractive girl he would scratch his head and inquire politely of the young lady if she could tell him how many sixpences there might be in his shilling. He never failed to bear off a conquest to the movies, where she could weep a sentimental tear over Greer Garson keeping her upper lip exquisitely stiff as Walter Pidgeon, in a battered raincoat, came back from Dunkirk, or moon over Bing Crosby dreaming of a White Christmas just the way Irving Berlin intended him to. Martha Raye, the soldier's soldier, was playing to acres of olive drab at the Palladium; Beatrice Lillie (who had just lost a son in action) was at His Majesty's Theatre in *Big Top;* and Vivien Leigh was at the Haymarket in *The Doctor's Dilemma*. At the Windmill, as always, there was the chorus line, the bravest and barest in the world.

In the country, pleasures were simpler if not necessarily quieter. Most places could boast what Staff Sergeant Edward J. Twohig described as "the surprisingly interesting stock met at some of the church parties." Conversely, the British were favorably impressed with the newcomers. Few of them withstood for long the ebullience of American spirits. The roster of Twohig's outfit carried nicknames like Silent Rapp, Skin Walbourne, Macadoo Machado, and Lightning Ruhberg, which startled the ears of the British, who confined themselves to time-hallowed familiarities no more daring than Dusty Miller or Chalky White. Herbert D. Bidgett and a buddy called Bowers from the 81st Seabee Battalion were standing around when they were greeted by a gentleman who looked "very English." He was wearing a stylish dark suit and a bowler hat and carried a slim umbrella. He invited the husky young men to join him for a drink at his club. Stifling their worst suspicions, they went along. "It was strictly male and strictly for drinking men," Bidgett recalled. "We were introduced all around and after a time Bowers wound up playing the piano, and that guy was one hot number. He could play boogie-woogie like you never heard, and all the Limeys really lapped it up, requesting songs they'd heard of and all. First thing you know old Bowers is just sweating and playing and all I have to do is accept drinks. He didn't even stop to drink. I'd just tip it up and he'd swallow. After a couple of weeks of this we were invited to join the club and did."

Many American units found themselves in British barracks, even, ironically, in the old red-brick quarters in Winchester normally occupied by the King's Royal Rifle Corps, which sometimes called itself (in memory of its foundation on Governors Island, New York, to deal with the rebel colonists) the 60th (Royal American) Rifles. Others, in villages and towns not garrisoned, trailed about with a sergeant and a policeman, being allotted in ones and twos to private homes. When Pfc. John J. Kenney of Wilmington, Minnesota, got to his billet the rain was dripping from his cap and his duffel bag was sodden black. The policeman knocked politely on the door and a gaunt woman opened it. She looked at Kenney and said "Oh, dear!" Not one to miss a nuance, John Kenney resolved that his behavior would be impeccable as long as he stayed in that house. It was. Before long Kenney joined the thousands of soldiers who, as members of the family, sat in front of the fire to listen to the B.B.C.'s nine o'clock news and explain why there was no ham in a hamburger, or to pop corn sent from home while their adopted mothers bustled about with tea and cookies.

There was not much food. An Englishman got two chops a week for his meat ration, two eggs if he was lucky, and a piece of cheese half the size of a pack of Lucky Strikes. Onions were as rare as pineapples. But many an American woke up on a Sunday morning with a plate of bacon and eggs by his bedside and toast made out of what was called "beetle bread." The bread was made from whole grain to save shipping space, and contained pieces of chaff from the wheat, which the G.I.'s darkly imagined, having been raised on the pure white blandness of store-bought loaves, were the wings of insects. The more imaginative soon

"Today on Omaha and Utah, ugly blockhouse ruins still yawn
toward the beaches....
There are patches in the sand still heavy with metal, shell fragments mixed
with rivets from ships sunk in the bay,
all oxidized a bright and symbolic red."

homed in on the fish-and-chips shops whenever they were open and carried off greasy packages of newspaper smelling strongly of vinegar. Others made occasional attempts to live off the country: George Marshall and some friends were recruited by the village kids to shoot rabbits, the children offering to act as beaters. "We took a chance," Marshall recalled. "They did scare up two of them and we blasted away with our M-1's at them, but no luck. I wish you could see the looks on those kids' faces when we missed."

The children were not the only ones to be dubious of the martial expertise of their allies. Winston Churchill had watched the first field exercises of the new divisions in North Carolina and asked the opinion of one of his aides, a general. "To put these troops against continental troops would be murder," the general said. Churchill, nevertheless, sensed the power of this raw material and guessed how quickly they would learn. Later, his judgment justified, he wrote: "Certainly two years later the troops we saw in Carolina bore themselves like veterans." But it took time to make a soldier. *As Time Goes By,* a slow, dreamy melody written eleven years before, was resurrected and seemed oddly appropriate. As Private Albert A. Turner put it, "The uncertain days stretched into uncertain weeks." Elsewhere, the plans to end the uncertainty had already been made.

The plans were given the code name Overlord. They were based on an American concept, and everything that happened in England was directed toward their execution. Overlord was the reason why the southwest of the island seemed to be sinking under the weight of foreign troops and foreign supplies; it was held up, people said, only by the barrage balloons. Though no one mentioned the name, Overlord caused hundreds of English families to leave their homes without knowing they would never see them again—by the time they were allowed to return, the walls had been pounded to rubble by American shells. Men like Colonel Robert T. Finn of La Jolla, California, moved in, building at Slapton Sands, three miles from the little port whence the *Mayflower* sailed, replicas of Omaha and Utah beaches so exact that later in Normandy a soldier could say to Finn: "Colonel, do you remember the damaged rowboat on the beach at the assault center? Well, I fell over the same damn boat last week during the real landing."

By May, Overlord had ground almost to its consummation. Opposite the French beaches the units were drawn up from east to west along the south coast of England in their order of battle, British on the left, Americans on the right. The assault troops had been funnelled into special camps called "sausages," a macabre term in connection with an operation some said

13

would be like a meat grinder. Churchill himself was doubtful, remembering Passchendaele and the Somme and Gallipoli. "It still seemed to me, after a quarter of a century," he revealed later, "that fortifications of concrete and steel armed with modern fire-power, and fully manned by trained, resolute men, could only be overcome by surprise in time or place, by turning their flank, or by some new and mechanical device like the tank." The British had in fact offered some of their new devices (armored bridge layers, flame throwers, and flails for the mine fields—collectively known as "the Funnies") to the Americans; but the latter to their cost used only amphibious tanks, which in the event mostly foundered in deep water.

When the Americans left their familiar villages for these camps, there had been weeping—more, one young medic thought, than when his draft contingent had left its home town in Iowa. Long afterward Mrs. Betty Hinde described what the British felt: "Somehow or other in the morning the whole place seemed quiet and eerie as if all the life had gone out of it. It really was quite uncanny." There was an awareness, everywhere. This was the last spin of the coin and everything depended on it. Mrs. Barbara Boyd heard soft boots stepping through the night and thought, "There were all our friends, all the people that we knew, going away to the real war, to the fighting war. We never knew if we'd see them again." Marching to his ship, Sergeant Harold E. Williams passed an old woman whose face was a mask of tears. She was repeating over and over, "Thank you, lads, for helping us out."

At the Stag's Head in Chilton Foliat the dart game was desultory. The locals drank their warm beer thoughtfully, missing their friends of the 101st Airborne Division who on most nights had accounted for most of the beer and nearly all of what little whisky there was. As the light faded in the long summer evening of June 5, they heard the planes. Sergeant Ivan T. Nielsen of Superior, Wisconsin, watched the paratroopers board. Twenty-five years later he could remember their expressions: even the young ones, the noisy ones who had shaved their hair into a single central brush in the Iroquois fashion, were not talking very much.

Over Normandy, they dropped in silence in utter darkness toward something they could not imagine. Suddenly they were in another world in which everything that had been familiar was immediately, terrifyingly, and mortally hostile. A hedgerow, they had always believed, was a place of ease, a molding of warm dirt and dry grass fitting the small of your back aching after harvest, giving off the slightly sour, faintly aromatic smell of sap from a broken leaf or a twig idly stripped of green. A hedgerow was a sanctuary; it was supposed to comfort you, not kill you. But these Norman hedgerows were monstrous, hiding the enemy so completely that you were close enough to feel the heat of his machine guns' firing before you saw him. General Maxwell D. Taylor landed quite alone and made his suspicious way toward one of those hedgerows. It was silent. He moved on. He began to wonder if he

*"The American military cemetery at
        St.-Laurent-sur-Mer in Calvados
lies atop the bluffs within view of the beach....
      It is green and beautiful and
immaculate, and about it broods the terrible,
        useless decorum of death."*

14

would ever find a single member of the division he commanded. He carried a cricket, as did each of his men, as a recognition signal, but it was a while before he decided to use it. After a long time he heard a faint sound, as of cattle grazing. He hazarded a click. It was answered. A figure rustled toward him, fully armed and confident, but helmetless. General Taylor's relief was so enormous that he found himself at a loss for words. Then he assumed command. "Soldier," he demanded, "where's your hat?"

Offshore, Lieutenant John E. Coleman, U.S.N.R., was catching a little sleep after being at sea in his tank-landing-craft for twenty-seven hours. A messenger woke him with "Mr. Coleman, the skipper says there's something you might like to see." Coleman joined his captain (who a few hours later would step out of his steel pilot house into a bursting shell) and watched the planes flying over. The sea was gray and misty, and chopped at the flat bottoms of the landing craft in a most uncomfortable manner. When Coleman began his run into the beach not a shot had yet been fired, though he could see warships with their great guns trained. One of the infantry officers he was about to land was uneasy. "It's too quiet," he muttered. The fleet opened up, slamming the air in great hot walls of sound over the boats slapping toward the sand. The Germans did not answer. Coleman was four hundred yards from the shore when they did. What he remembered after that was dying men.

There is no coherent picture of what happened on Omaha Beach during the first hours of June 6, 1944, because it was not a coherent battle. The men who were there remember incidents only, so the true picture recollected is as if lit by flashes. At low tide it was a flat, wide stretch of sand crossed by shallow channels. This was spread with ranks of explosive devices of various kinds. At about highwater mark a bank of pebbles, in places nine feet high, ran the length of the beach. Beyond this shingle there was flat, marshy ground two or three hundred yards across at its widest,

CONTINUED ON PAGE 100

This striking oil painting of the NC-4 banking over Drake's Waters off Plymouth Hoe, England, was rendered by Henry Reuterdahl, one of two American artists assigned by the Navy to cover the flights of the NC boats.

FIRST TO FLY the ATLANTIC

The commander of the NC-4 called the trip "uneventful," but the men in the other planes of the mission could not quite agree

By BERNARD A. WEISBERGER

Half a century ago, heavier-than-air flight was less than sixteen years old, but men were already using their frail new wings for nothing less ambitious than leaping an ocean. In 1919, the Atlantic was vaulted three times in three consecutive months, first by a team of American naval airmen in a flying boat, then by two Englishmen in a conventional bomber, and finally by the crewmen and officers of a British dirigible. The exploits of the aerial adventurers provided hope in an otherwise uneasy postwar springtime. The American public followed every mile of the transoceanic hops in the headlines. It was so enthralled by the drama that it scarcely noticed the abrupt passing of one of the basic certainties of its national identity—physical remoteness from the Old World. Nor did one in a hundred grasp the full import of the flights vis-à-vis the cherished ideal of individualism. As one designer of the American planes involved pointed out, the achievement was essentially collective and technical; success was due to "organized engineering, which takes the place of invention and makes use of the special knowledge of many people."

From the beginning, aviation had had two faces. It was both scientific advance and adventure. It was brought to birth by a strange alliance of meticulous engineers, rich sportsmen, thrill seekers, daydreamers, cranks. Its growth was a miracle. In December of 1903 the Wright brothers' plane barely cleared the ground and wobbled 120 feet in twelve seconds, pushed into a twenty-five-mile-an-hour wind by a twelve horsepower engine. Less than six years later, Voisin, Farman, and Curtiss biplanes were flying for an hour or more, climbing as high as a thousand feet, and achieving ground speeds of forty miles an hour. By 1914 specially souped-up models had, astonishingly, attained an altitude of 25,755 feet, a speed of 128 miles an hour, and a nonstop distance of over 1,100 miles. Trophy-winning superplanes were built one by one, primarily with private funds, in shops that were no more than glorified garages. Aviation still belonged to enthusiasts sustained by their own time and money.

World War I changed that. All of the major combatants poured into the laps of aeronautical engineers enough money to build whatever their imaginations conceived, provided it was deadly. The fundamental wartime revolution in aeronautics was the shift to mass production of planes designed by committees of military and technical experts. The United States alone produced forty-three aircraft in 1914 and more than 14,000 in 1918. The romantic, mile-high tournaments-in-the-clouds of the combat pilots—the Guynemers, Foncks, Boelckes, Bishops, Richthofens, and Rickenbackers, costumed in riding breeches, scarves, and goggles—obscured the fact that the aces were less important to the future than were their machines. Each year the fighting craft grew in muscle and sophistication. The state's quest for killing power had been an effective stimulant to aeronautic ingenuity.

In the spring of 1919 aviation's leaders were anxious to prove that the precocious adolescent could do man's work in peacetime, too. Veterans of the prewar sporting years of aeronautics yearned to try powerful new machines against fresh obstacles of distance and time. In the first five months of 1919, French aviators easily

17

On the left above are some of the NC-4's crew. They are, from left, Eugene Rhoads, chief mechanic's mate; Lieutenant James Breese, engineer; Lieutenant (j.g.) Walter Hinton and Lieutenant Elmer Stone, pilots; and Lieutenant Commander Albert C. Read, flight commander. Shortly after the last leg of the flight Read was posing (far right) in front of

hopped from southern France to Algeria, took seventeen passengers on a round trip from Paris to Brussels and back in half a day, and began airmail service from Paris to Bordeaux and Marseilles. A British blimp cruised for four days in an uninterrupted patrol over the North Sea. Four American army planes made a four-thousand-mile transcontinental mapping and pathfinding tour, and another sped from California to Georgia and back in forty-four hours' flying time. Winged shadows darted across Alpine peaks as the Italians risked airmail deliveries from Padua to Vienna. Even the Germans, their wings clipped by the armistice agreements, set a record with a nonstop flight between Berlin and Stockholm—about 570 miles in seven hours.

But of all the tests of the airplane's new-found strength, the most challenging was the North Atlantic. Winston Churchill, Britain's Secretary for War and Air in 1919, called it a "terrible waste of desolate waters, tossing in tumult in repeated and almost ceaseless storms, and shrouded with an unbroken canopy of mist." So it was, but it was also the most vital highway of nineteenth and early twentieth-century Western civilization, most of whose capitals were located relatively near its shores. To span the Atlantic was a minimum requirement of aviation if it was to play any significant role in transportation. But the fliers who first tried it would be at every moment, in Churchill's words, threatened with "destruction from a drop of water in the carburetor, or a spot of oil on their plugs, or a tiny grain of dirt in their feed pipe, or from any of the other hundred and one indirect causes" which,

in those days, "might drag an aeroplane to its fate."

Despite these risks, pilots and designers had been dreaming of transatlantic flight since before the war. In 1913 Alfred Harmsworth, Baron Northcliffe, publisher of the London *Daily Mail,* announced that he would award ten thousand pounds—a genuine treasure in that time of low-taxed incomes—to the first aviator or aviators to cross the ocean. It was a tempting enticement, but it seemed impossibly remote. Few planes then had a range of more than two hundred miles. A flight from America to Europe by any route would require, for safety's sake, an ability to cover 1,500 miles without a stop, which would be possible only if tons of fuel could be carried. But air-minded engineers enjoyed the paper solution of "impossible" equations, and the Northcliffe offer set pencils to scribbling figures and tracing curves in every flying club on both sides of the ocean.

By June, 1914, in the little New York town of Hammondsport, on Keuka Lake, a twin-engined red flying boat rose and settled on the water again and again in preliminary tests. She was the *America,* and her builder was Glenn H. Curtiss, a native of Hammondsport. Among the curiosity seekers and reporters attracted to the lake was an observer sent by the United States Navy, Lieutenant John H. Towers, a Georgian and an Annapolis graduate of the class of 1906. Just twenty-nine years old, he was nevertheless a veteran flier, the third official American naval aviator. Curtiss had been his teacher. The outbreak of world war cancelled any attempts for the North-

18

the House of Commons with, among others, Edward, then Prince of Wales (left); Winston Churchill, Secretary for War and Air (right); and, next to Churchill, Lord Birkenhead (Frederick Edwin Smith), Lord Chancellor of England. In November, 1918, the NC-1 *had carried a record fifty-one passengers; a sizable crowd (center) witnessed the stunt.*

cliffe prize, but Towers and Curtiss would—five years later—furnish the planes and leadership that would finish the work under way that June.

By the summer of 1917 the United States was in the war, Curtiss was building planes for the Navy, and Towers, by then a lieutenant commander, was on duty in Washington, D.C. On an August day in 1917, Rear Admiral David W. Taylor, the Navy's chief constructor, called in two of his assistants for aeronautics, Jerome C. Hunsaker and G. C. Westervelt, to discuss the implementation of a memorandum he had just prepared. "It seems to me," he had written, "the submarine menace could be abated, even if not destroyed, from the air." This could be accomplished by large, flying boats, which could carry heavy depth charges and machine guns on long ocean hunts. To save valuable shipping space in delivery, they should be able "to fly the Atlantic under their own power." In effect, the Admiral told Hunsaker and Westervelt, the Navy was committing itself, as a matter of military logic, to performing what had previously been considered a stunt. They were to get the project in motion. The two junior officers reached immediate accord on the first step: they wired to Curtiss to come down to Washington.

Curtiss was not just another manufacturer. He was to aviation what Ford was to the automobile: a founding father, a prophet, an evangel, a worker of miracles who could assemble the cash and equipment to turn the spidery drawings of inventors (himself included) into finished hardware. Born in 1878, he belonged to the generation of young Americans who seized the gasoline engine and raced exuberantly with it into the twentieth century. Like the Wright brothers, he tinkered first with bicycles and then discovered the lively possibilities of hitching motors to them. When he was in his twenties he set a world motorcycle speed record of 137 miles an hour. But airplanes held an even greater promise of speed and freedom, and he began in 1909 to build them from his own designs. (Not altogether his own, according to the Wright brothers, who successfully sued him for patent infringement in his use of ailerons too much like theirs.)

Curtiss, who was deceptively unassertive-looking, raced like a demonic wind in planes with saucy names —the *June Bug*, the *Red Wing*, the *Silver Dart*. He went to Europe and raced and beat the continent's best fliers as if they were Hammondsport slowpokes. The list of his awards was a bluebook of aviation's early sponsors: the Scientific American Trophy, the Cortland F. Bishop Prize, the Gordon Bennett Cup, the Robert J. Collier Trophy, the W. E. Kelly Cup, the Grand Prix Passenger Prize, and the Langley Medal of the Smithsonian. He flew faster and higher than anyone. And his imagination kept suggesting new airplanes and airplane uses, which his business sense turned into production models. He invented the flying boat, or hydroplane, pioneered water landings and take-offs, sold his seagoing flying machines to the Navy, and personally taught blue-water sailors to fly them. By 1914 he had created the Curtiss Motor Company and the Curtiss Aeroplane Company, worth nearly ten million dollars; they would build more than 200 kinds of aircraft, using sixty-seven of Curtiss' patents.

Curtiss and his engineering staff began to work with the Navy's Bureau of Construction experts on the development of four ocean-going superplanes that would make the impossible possible, the technological game twentieth-century man has played so brilliantly. Step by step, out of conferences, arguments, scribbled notes, sketches, long sessions over drawing boards, mounting piles of empty coffee cups and cigarette butts, the regular Navy scientists, the physics professors in reservists' uniforms, the Curtiss production men, and the experienced aviators worked out the equations of success. They whittled fantasy down to limits that reality could nearly embrace, and then stretched reality until it did. Commander Holden C. Richardson was told to design a hull that would be independently seaworthy, light as air-borne wood could be, and sturdy enough to survive slamming into a wave while landing at sixty miles an hour loaded with twelve tons. Patient, skilled, and a twenty-year veteran of naval construction, Richardson produced a V-bottomed boat forty-five feet long and ten feet wide, with double planking sandwiching a waterproof layer of glued muslin. It weighed only 2,800 pounds empty. Richardson, Hunsaker, and Westervelt protected the tail surfaces against the beating of huge ocean waves by mounting them on hollow wooden spars well above the water. The emerging aircraft took on a curious appearance of a wing-and-tail assembly mated to a hull yet not integrally part of it—like some monster dragonfly pouncing on a fish. The original plan called for three twelve-cylinder Liberty engines, but weight-to-horsepower ratios showed that a fourth engine would lift two pounds for every one added by its own weight. So the planes would have four engines, one on each wing and two in tandem on the center line, and would fly with a total weight of 28,000 pounds. Six of those fourteen tons could be useful load, over the weight of the empty plane—enough for 1,800 gallons of gasoline (in nine tanks), spare parts, oil, radio equipment, and six-man crews.

Day by day hotly discussed hunches were checked by slide rule, towing basin, and wind tunnel. Month by month the first plane took shape. It was to be called the *N* (Navy) *C* (Curtiss) *1* (first of a series.) It would be a joint product; many of its parts would be subcontracted out to keep from overwhelming Curtiss' facilities and to give more of the American aircraft industry a stake in it. Its upper wing would span 126 feet, half a Manhattan Island block, and would have a chord of 12 feet. From nose to tail it would be just under seventy feet, and it would stand twenty-five feet high. Its wing panels were moved from Curtiss' Garden City, Long Island, assembly plant to the Naval Air Station at Far Rockaway in trucks ordinarily used for hauling theatrical scenery. At Rockaway the plane required a special hangar and, later on, railroad tracks and tractor engines to move it into the water. In October of 1918 it was completed, with the *NC-2, -3,* and *-4* in various stages of construction.

These scenes were painted by the Navy artist C. E. Ruttan. The planes left Newfoundland the evening of May 16. That night a chain of destroyers helped to light their way (center), but early the next morning the NC-1 and the NC-3 landed in mid-Atlantic fog. The NC-3

By then it was clear that the end of the war was only weeks away, and that there would be no military use for the planes. The contracts for the uncompleted three would probably be cancelled. The prospect was wormwood to Commander Towers. He pleaded with his superiors to let the planes prove their transoceanic capabilities. The United States, he wrote, had built the first airplane and the first seaplane. It should not miss another opening. The first flight across the Atlantic would be sure to "go down in history as an epoch making event." He asked for command of the expedition as "the senior aviator, in point of aviation service, on aviation duty," and added, "I believe that I could quickly get the project organized without interference with my present duties." It was a promise he would make good on.

Towers had thought more about such a flight than any other man in the Navy. His service record was virtually the story of early naval aviation, with its crises, lean years, and improvisations. He had flown every kind of craft, taught other men to fly, organized air stations, supervised purchases, designed improvements, and fitted them to planes with his own calloused, greasy hands. And he had constantly risked his life. Once he was in a plane with another officer when it spun out of control. There were no safety belts then, and both men were pitched out of their seats. The other fell to his death. Towers caught a strut, hung on, and survived the crack-up. It was all in the day's work for the fathers of military flight.

Moreover, Towers' request was well timed. The Secretary of the Navy, Josephus Daniels, was a North Carolina editor and politician with a deep concern for public relations. The assistant secretary, Franklin D. Roosevelt, was an enthusiastic amateur sailor, whose passion for the Navy was matched by an appetite for novelties. Both men were undoubtedly impressed when the *NC-1*, on November 27, 1918, swallowed fifty-one sailors and civilian workers (including one stowaway) and set a world's passenger-carrying record. Bannered in the press, such feats carried weight with the public and with Congress.

Early in February, 1919, Towers got his wish. But from the start, the Navy officials made every effort to give the flight the character of a carefully planned military operation rather than a theatrical gamble unworthy of the attention of admirals. The *Daily Mail* had renewed its offer of ten thousand pounds, but the Navy fliers were forbidden to compete for it. Every element of risk was compressed to minimum dimensions. The Navy's planners decreed that the four planes should fly together, each with a navigator, two pilots, a radioman, and two engine specialists. They loaded each craft with lifesaving communications equipment: a transmitter that could send a distress call squeaking over 250 miles, a short-range set to talk to other planes up to twenty-five miles away, receivers whose radio eardrums could pick up messages and orders from stations several thousand miles away, and a radio compass to locate the source of signals from

CONTINUED ON PAGE 101

eventually drifted and taxied to the Azores, but the NC-1, *after the rescue of her crew (left) and a futile towing effort, was left to sink. The* NC-4's *arrival in the Azores is shown at right. Both Ruttan and Reuterdahl made sketches from which they later did their paintings.*

By nightfall of December 7, 1941—the day Pearl Harbor was attacked—F.B.I. agents on the West Coast had arrested 1,300 "potentially dangerous" enemy aliens. During the next few weeks the western edge of the country underwent a panic that is hard to understand even in retrospect. Sporadic acts of violence against Japanese, alien and native-born, began to occur. A California state legislator demanded the mass evacuation of "all persons of Japanese ancestry," and the cry reverberated in the press. By mid-February of 1942 the California attorney general, Earl Warren, was calling for military action to "protect this state from the Japanese situation." On February 19, President Roosevelt signed the executive order that made such action possible. Many Japanese-Americans who could afford the price of a ticket accepted "voluntary deportation" to other areas of the country. On April 30, the long-expected final order of exclusion came through.

All persons of Japanese descent in the three coastal states were required to report to so-called assembly centers; they were to bring bedding and linen, toilet articles and clothing, knives, forks, spoons, plates, bowls, and cups. Nothing else.

In the end, the evacuee figure came close to 110,000. There were old and young, sick and well, mothers, grandmothers, infants, aging veterans of other U.S. wars. Half of them were under twenty years old; many neither spoke nor read Japanese. All were forced to leave their homes, lands, and businesses. They were herded into hastily built barracks, surrounded by barbed wire, in remote, often isolated areas of California, Arizona, Utah, Wyoming, Idaho, Colorado, and Arkansas.

In 1945, when the Japanese were permitted to return, Earl Warren was governor of California and Robert Walker Kenny was attorney general. Kenny and Warren were political rivals. Both were frequently mentioned as possible presidential nominees for, respectively, the Democratic and Republican parties. It was the attorney general, not the governor, who had to handle the politically sensitive task of the peaceful return of the Japanese to California. In a recent interview with his biographer, Janet Stevenson, Kenny recalled that process and the events leading up to it.

BEFORE THE COLORS FADE:

In 1945 Robert W. Kenny fought for the rights of Japanese-Americans re-entering California.

One of the strange things about the whole episode of the so-called relocation was that there really wasn't much anti-Japanese sentiment in California at the time of Pearl Harbor. Nor even afterward. It had to be whipped up. It took a number of weeks to do it.

I was in the state senate in December, 1941, and I remember we had a resolution offered to the effect that all Japanese-Americans should be barred from civil service employment. Well, it just didn't get any takers. The thing was referred to committee—which is to say, it got lost.

And Governor Culbert L. Olson (who changed his mind a few weeks later) was making statements about how we should not regard the Japanese in California as responsible for what had happened in Hawaii; they were just as much victims as we Caucasians. . . . I remember going up in an elevator in the State Building

By JANET STEVENSON

The Return of the Exiles

Today the former state attorney general is a judge of the superior court in Los Angeles.

in Los Angeles. There were two Nisei [native-born Japanese-Americans] aboard, and everybody took the occasion to wish them well. Everybody was sorry for them. That was no more than two weeks after Pearl Harbor.

But then the newspapers got going, especially the Hearst papers. People began reading those crazy headlines about sabotage—arrow-shaped forest fires pointing at our cities—and spies standing on the beach signalling to submarines. By February they had us so jumpy we couldn't read our own radar. Somebody in Los Angeles picked up a false signal from a weather balloon, and we had a whole night of ack-ack. The point is that all this had to be fomented.

Didn't California have a long history of anti-Japanese prejudice?

Back in the twenties, in Hiram Johnson's time. From 1914 on, a California politician who wanted to get elected had to be just as racist on the Japanese as a Democratic politician in the South had to be on the Negro.

But by 1940 that was gone. Well, maybe not in some of those rural communities where there was real jealousy of the Japanese farmers. But for the most part the Japanese had become settled, respectable, useful citizens. The people we were down on by 1940 were the Filipinos, who were the latest immigrants to arrive and to start competing for jobs. Of course, during the war we couldn't express that feeling because here were the Filipinos fighting along with MacArthur at Bataan. And since we apparently have to hate somebody, we reverted to our old, bad habits about the Japanese. But it took an effort. It could only have been done in an atmosphere of war nerves.

Once the Japanese had been evacuated, did the feeling against them die down?

Not everywhere. Not in those rural communities—Placer County, Nevada County, Fresno, Orange. You see, there were all these organizations dedicated to keeping it up. Like the California Joint Immigration Committee. That's "joint" because it was composed of the American Legion, the Native Sons of the Golden West, the state Grange, and—for a while, at least—the state Federation of Labor. Their program had always been "Get the Japanese out of California." Now they had what they wanted, and they were working overtime to make sure it stuck.

Even a liberal newspaper like the Sacramento *Bee* was involved. All during the war I remember really shocking advertisements appearing in the *Bee*. Some outfit that called itself the Home Front Commandoes was offering to pay "volunteers" to work on their "Deport the Jap" campaigns.

It wasn't just the lunatic fringe, either. I was no longer in the senate by this time, but I remember being told that a Presbyterian minister had testified that after prayer and fasting he'd concluded it was our Christian duty to keep the Japanese out of the Western world. He was for deporting them right off the continent!

Of course, we were at war with Japan all this time. People were losing sons and husbands in those battles in the Pacific. That tended to delay our sobering up from this racist binge.

Were we still at war with Japan when the Exclusion Order was revoked?

Yes indeed. Recall the order of events here. Pearl Harbor was December 7, 1941. The evacuation began in April, 1942. By the time I became attorney general in 1943, the Japanese were gone. Ex parte *Endo*—the U.S. Supreme Court decision that opened up the concentration camp gates—was December 18, 1944. The first returnees must have hit California in late January, 1945. We were still fighting for Iwo Jima and Okinawa in February and March. Roosevelt died in April. V-E Day was May 7, 1945. We dropped the bomb on Hiroshima on August 6, and Japan surrendered on the fourteenth. By that time we only had a few thousands of our returnees. They were still coming in as late as December.

When did you first hear about the return?

Just a few days before *Endo* was handed down. I was in Washington, and a high official in the Department of the Interior called to tip me off. The War Relocation Authority, which had the unpleasant job of running the camps in which the Japanese were held, was part of Interior. So I got a little advance warning—about a week as I recall—to begin making preparations for the orderly reception of these people. Warren, as governor, was tipped off too. But as the chief law enforcement officer of the state, it was mainly my concern.

Was there an obvious possibility of trouble?

I think so. Not all the people we'd sent out of California would be coming back. Some had left the camps and settled in less hostile parts of the country. The Midwest, the East. Particularly the professionals—doctors, lawyers. Some had gone into the armed services. Some had decided to renounce their citizenship and go to Japan, when that became possible.

But the chances were that something close to 50,000 people who had been stripped of virtually all their possessions and locked up for two years were going to be turning up before long. Sure there were going to be problems.

Were you expecting them all to turn up at once?

No. There were complicated procedures involved—processing, transportation. Of course, they were all free to return from the day of *Endo*, or whenever it was the Army revoked its Exclusion Order. But I think if we had expected them all back at once—the way they were sent away—we would have been even more alarmed.

How did you go about making preparations for their "peaceful and orderly return"?

Well, I came back to Sacramento and talked it over with Governor Warren. The one experience we had
CONTINUED ON PAGE 96

24

WARTIME HYSTERIA

The "relocation" of Japanese-Americans during World War II was a shocking suspension of the civil rights guaranteed by the Fourteenth Amendment. They were deprived of liberty and property without due legal process and were denied the "equal protection of the laws" afforded other citizens. The photographs on these pages can only start to suggest what the Japanese-Americans had to endure. Below, a group of Angelenos queue up to register for evacuation. The storefront above was in the Little Tokyo section of Los Angeles;

ALL: LIBRARY OF CONGRESS

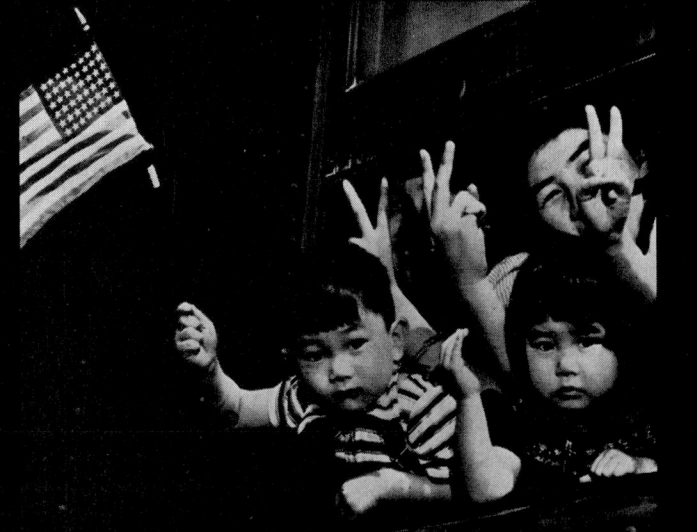

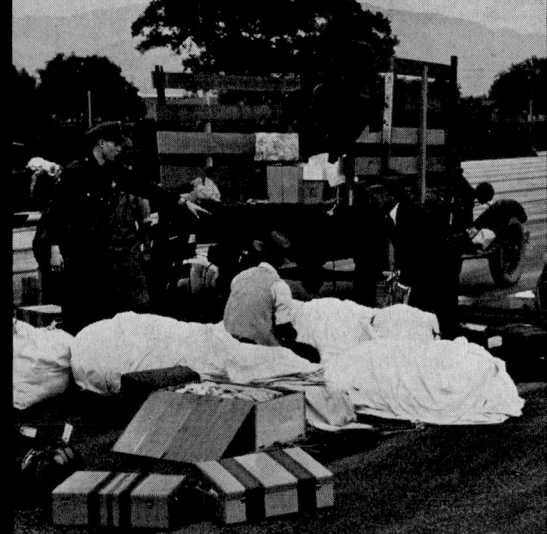

CITIZENS INTERNED

despite the patriotic protestations in the window, the owner—like thousands of others—had to sell out and get out. Many families declared their allegiance even as they entrained for barbed-wire camps. The Santa Anita Racetrack in Arcadia, California, served as one of the assembly centers. There, evacuees were ordered to open their baggage for inspection, and then were processed by a registrar. Their final destination was a dusty, desolate, windswept internment camp of crude barracks, like the one below at Tule Lake, California.

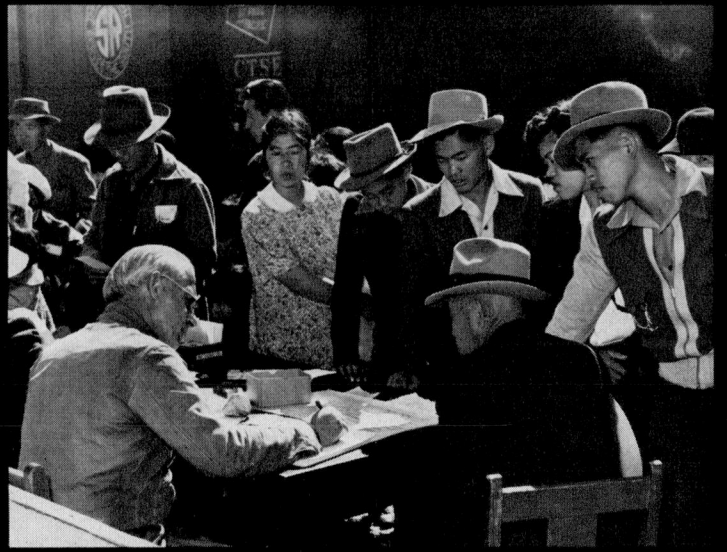

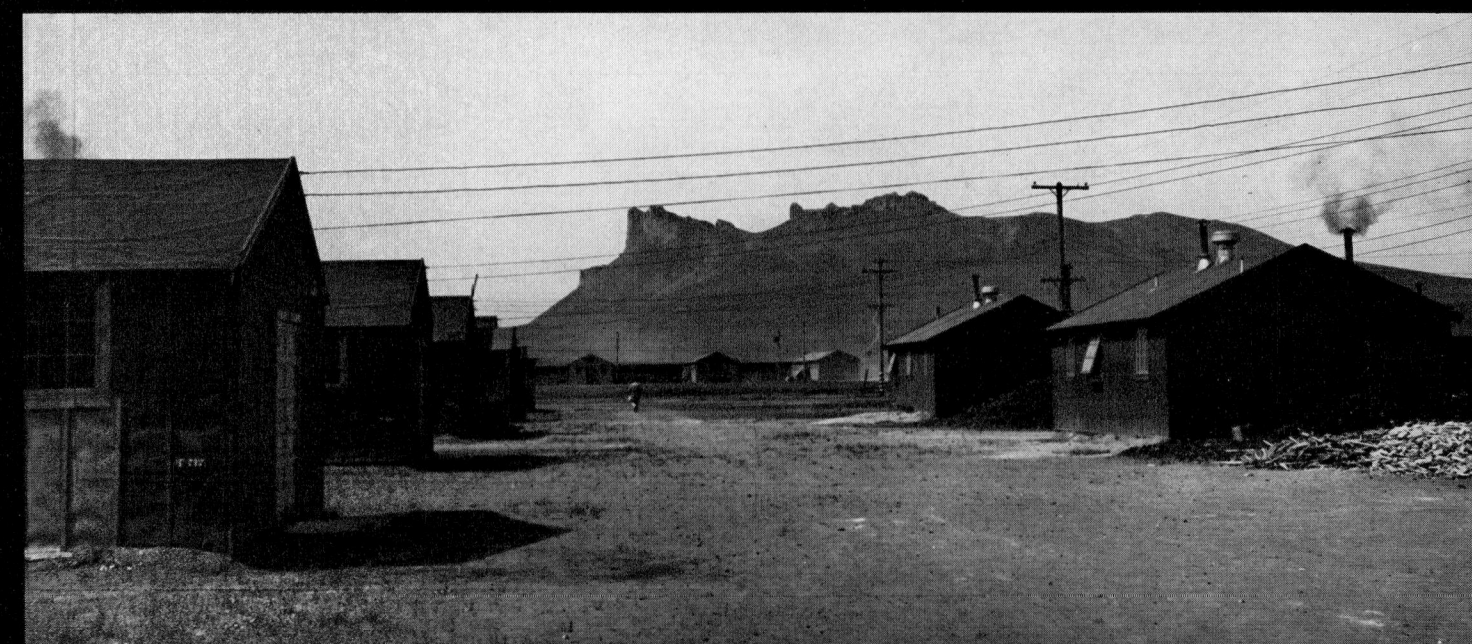

DRAWN FOR AMERICAN HERITAGE BY MICHAEL RAMUS

THE LAST LEAF

They were usually corrupt and often inefficient, but the old-style politicians had their uses. Now almost all are gone

THE POLITICAL MACHINE I: RISE AND FALL
THE AGE of the BOSSES

By WILLIAM V. SHANNON

The big city and the political boss grew up together in America. Bossism, with all its color and corruption and human drama, was a natural and perhaps necessary accompaniment to the rapid development of cities. The new urban communities did not grow slowly and according to plan; on the contrary, huge conglomerations of people from all over the world and from widely varying backgrounds came together suddenly, and in an unplanned, unorganized fashion fumbled their way toward communal relationships and a common identity. The political bosses emerged to cope with this chaotic change and growth. Acting out of greed, a ruthless will for mastery, and an imperfect understanding of what they were about, the bosses imposed upon these conglomerations called cities a certain feudal order and direction.

By 1890 virtually every sizable city had a political boss or was in the process of developing one. By 1950, sixty years later, almost every urban political machine was in an advanced state of obsolescence and its boss in trouble. The reason is not hard to find. Some of the cities kept growing and all of them kept changing, but the bosses, natural products of a specific era, could not grow or change beyond a certain point. The cities became essentially different, and as they did, the old-style organizations, like all organisms which cannot adapt, began to die. The dates vary from city to city. The system began earlier and died sooner in New York. Here or there, an old-timer made one last comeback. In Chicago, the organization and its boss still survive. But exceptions aside, the late nineteenth century saw the beginning, and the middle twentieth, the end, of the Age of the Bosses. What follows is a brief history of how it began, flourished, and passed away.

Soft-spoken Irish farmers from County Mayo and bearded Jews from Poland, country boys from Ohio and sturdy peasants from Calabria, gangling Swedes from near the Artic Circle and Chinese from Canton, laconic Yankees from Vermont villages and Negro freedmen putting distance between themselves and the old plantation—all these and many other varieties of human beings from every national and religious and cultural tradition poured into America's cities in the decades after the Civil War.

Rome and Alexandria in the ancient world had probably been as polyglot, but in modern times the diversity of American cities was unique. Everywhere in the Western world, cities were growing rapidly in the late nineteenth century; but the Germans from the countryside who migrated to Hamburg and Berlin, the English who moved to Birmingham and London, and the French who flocked to Paris stayed among fellow nationals. They might be mocked as country bumpkins and their clothes might be unfashionable, but everyone they met spoke the same language as themselves, observed the same religious and secular holidays, ate the same kind of food, voted—if they had the franchise at all—in the same elections, and shared the same sentiments and expectations. To move from farm or village to a big European city was an adventure, but one still remained within the reassuring circle of the known and the familiar.

In American cities, however, the newcomers had nothing in common with one another except their poverty and their hopes. They were truly "the uprooted." The foreign-born, unless they came from the British Isles, could not speak the language of their new homeland. The food, the customs, the holidays, the politics, were alien. Native Americans migrating to the cities from the countryside experienced their own kind of cultural shock: they found themselves competing not with other Americans but with recently arrived foreigners, so that despite their native birth they, too, felt displaced, strangers in their own country.

It was natural for members of each group to come together to try to find human warmth and protection in Little Italy or Cork Hill or Chinatown or Harlem. These feelings of clannish solidarity were one basis of strength for the political bosses. A man will more readily give his vote to a candidate because he is a neighbor from the old country or has some easily identifiable relationship, if only a similar name or the same religion, than because of agreement on some impersonal issue. Voters can take vicarious satisfaction from his success: "One of our boys is making good."

With so many different races and nationalities living together, however, mutual antagonisms were present, and the opportunity for hostility to flare into open violence was never far away. Ambitious, unscrupulous politicians could have exploited these antagonisms for their own political advantage, but the bosses and the political organizations which they developed did not function that way. If a man could vote and would "vote right," he was accepted, and that was the end of the matter. What lasting profit was there in attacking his religion or deriding his background?

Tammany early set the pattern of cultivating every bloc and faction and making an appeal as broad-based as possible. Of one precinct captain on the Lower East Side it was said: "He eats corned beef and kosher meat with equal nonchalance, and it's all the same to him whether he takes off his hat in the church or pulls it down over his ears in the synagogue."

Bosses elsewhere instinctively followed the same practice. George B. Cox, the turn-of-the-century Republican boss of Cincinnati, pasted together a coalition of Germans, Negroes, and old families like the Tafts and the Longworths. James M. Curley, who was mayor of Boston on and off for thirty-six years and was its closest approximation to a political boss, ran as well in the Lithuanian neighborhood of South Boston and the Italian section of East Boston as he did in the working-class Irish wards. In his last term in City Hall, he conferred minor patronage on the growing Negro community and joined the N.A.A.C.P.

The bosses organized neighborhoods, smoothed out antagonisms, arranged ethnically balanced tickets, and distributed patronage in accordance with voting strength as part of their effort to win and hold power. They blurred divisive issues and buried racial and religious hostility with blarney and buncombe. They were not aware that they were actually performing a mediating, pacifying function. They did not realize that by trying to please as many people as possible they were helping to hold raw new cities together, providing for inexperienced citizens a common meeting ground in politics and an experience in working together that would not have been available if the cities had been governed by apolitical bureaucracies. Bossism was usually corrupt and was decidedly inefficient, but in the 1960's, when antipoverty planners try to stimulate "community action organizations" to break through the apathy and disorganization of the slums, we can appreciate that the old-style machines had their usefulness.

When William Marcy Tweed, the first and most famous of the big-city bosses, died in jail in 1878, several hundred workingmen showed up for his funeral. The *Nation* wrote the following week:

Let us remember that he fell without loss of reputation among the bulk of his supporters. The bulk of the poorer voters of this city today revere his memory, and look on him as the victim of rich men's malice; as, in short, a friend of the needy who applied the public funds, with as little waste as was possible under the circumstances, to the purposes to which they ought to be applied—and that is to the making of work for the working man. The odium heaped on him in the pulpits last Sunday does not exist in the lower stratum of New York society.

This split in attitude toward political bosses between the impoverished many and the prosperous middle classes lingers today and still colors historical writing. To respectable people, the boss was an exotic, even grotesque figure. They found it hard to understand why anyone would vote for him or what the sources of his popularity were. To the urban poor, those sources were self-evident. The boss ran a kind of ramshackle welfare state. He helped the unemployed find jobs, interceded in court for boys in trouble, wrote letters home to the old country for the illiterate; he provided free coal and baskets of food to tide a widow over an emergency, and organized parades, excursions to the beach, and other forms of free entertainment. Some bosses, such as Frank Hague in Jersey City and Curley in Boston, were energetic patrons of their respective city hospitals, spending public funds lavishly on new construction, providing maternity and children's clinics, and arranging medical care for the indigent. In an era when social security, Blue Cross, unemployment compensation, and other public and private arrangements to cushion life's shocks did not exist, these benefactions from a political boss were important.

In every city, the boss had his base in the poorer, older, shabbier section of town. Historians have dubbed this section the "walking city" because it developed in the eighteenth and early nineteenth centuries, when houses and businesses were jumbled together, usually near the waterfront, and businessmen and laborers alike had to live within walking distance of their work. As transportation improved, people were able to live farther and farther from their place of work. Population dispersed in rough concentric circles: the financially most successful lived in the outer ring, where land was plentiful and the air was clean; the middle classes lived in intermediate neighborhoods; and the poorest and the latest arrivals from Europe crowded into the now-rundown neighborhoods in the center, where rents were lowest. Politics in most cities reflected a struggle between the old, boss-run wards downtown and the more prosperous neighborhoods farther out, which did not need a boss's services and which championed reform. The more skilled workingmen and the white-collar workers who lived in the intermediate neighborhoods generally held the balance of power between the machine and the reformers. A skillful boss could hold enough of these swing voters on the basis of ethnic loyalty or shared support of a particular issue. At times, he might work out alliances with business leaders who found that an understanding with a boss was literally more businesslike than dependence upon the vagaries of reform.

But always it was the poorest and most insecure who provided the boss with the base of his political power. Their only strength, as Professor Richard C. Wade of the University of Chicago has observed, was in their numbers.

These numbers were in most cases a curse; housing never caught up with demand, the job market was always flooded, the breadwinner had too many mouths to feed. Yet in politics such a liability could be turned into an asset. If the residents could be mobilized, their combined strength would be able to do what none could do alone. Soon the "boss" and the "machine" arose to organize this potential. The boss system was simply the political expression of inner city life.

At a time when many newcomers to the city were seeking unskilled work, and when many families had a precarious economic footing, the ability to dispense jobs was crucial to the bosses. First, there were jobs to be filled on the city payroll. Just as vital, and far more numerous, were jobs on municipal construction projects. When the machine controlled a city, public funds were always being spent for more schools, hospitals, libraries, courthouses, and orphanages. The growing cities had to have more sewer lines, gas lines, and waterworks, more paved streets and trolley tracks. Even if these utilities were privately owned, the managers needed the goodwill of city hall and were responsive to suggestions about whom to hire.

The payrolls of these public works projects were often padded, but to those seeking a job, it was better to be on a padded payroll than on no payroll. By contrast, the municipal reformers usually cut back on public spending, stopped projects to investigate for graft, and pruned payrolls. Middle- and upper-income taxpayers welcomed these reforms, but they were distinctly unpopular in working-class wards.

Another issue that strengthened the bosses was the regulation of the sale of liquor. Most women in the nineteenth century did not drink, and with their backing, the movement to ban entirely the manufacture and sale of liquor grew steadily stronger. It had its greatest support among Protestants with a rural or small-town background. To them the cities, with their saloons, dance halls, cheap theatres, and red-light districts, were becoming latter-day versions of Sodom and Gomorrah.

Many of the European immigrants in the cities, however, had entirely different values. Quite respectable

Germans took their wives to beer gardens on Sundays. In the eyes of the Irish, keeping a "public house" was an honorable occupation. Some Irish women drank beer and saw no harm in going to the saloon or sending an older child for a bucketful—"rushing the growler," they called it. Poles, Czechs, Italians, and others also failed to share the rage of the Prohibitionists against saloons. Unable to entertain in their cramped tenements, they liked to congregate in neighborhood bars.

The machine also appealed successfully on the liquor issue to many middle-class ethnic voters who had no need of the machine's economic assistance. Thus, in New York in 1897, Tammany scored a sweeping victory over an incumbent reform administration that had tried to enforce a state law permitting only hotels to sell liquor on Sundays. As one of the city's three police commissioners, Theodore Roosevelt became famous prowling the tougher neighborhoods on the hunt for saloon violations, but on the vaudeville stage the singers were giving forth with the hit song, "I Want What I Want When I Want It!" As a character in Alfred Henry Lewis' novel *The Boss* explained it, the reformers had made a serious mistake: "They got between the people and its beer!"

In 1902, Lincoln Steffens, the muckraker who made a name for himself writing about political bossism, visited St. Louis to interview Joseph W. Folk, a crusading district attorney. "It is good businessmen that are corrupting our bad politicians," Folk told him. "It is good business that causes bad government in St. Louis." Thirty-five years later, Boss Tom Pendergast was running the entire state of Missouri on that same reciprocal relationship.

Although many factory owners could be indifferent to politics, other businessmen were dependent upon the goodwill and the efficiency of the municipal government. The railroads that wanted to build their freight terminals and extend their lines into the cities, the contractors who erected the office buildings, the banks that held mortgages on the land and loaned money for the construction, the utility and transit companies, and the department stores were all in need of licenses, franchises, rights of way, or favorable rulings from city inspectors and agencies. These were the businesses that made the big pay-offs to political bosses in cash, blocks of stock, or tips on land about to be developed.

In another sense, profound, impersonal, and not corrupt, the business community needed the boss. Because the Industrial Revolution hit this country when it was still thinly populated and most of its cities were overgrown towns, American cities expanded with astonishing speed. For example, in the single decade from 1880 to 1890, Chicago's population more than doubled, from a half million to over a million. The twin cities of Minneapolis and St. Paul tripled in size. New York City increased from a million to a million and a half; Detroit, Milwaukee, Columbus, and Cleveland grew by sixty to eighty per cent.

Municipal governments, however, were unprepared for this astonishing growth. Planning and budgeting were unknown arts. City charters had restrictive provisions envisaged for much smaller, simpler communities. The mayor and the important commissioners were usually amateurs serving a term or two as a civic duty. Authority was dispersed among numerous boards and special agencies. A typical city would have a board of police commissioners, a board of health, a board of tax assessors, a water board, and many others. The ostensible governing body was a city council or board of aldermen which might have thirty, fifty, or even a hundred members. Under these circumstances, it was difficult to get a prompt decision, harder still to co-ordinate decisions taken by different bodies acting on different premises, and easy for delays and anomalies to develop.

In theory, the cities could have met their need for increased services by municipal socialism, but the conventional wisdom condemned that as too radical, although here and there a city did experiment with publicly owned utilities. In theory also, the cities could have financed public buildings and huge projects such as water and sewer systems by frankly raising taxes or floating bonds. But both taxes and debt were no more popular then than they are now. Moreover, the laissez-faire doctrine which holds that "that government is best which governs least" was enshrined orthodoxy in America from the 1870's down to the 1930's.

As men clung to such orthodox philosophies, the structures of government became obsolete; they strained to meet unexpected demands as a swelling number of citizens in every class clamored for more services. In this climate the bosses emerged. They had no scruples about taking shortcuts through old procedures or manipulating independent boards and agencies in ways that the original city fathers had never intended. They had no inhibiting commitment to any theory of limited government. They were willing to spend, tax, and build—and to take the opprobrium along with the graft. Sometimes, like Hague in Jersey City, Curley in Boston, and Big Bill Thompson in Chicago, they got themselves elected mayor and openly assumed responsibility. More often, like Pendergast in Kansas City, Cox in Cincinnati, the leaders of Tammany, and the successive Republican bosses of Philadelphia, they held minor offices or none, stayed out of the limelight, and ran city government through their iron control of the party organization. In ruling Memphis for forty years, Ed Crump followed one pattern and then the other. Impeached on a technicality after being elected three times as mayor, Crump retreated to the back rooms and became even more powerful as the city's political boss.

What manner of men became political bosses? They were men of little education and no social background, often of immigrant parentage. A college-educated boss like Edward Flynn of The Bronx was a rarity. Bosses often began as saloonkeepers, because the saloon was a natural meeting place in poorer neighborhoods in the days before Prohibition. They were physically strong and no strangers to violence. Seventy-five years ago, most men made their living with brawn rather than brain, and a man who expected to be a leader of men had to be tough as well as shrewd. Open violence used to be common at polling places on Election Day, and gangs of repeaters roamed from one precinct to another. Although the typical boss made his way up through that roughneck system, the logic of his career led him to suppress violence. Bloody heads make bad publicity, and it is hard for any political organization to maintain a monopoly on violence. Bosses grew to prefer quieter, more lawful, less dangerous methods of control. Ballot-box stuffing and overt intimidation never disappeared entirely, but gradually they receded to the status of weapons of last resort.

Political bosses varied in their idiosyncrasies and styles. A few, like Curley, became polished orators; others, like the legendary Charles Murphy of Tammany Hall, never made speeches. They were temperate, businesslike types; among them a drunk was as rare as a Phi Beta Kappa. If they had a generic failing it was for horses and gambling. Essentially they were hardheaded men of executive temper and genuine organizing talents; many, in other circumstances and with more education, might have become successful businessmen.

They have disappeared now, most of them. Education has produced a more sophisticated electorate; it has also encouraged potential bosses to turn away from politics toward more secure, prestigious, and profitable careers. A young man who had the energy, persistence, and skill in 1899 to become a successful political boss would in 1969 go to college and end up in an executive suite.

The urban population has also changed. The great flood of bewildered foreigners has dwindled to a trickle. In place of the European immigrants of the past, today's cities receive an influx of Negroes from the rural South, Puerto Ricans, Mexicans, and the white poor from Appalachia. As they overcome the language barrier and widen their experience, the Puerto Ricans are making themselves felt in urban politics. New York City, where they are most heavily concentrated, may have a Puerto Rican mayor in the not too distant future.

But the other groups are too isolated from the rest of the community to put together a winning political coalition of have-nots. The Mexicans and the ex-hillbillies from Appalachia are isolated by their unique cultural backgrounds, the Negroes by the giant fact of their race. Inasmuch as they make up a quarter to a third of the population in many cities, are a cohesive group, and still have a high proportion of poor who have to look to government for direct help, the Negroes might have produced several bosses and functioning political machines had they been of white European ancestry. But until Negroes attain a clear numerical majority, they find it difficult to take political power in any city because various white factions are reluctant to coalesce with them.

Regardless of the race or background of the voters, however, there are factors which work against the old-style machines. Civil service regulations make it harder to create a job or pad a payroll. Federal income taxes and federal accounting requirements make it more difficult to hide the rewards of graft. Television, public relations, and polling have created a whole new set of political techniques and undermined the personal ties and neighborhood loyalties on which the old organizations depended.

The new political style has brought an increase in municipal government efficiency and probably some decline in political corruption and misrule. But the politics of the television age puts a premium on hypocrisy. Candor has gone out the window with the spoils system. There is still a lot of self-seeking in politics and always will be. But gone are the days of Tammany's Boss Richard Croker, who when asked by an investigating committee if he was "working for his own pocket," shot back: "All the time—same as you." Today's politicians are so busy tending their images that they have become incapable of even a mildly derogatory remark such as Jim Curley's: "The term 'codfish aristocracy' is a reflection on the fish."

Curley entitled his memoirs *I'd Do It Again*. But the rough-and-tumble days when two-fisted, rough-tongued politicians came roaring out of the slums to take charge of America's young cities are not to come again.

William V. Shannon is on the editorial board of the New York Times. *He is the author of* The American Irish *and of* The Heir Apparent, *a study of the late Senator Robert F. Kennedy, both published by Macmillan.*

THE POLITICAL MACHINE II: A CASE HISTORY
"I AM THE LAW"

By THOMAS J. FLEMING

He came out of the Horseshoe, a teeming slice of downtown Jersey City that owed its name to a gerrymander of earlier decades. From the brutal poverty of those narrow waterfront streets crammed with saloons and slum tenements, Frank Hague rose to plush accommodations at the Plaza and a mansion on Biscayne Bay, to dinners at the White House and at the homes of the wealthy, to annual trips to Europe in the royal suites of luxury liners, to made-to-order shirts and silk underwear from A. Sulka & Company. A few years before his death he secretly acknowledged that he was worth eight million dollars. The lawyer who extracted this figure, a former attorney general of New Jersey, says: "The real amount was probably ten times higher."

But it was not just his wealth that made Hague unique—it was the totality of his power and the ferocity with which he exercised it. For thirty years he reigned as mayor of Jersey City and ruler of New Jersey. Judges and district attorneys, senators and congressmen, governors and presidential candidates, respected—or at least feared—his name. Those who opposed him, especially on his home grounds, frequently ended up in jail or in the hospital. "I am the law!" he bellowed once in a moment of unguarded candor. Though he could claim, with some justice, that his enemies had distorted the circumstances in which he said it—he was trying to keep some delinquent boys out of jail—even his friends had to admit that, inside Jersey City's 8,320 grubby acres, it was the literal truth.

How Hague achieved this wealth and power is an American saga, rich in irony and symbolic overtones still significant today. Born in 1876, he was expelled from school at the age of thirteen as a hopeless incorrigible; he acquired his real education in the brawling streets of the Horseshoe in the 1890's. Along with a taste for violence, he acquired from his boyhood a deep infusion of Irish Catholicism in its most puritanical form. The infusor was his mother, Margaret Hague. Her husband, John Hague, was a quiet cipher. Mrs. Hague is recalled by one old Jerseyite as "a bitch on wheels." She turned Hague's younger brother, Jimmy, into a mamma's boy so effeminate he never married. Her son Frank, made of tougher stuff, emerged from her stern tutelage ideally equipped to march to power flaunting the banner of a Catholic reformer. The two words are of equal importance in Frank Hague's rise.

Religion was as divisive to the slum dweller of 1900 as race is to the slum dweller of 1969. The Anglo-Saxon Protestants on Jersey City's affluent Heights had the money, and they were haughtily determined to convert or browbeat into submission the immigrant Catholics downtown. From his earliest days, Frank Hague was a devout Catholic, and he could always draw on this simmering sense of discrimination as part of his political weaponry.

His psychological combination of Irish puritanism and hypochondria also guaranteed him a "clean" image. He had no interest in fast women or in drinking the saloons dry. Until the age of twenty-seven he lived at home with his mother and frequently accompanied her to church on Sunday. Then he married Jennie Warner, a prim, shy, retiring girl who never played the slightest role in his political life.

The reform side of Hague's image has been almost totally forgotten today. But it is one of the two things—the other is his technique of holding power—that makes his story worth recalling.

When the lean, red-headed six-footer won his first election, to the post of constable in 1897, New Jersey was called The Traitor State by despairing reformers. Hague's campaign, which consisted of borrowing seventy-five dollars from saloonkeeper Nat Kenny to "make friends" in the Horseshoe's ubiquitous bars, was typical of New Jersey's seamy political life. The political boss of Newark, James Smith, Jr., and the boss of Jersey City, Robert Davis, had auctioned off the state to the burgeoning railroads and utilities in return for juicy stock options and side deals. Thirty per cent of Jersey City's land was owned by the railroads, and they were assessed at only $3,000 an acre while other properties were evaluated as high as $18,000 an acre.

Backed by his self-organized "Tammannee Club"—a name that revealed little originality but much ambition—

COLLECTION OF WILLIAM MAYER, JR.

The affluence of Hague's political career contrasted vividly with the poverty of his youth. At eleven, the future mayor (center) worked as a helper on an express wagon and sold bags of discarded clothes at fifty cents each.

Opposite: Frank Hague of Jersey City in 1938, when he was sixty-two years old

Hague swiftly became the leader of the Horseshoe's second ward. Having antagonized Davis, Hague promptly formed an alliance with H. Otto Wittpenn, a reform Democrat who was committed to fighting bossism and the "interests," as the big corporations were called. When Davis died in 1910 and Wittpenn attempted to assume his mantle as Democratic leader, Hague turned on him and smeared him with the "boss" label. Meanwhile, Woodrow Wilson became an aggressive reform governor of New Jersey, ramming through a series of bills aimed at returning the control of the government to the people. No one supported him more vociferously than Hague, especially when the Governor attacked and all but destroyed Boss Smith of Newark.

In 1911, Hague became the street and water commissioner of Jersey City. He instantly cut his department's budget from $180,000 a year to $110,000 and "for economy reasons" fired half the men. Later in the year he quietly replaced them with his own followers, and at his *sotto voce* request the city council restored his budget cuts. He had more than made his point—he was a tough administrator who meant business when he cried "reform."

On New Year's Day, 1939, Hague's constituents queued up, as they did annually, to shake the Mayor's hand and thank him for real or imagined favors.

ton, Texas, in 1900. It was supposedly superior to the mayor-council form because each commissioner was directly responsible to the people for the operation of his department. The so-called reform (Jersey City returned to the mayor-council pattern in 1961) won massive approval in a referendum, and candidates blossomed by the dozen for the first election, in the spring of 1913. Wittpenn entered a slate of followers

One promise Hague more than fulfilled was his offer of first-class medical treatment. His multimillion-dollar Medical Center, which dominates the center-city skyline, prompted the slogan: "Have your baby or your operation on Mayor Hague."

Now Hague pulled out all the stops for one of Governor Wilson's pet reform measures—city commission government. This new style in city government had been inspired by the superb job a commission of citizens had done resuscitating hurricane-wrecked Galves-

but did not run himself because he was campaigning to succeed Wilson, now President, as governor. Hague, running for commissioner, turned his campaign into a crusade against the so-called Wittpenn "machine."

The second-ward leader's bellows on

behalf of reform won him wide support. On June 9, 1913, the local *Jersey Journal* ran a cartoon showing the city awakening from a long slumber. Beside it was an editorial urging the voters to "kill machine rule forever." The voters responded by choosing Hague as one of the commissioners. A pioneer Republican reformer, Mark Fagan, ran first with 21,379 votes, and was made mayor, while Hague became commissioner of public safety. Shortly thereafter, the Hudson County Democratic Committee, under Hague's leadership, rescinded an earlier vote endorsing Wittpenn for governor and urged the election of James Fielder, his opponent in the approaching Democratic primary. This about-face meant that Hague was the acknowledged, unopposed leader of the Democratic party in Hudson County.

One of the unrealized dreams of Hague's political life was to create a "Greater Jersey City" out of the hodgepodge of municipalities that made up Hudson County. Besides Jersey City, with about half of the county's 538,000 population, there were Bayonne, at the end of the peninsula formed by New York and Newark bays; Hoboken to the north; and a number of smaller enclaves such as Weehawken, North Bergen, Secaucus, Kearney, and West New York. All of these places could, at times, become very jealous of their independence. That made for political headaches, but it also had its advantages.

The multiplicity of governments, each with its own police, fire, and other city departments, created a remarkable number of political jobs. The county itself, with its courts of justice, its own police department, hospitals, jails, and other institutions, was also a hive of political patronage. Moreover, the man who controlled Jersey City inevitably ruled Hudson County, and with it the grand juries that had the power to investigate graft. The politicians of the smaller cities were therefore almost certain to fall into line behind the Jersey City leader.

The scent of total power inspired Hague to tackle his public duties with passionate ferocity. He needed all the energy he could muster; his new job plunged him into a violent conflict

BY PERMISSION OF NEW YORK *Post*; COURTESY CULVER PICTURES

WHEN GABRIEL BLOWS HIS HORN

with Jersey City's police and fire departments. The police had been a municipal disgrace for decades. Robert Davis had run Jersey City as a wide-open town. Red-light districts flourished, saloons served liquor into the dawn, and gambling was uninhibited. Such an atmosphere made the moral decay of the police force inevitable.

Hague launched an all-out assault on police laxity. His motive was twofold. First, it was vital for him to protect his reform image in the shadow of Mayor Mark Fagan, who had achieved national fame in this role. Second was the opportunity to open an unparalleled number of jobs to his dispensation. As many as 125 men were put on trial in just one day for violating departmental regulations. Hundreds of police officers were ruthlessly demoted or dismissed. Into the decimated ranks Hague poured his tough young Horseshoe followers, from whom he culled an elite squad of plainclothesmen, called Zeppelins, who wove a web of secret surveillance around the entire force. Soon not a cop in the city dared to accept petty graft. They began enforcing for the first time city laws against prostitution and after-hours drinking. Women were barred from every one of Jersey City's thousand saloons, and any saloonkeeper

UPI

When state investigators tried to examine the 1937 election records, Hague's men arranged for the documents to be sealed and the vault guarded by police.

who violated this puritanical ordinance was threatened with fines, loss of his license, and less legal kinds of punishment. The result, to the average voter in Jersey City, seemed almost miraculous. Public Safety Commissioner Hague had literally cleaned up the city.

Hague's organization now demonstrated its political prowess by winning its first county-wide contest: Hague's deputy commissioner of public safety, James F. Norton, was elected to the potent post of surrogate. Next came a more crucial test—the gubernatorial election of 1916. Running with the endorsement of President Wilson, Wittpenn, now Hague's avowed enemy, had won the Democratic nomination for governor. Coolly, Hague reversed the engine of the county Democracy and wrecked Wittpenn by giving him the smallest majority a Democratic gubernatorial candidate had received from the Hudson County bastion in decades —a puny 7,430 votes, in contrast to the 25,959 the organization had rolled up for Governor Fielder in 1913.

Time was running out for the anti-Hague men in Jersey City, and they knew it. The mayoralty election of 1917 found them in a frantic mood. Wittpenn and Mayor Fagan both begged President Wilson for help, but they could not agree on a united front. Wittpenn entered a slate of so-called regular Democrats, and Mayor Fagan headed a group of Republicans. Hague, with a prominent ex-Wittpennite, A. Harry Moore, firmly wedded to his standard, dubbed his Democratic slate "The Unbossed."

Hague and his four candidates won easily. His style of reform—the swept sidewalk, the honest cop, the clean saloon, all of which the citizen could see with his own eyes—had won. The other reformers never had a chance. Moore ran slightly ahead of Hague— 19,883 to 18,648—in the final count. But when the city commission met to organize for the new administration, they ignored the tradition that the man with the most votes had the first call on the mayor's job. In a tumultuous scene in the City Hall council chamber, which was packed with howling Horseshoe supporters, Hague was unanimously elected mayor. Three

35

A NURSERY RHYME

NEW YORK Post CARTOON BY STAN MACGOVERN © 1938, NEW YORK Post CORPORATION

1. This is the house that JACK built.

2. This is the janitor who drags down — twenty-six hundred in Hague's home town — to work in the house that JACK built.

3. This is the porter, at twenty-four, who's supposed to sweep the floor, and help the janitor (hawl hawl hawl) at work in the house that JACK built.

decades would pass before another man stood there to receive similar acclaim.

The man thus poised on the threshold of state power had, at first glance, some curious personal defects. He was still almost totally uneducated; some of his surviving enemies insist to this day that Hague could not read more than the headlines in the daily paper. Immediately after he became mayor he took some lessons in public speaking, but he never mastered the complexities of English grammar. He remained likely to declare: "One hundred ten thousand voters has endorsed my administration," or to remark that the city commission "has went on record" regarding a particular issue. He once called Jersey City "the most moralest city in America." Closing a radio address he said, "And thank you, ladies and gentlemen, for the privilege of listening to me."

Nor was Hague personally popular, much less beloved, in the James Michael Curley *Last Hurrah* tradition. The stern aura of the reformer, the protector, the tough taskmaster who got results, was more in keeping with his personality. Even his closest legal adviser, John Milton, wryly called him "the Commissar."

As the years passed, Hague became more arbitrary about inflicting his likes and dislikes on subordinates. Each year, he took the office workers of City Hall to Dinty Moore's in New York for a banquet. Not a man was allowed to touch a drop of liquor as long as the Mayor sat at the table. Once he left, it was tacitly acknowledged that drinking could begin. In his later years, Hague even treated non-New Jerseyites this way. Once Dan Finn, a powerful Tammany politician, called on Hague for a New Jersey favor. The Mayor was lunching alone in New York City at the Plaza Hotel. Hague asked Finn if he would like to order anything. "I'll have a Scotch and soda," the chieftain said. "Not at my table you won't," snapped Hague.

Hague's taste for personal violence was another unendearing trait. He was prone to punch, kick, and batter people who disagreed with him. He reportedly knocked one of his commissioners, Michael I. Fagen, cold on the mayoral carpet one day in 1929. Once, during one of his long walks around the city (always accompanied by bodyguards, at a discreet distance) Hague called an ambulance to see how quickly it would respond. It took fifteen minutes, and Hague began excoriating the interne in charge. "It took me a while to wake up," the young man said insolently. Hague belted him into the gutter.

He was equally willing to condone violence on the part of the cops. He guaranteed their loyalty by making the police force the largest (for cities of comparable size) and best paid in the country. Jeff Burkitt, a cheerful Alabamian who fought Hague for almost a decade, was beaten up so many times that he finally went to the Mayor, his head wrapped in bandages, to ask Hague to be "a good sport" and let him have two or three street corners where it would be understood that the cops would not club him.

Hague began roaring with laughter. The battered Burkitt looked puzzled. "I'm sorry," the Mayor said, his eyes streaming, "I just can't help it. You look so goddamn funny with all those bandages on your head."

But Hague did not win all his elections with night sticks. Although he obviously enjoyed violence (boxing was far and away his favorite sport), he reserved it for emergencies. The election of 1920 fell into that category. The country was tired of Wilsonian idealism. Even before Election Day, it became obvious that the entire Hudson County ticket was going to go down the drain. An order went out from City Hall—"Save Madigan." Thomas "Skidder" Madigan was an old Horseshoe crony who was blithely running for sheriff of Hudson County, ignoring a disability that would have been considered something of a handicap by the average candidate: the Skidder could not read or write. His campaign slogan was unique, even for Jersey City—"He was good to his mother."

As sheriff, Skidder would control an absolutely vital function in the Hague scheme of things—the selection of grand juries. All other candidates were abandoned to their fates. Using every electioneering technique at their disposal, including physical force, Hague's lieutenants carried Madigan, the lone survivor of that terrible debacle, into office with a majority that was one hundred per cent stolen.

On the other hand, when Hague knew he had an election sewed up, he was a model of decorum. In 1929, Republicans made an all-out effort to unseat him as mayor. On election eve there were frantic predictions that Hague was assembling hoodlums and phony voters by the busload. At the end of the voting day, the Republican prosecutor grudgingly had to admit that it had been the cleanest election in Jersey City in decades. Hague coasted to victory by 25,000 votes.

Contrary to myth, the paper ballot and the graveyard vote did not fully account for Hague's success. Wherever they could get away with it, Hagueites voted the cemeteries and the names of those who had long since moved out of the county. The state's permanent registration law offered an irresistible opportunity for fraud, especially when the local election bureau was lackadaisical about keeping track of the dead and departed. Hague guaranteed their laxity by making sure those appointed to the local election bureau were "Hague Republicans"—men who had nominal allegiance to the GOP but were keenly aware that their jobs had come from Hague. But in the 1940's, when the Republican-controlled state legislature inflicted voting machines and genuine Republican watchdogs in the election bureau, Hague's majorities were almost as huge as ever.

Hague's three decades of success as a political leader were, above all else, a triumph of executive ability. With the same driving energy he had exhibited in cleaning up the police department, Hague completely overhauled the structure of the Democratic organization in Hudson County. Not loyalty alone but also efficiency became the hallmarks of Hague Democracy. The city was divided into twelve wards, and these wards were subdivided into districts. Each ward and each district had a male and a female leader. There were ward committees and district committees. Hague knew from personal observation that thousands of Hudson County residents stayed home on each Election Day. Most of them were immigrants—the Poles, Italians, Czechs, and Slovaks who had followed the Irish into the slums—and they often did not know enough English to comprehend the era's tumultuous politics in the newspapers. Hague grimly decided that these people were going to vote. Whether they had to be bullied or cajoled, bribed or frightened to the polls, they were his secret weapon in Hudson County.

In every election every district was canvassed—which meant that every voter was personally asked to come out and vote on every Election Day. Lists of the aged and infirm were carefully compiled, and fleets of cars were at the disposal of every ward leader, to transport even the dying to the polls. Names were carefully checked off as people entered the polling booths, and the final hours of each Election Day were devoted to telephoning and even visiting those who had not yet voted to ask them why. Ward and district leaders were rewarded—or punished—strictly on the basis of their turnouts.

Simultaneously, Hague never abandoned his clean-city policy. He could boast, with considerable pride, that throughout the twenties, when hoodlums were shooting up Chicago and other cities, no gangster's corpse was found within Jersey City's borders. As usual, Hague's methods were not always orthodox. City detectives, disguised as bums, loitered in the stations of the Hudson & Manhattan Railroad and at the ferry slips. Anyone they considered undesirable was likely to be sent back to New York on the next train or ferry.

Hague's political technique was a blend of violence and benevolence. At Christmastime each ward leader distributed thousands of food baskets to the poor. Every ward had a boat ride or a picnic or both each summer. But for Hague, the ultimate charity was free hospital care. He poured millions into a medical center, hired top-notch doctors to run it, and supervised it in fanatical detail. He maintained a suite of offices there, and was ever roaming the corridors picking up stray bits of paper and checking the meat in the kitchen.

Once a Republican prober accused Hague of allowing the affluent as well as the poor to have their babies and operations free. With oracular sincerity

4. The assistant porter, at twenty-two, has a hell of a time finding things to do, to help the porter, at twenty-four, who's supposed to sweep the floor and aid the janitor (haw! haw! haw!) at work in the house that JACK built.

5. The cleaner also gets twenty-two, to help the assistant porters through the work that they're supposed to do in helping the porter, at twenty-four, who's supposed to sweep the floor and aid the janitor (haw! haw haw!) at work in the house that JACK built.

6. The cleaner's helper gets paid too, eighteen hundred, with nothing to do, but help the cleaner, at twenty-two, who helps the assistant porter too, looking around for work to do in helping the porter, at twenty-four, who's supposed to sweep the floor and help the janitor (haw! haw! haw!) at work in the house that JACK built.

the Mayor proclaimed: "If they say they cannot pay, that is good enough for me.... We do not argue with a sick person."

"If the patient is trying to get something for nothing," the prober demanded, "notwithstanding his ability to pay?"

"My God, he is welcome to be restored to health!"

"At the expense of the other taxpayers?"

"Of anybody, of anybody. When you give me a sick man I will restore him to health at anyone's cost."

It all dovetailed neatly with the reform aura that created Hague's initial power. He was barely ensconced as mayor when he demonstrated that he could war on "the interests" far more ferociously than a Fagan or a Wittpenn. Where previous reformers had raised corporate tax assessments to levels they thought were reasonable and yet would not produce violent counterattack by the companies, Hague went all out. In 1917 and 1918, he increased the tax assessments on the Standard Oil Company from $1,500,000 to $14,000,000, on the Public Service Corporation from $3,000,000 to $30,000,000, and on the railroads from $67,000,000 to $160,000,000. The corporations rushed to the state Board of Taxes and Assessments in Trenton. The board cancelled all Hague's escalations.

Hague furiously denounced the board members as tools of the interests, and summoned his Hudson legions to elect a Democratic governor, who would appoint a new tax board. He soon found his candidate, Edward I. Edwards, president of the First National Bank of Jersey City. Edwards won by 14,510 votes, aided by the huge majority—58,527 to 23,009—Hague delivered for him in Hudson County.

Bucking a national Republican era, Hague proceeded to elect three governors in succession (the law then prohibited a governor from serving two consecutive three-year terms); his third, Jersey City's A. Harry Moore, boomed into Trenton in 1926 atop a Hudson County avalanche of 103,000 votes. In eight short years, Hague had quadrupled the standard Hudson County majority. Even subtracting the extra votes he garnered from woman suffrage, it

Hague's annual itinerary included voyages to Europe in the royal suites of the best liners. His seldom-photographed wife is stylishly attired in 1925.

was still a remarkable achievement.

During this nine-year period, Hague exultantly concentrated on appointing Democrats to the state Board of Taxes and to a breathtaking number of other jobs that the New Jersey governor had in his power. Between 1900 and 1910, the state had espoused the reform idea of the short ballot, and had eliminated scores of jobs that had theretofore been elective. The governor had the power to appoint almost every officer in the state government, ranging from the attorney general and the treasurer down to the prosecutors of the individual counties. There were more than eighty different boards and commissions, plus judgeships in fourteen court systems.

Most important were the judgeships. They were reserved for men with proved loyalty to Frank Hague. The Mayor's attitude toward these vital figures is summed up in an argument he had in the 1940's with Governor Charles Edison when the two men differed over a judicial appointment. Edison insisted that his preference was a man of integrity. "The hell with his integrity, Charlie," Hague roared. "What I want to know is, can you depend on the S.O.B. in a pinch?"

Another politician recalls Hague's wheeling and dealing to execute his greatest judicial coup, the installation of his former corporation counsel,

Most of his time away from Jersey City was spent in Miami, where he lived lavishly and played golf with, among others, theatrical producer John Golden.

Thomas Brogan, as chief justice of the New Jersey Supreme Court. For all Hudson's clout, Hague never won control of the New Jersey legislature; Brogan's appointment had to be confirmed by the Republican-dominated state senate. Hague traded jobs by the dozen to Republican politicians in return for their votes.

The senate confirmed Brogan's appointment. He proved he could deliver in the pinch, more than once. Outraged Republican investigators tried to subpoena the voting records in Hudson County after the gubernatorial election of 1937, another emergency in which Hague needed every nightstick and graveyard vote he could find to squeak A. Harry Moore into his third term as governor. Chief Justice Brogan listened to stories of people being beaten up and thrown out of polling places, of men voting from insane asylums, and solemnly ruled on the great principle of the law, *Quod non apparet non est.* Since there was no evidence of corruption in the election, there was no basis for granting a subpoena of the voting records.

Hague penetrated the Republican party, not only by astute job trading, but also by occasionally helping the Republicans select their candidates. He first performed this bit of legerdemain in the 1928 gubernatorial primary. The man favored to get the Republican nomination was Robert Carey, a former Jersey City judge and a fierce critic of Hague and the organization. On primary day, some 20,000 "instant Republicans" flowered in Hudson County, and not one voted for Carey. All their enthusiasm—and the nomination—went to a colorless state senator from Middlesex County named Morgan Larson.

Worse, the galled Republicans discovered the ploy was perfectly legal. Hague's lawyers had spotted a loophole in the election law that permitted a man who had not voted in a previous year's primary to switch his party affiliation without penalty. Like a shrewd general, Hague had simply ordered 20,000 loyalists to skip a primary and stand by, on reserve status, to name the Republican of his choice.

In the beginning New Jersey Republicans could not quite believe what was happening in Hudson County. The only answer they could produce to match Hague's maneuvers was a gimmick to pin the state closer to the coattails of the national Republican ticket, which still looked like a winner. They called for a referendum to lengthen the governor's term to four years, and to elect him in presidential years. In a special election in September, 1925, the proposal was defeated 200,716 to 135,288. Of the No votes, 100,002 were from Hudson County. This was only 3,000 fewer votes than

Hague usually avoided the spotlight, but when he and Mayor Edward Kelly of Chicago (left) toured the Warner Brothers studio in 1935, they were greeted by, from left, Joan Blondell, Marion Davies, and William Randolph Hearst.

Hudson's huge gubernatorial turnout the next year for favorite son Moore. Such a vote on an issue so tenuous to the average voter struck the state as little short of miraculous. As one politician to another, New Jersey's Republican senator, Walter Edge, congratulated Hague for an unsurpassed performance.

The almost incredible solidarity Hague had created in Hudson County was partly based on his reformer's war with the corporations. It injected a priceless element of drama into the humdrum lives of those nondescript thousands on Jersey City's downtown streets. On their behalf, Hague thundered defiance of the once all-powerful railroads, Public Service, and Standard Oil. He created a kind of inverted arrogance in his followers, the feeling that John L. Sullivan excited with his famous shout, "I can lick any man in the house." With Hague at their head, each election day they marched, like an army with banners, into the heart of the state, flattening those arrogant Protestant Republicans who had for so long looked down their aristocratic noses at the Irish and their fellow immigrants.

Taxes were only one weapon used by Hague in his continual war with the corporations. During the winter of 1926, a coal strike caused severe hardship among Jersey City's poor. Cries for help poured into City Hall. Hague knew, without even bothering to check, that there were thousands of railroad cars full of coal standing in Jersey City's railyards, waiting for shipment across the Hudson River to Manhattan. The denizens of the Horseshoe had stolen their fuel from these cars for decades. The Mayor called the chief of police and ordered: "Don't allow a scuttle of coal to go out of this city."

The coal company screamed that the Mayor was interfering with interstate commerce. The Mayor said he had the authority "by virtue of my office as Mayor."

"That is not enough," shouted the manager of the coal company.

"By the law at the end of a night stick," roared the Mayor. "How do you like that one?"

The coal company capitulated and sent ten tons of coal to each police and fire station, where city residents were able to get it for little or nothing.

Hague's antibusiness stance was a distinct break in the boss tradition in the United States. Most bosses made their money through seemingly legiti-

Jersey Journal

Within ten years of becoming Jersey City's $7,500-a-year mayor, Hague paid out close to $400,000 in cash for real estate, including this $125,000 summer home near the ocean in Deal, a fashionable resort community on the New Jersey shore.

mate business fronts, co-operating behind the scenes with the powerful corporations. Not Frank Hague: his money came from other sources.

Each year, every officeholder in Hudson County had to contribute three per cent of his salary to City Hall, supposedly to finance the organization's political battles. A third or half of every raise a man received went to City Hall. So did perhaps half the salary a man was paid for nominal work on a state board or commission. No accounting was made of this river of cash—which swelled to at least $500,000 and probably $1,000,000 a year.

39

Then there were the real-estate deals. Dummy corporations headed by shadowy figures in New York bought land shortly before Jersey City or Hudson County condemned it, and resold it at fabulous prices. One of these operations cleared a profit of $628,145 between 1919 and 1924.

Most lucrative of all was the gambling take. Among the sports columnists and betting fraternity, Hague's Jersey City quickly became known as "the Horse Bourse." In the downtown tenements, under Hague's careful control, major bookmakers set up a system of telephone and telegraph connections that handled the enormous quantities of off-track betting on races all over America and Canada. Beside this golden stream flowed the by no means inconsiderable pay-offs of the numbers racketeers. These too were carefully controlled by the organization. Finally, each ward was given the O.K. for a carefully regulated number of card and dice games, each of which paid a monthly slice of its "handle."

Hague supported the Democratic presidential candidate, John Davis, in 1924.

Inevitably, Hague's personal habits began to change. He moved out of the Horseshoe into a fourteen-room apartment on fashionable Hudson County Boulevard, bought a mansion in even swankier Deal, on the New Jersey shore, and acquired other property in Jersey City. In seven years he laid out a grand total of $392,910.50 for real estate, a remarkable performance for a man supposedly living on a salary of $7,500.

This, of course, was only the tip of the iceberg, the portion visible in New Jersey. In New York and elsewhere, vastly larger sums of cash were being invested in stocks or stored in savings banks. A still-active Jersey City politician recalls how, as a young man just out of the Army, he got a job in the city finance department. On one of his first assignments he was given an old suitcase and told to make a series of stops at brokerage houses and banks in New York, where the suitcase was taken into back rooms and then politely returned to him, considerably lightened.

"What the hell is in that thing?" he finally asked. "Money," he was told.

But Hague's ostentatious display of wealth was to be his Achilles heel. Each winter he was a familiar figure at Florida's racetracks, where he displayed an almost childish fondness for flashing thousand-dollar bills. Summer cruises to Europe became part of his routine. At World Series games and other major sporting events, the Mayor always entertained a contingent in the more expensive seats. In 1929, a committee from the New Jersey legislature, convened to investigate election irregularities in Hudson County, asked Hague some questions about his personal finances. He declined to answer. He defied not only the committee but both houses of the New Jersey legislature, assembled in righteous panoply.

Hague supported Al Smith in 1928 and was his convention manager in 1932.

The legislature charged him with contempt, and he was still defiant. Eventually, the state supreme court decided in Hague's favor, accepting his lawyers' argument that the legislature did not have the judicial power to probe for felonies: that function belonged to the courts and their grand juries. But it was a barren, legalistic victory. It ruined Hague's image as a reformer forever. The Newark *Evening News* summed up the public sentiment in the state: "If Mr. Hague himself would come clean; if he would tell the truth and shame his enemies with the truth, what a triumph would be his! A man who has nothing to conceal, a man whose life is an open book, does not fall back on right of privacy or other technical safeguards when his reputation is at stake."

There was, at that point, some ground for wondering if Hague could last much longer. The Republican-controlled legislature was still in furious pursuit of him, and a hefty two-fifths of the voters in his Jersey City bailiwick had turned against him in the May, 1929, mayoralty election. *Time* magazine predicted that he would soon imitate several former leaders of Tammany Hall by taking refuge in Europe. Then an event occurred across the river in New York that transformed the politics of the entire nation. The bottom dropped out of Republican prosperity, and with a shock that was felt around the world, the stock market crashed. The gray, dismal years of the Depression settled on the nation. They were made to order for Hague.

As the private sector of the economy shrank, thousands found themselves unemployed, and Hague was transformed from a politician on the run to a titan of steadily swelling power. He alone, by executive fiat, could ignore economic reality and maintain his padded payrolls intact. A city job became not merely a way out of the slums but a source of salvation for those who thought they had achieved the mythical security of the American middle class. Many of the older, wealthier Protestant families, who had been the backbone of Hague's Jersey City opposition, were totally ruined.

His new Depression-spawned power made Hague meaner and tougher. For the next two decades, his operation became an exercise in the retention of power for its own sake. Having double-crossed the two leaders who had given him his start, Hague trusted no one. Phones were tapped regularly. "Every night," declares a man who is still an important Hudson County official, "a police lieutenant sat in the Western Union telegraph office in Journal Square and read every telegram that

Having denounced F. D. R. before the nomination, Hague moved quickly to join up with the victors, a reconciliation that the press viewed with derision.

came in and went out of Jersey City that day." Hague spies in the U.S. Post Office maintained similar surveillance on the mail of all those who were labelled untrustworthy. There were informants in every bank in Jersey City, quick to alert City Hall to any unusual surplus in a man's account.

Throughout the twenties, when Hague had been blasting the corporations, he had maintained a warm alliance with labor unions. Theodore "Teddy" Brandle, head of the Ironworkers Union, loaned Hague $60,000 when the Bureau of Internal Revenue gave the Mayor a tap on the wrist in 1930. Three years later, Brandle was called a hoodlum and a crook by Hague, and driven out of the labor movement. Every other union in Hudson County was invaded by Hague's "reporters" and reduced to docility. "Everything for industry" became Jersey City's slogan, and Hague lured companies to Jersey City by promising them "perfect" labor relations.

Hague was equally adept at instilling fear or proferring favor. "Play ball with me and I'll make you rich," he would tell those who fought him. A distressing number of them took him at his word, and quietly accepted a judgeship or a commissionership in the state, county, or city government. The churches, a potential source of moral censure for an ex-reformer, were mopped up with extensive favor-doing and giving. Hague helped Roman Catholic Archbishop Thomas Walsh of Newark raise millions for Darlington Seminary. The Mayor donated a $50,000 altar to Saint Aedan's, his own parish church. At least fifty-four priests, ministers, and rabbis were on the government payroll as chaplains to hospitals, police, fire, and other city and county departments.

Massive majorities were demanded in every election, no matter how trivial, to awe and discourage potential rebels. The zenith was reached in 1937, when Hague was re-elected mayor for the sixth time, by 110,743 to 6,798. Each year, in a final rally at the uptown auditorium known as The Grotto, Hague would exhort the faithful as if Armageddon were at hand. "Three hundred and sixty-four days a year I work for you," he would cry. "Now this one day I ask you to work for me." In 1941, Hague needed, under the Walsh Act, only 766 signatures to nominate him for his seventh term as mayor. The organization collected 125,371. "It is very gratifying," the Mayor said as truckmen staggered into City Hall with bushels of the signed petitions.

Then there was the ritual of January 1. No matter how hung-over he may have been by year-end whoopee, every faithful job holder dragged his bones into the cold to stand in an immense line, which wound around City Hall three or four times, inching slowly forward into the lobby and up the steps to the Mayor's office. There the Mayor and the commissioners, in morning coats and striped pants, received handshakes and earnest good wishes for the coming year. A man who failed to appear was practically saying that he was no longer interested in promotions or favors. He was all but declaring his intention to leave the city.

Even while Hague thus assumed almost total power inside Hudson County, he revealed a weakness that was to embarrass him and his followers again and again in the next two decades of his reign. He was singularly unable to grasp the psychology of the average voter outside the county.

This defect plus an almost insane arrogance bred by an excess of power might explain why he had Governor Moore appoint thirty-two-year-old Frank Hague, Jr., a likeable playboy who had failed to get through two

Hague made up with the party candidate at a huge rally in Sea Girt, New Jersey.

Hague supported President Truman in 1948, but not before the convention.

41

law schools (yet had miraculously passed the New Jersey bar exam on his first try) to the Court of Errors and Appeals, New Jersey's highest judicial body. Bar associations fulminated, newspapers across the country decried, but Governor Moore only replied: "I know this appointment will make his Dad happy."

On the level of national politics, Hague was even more obtuse. In 1932 he blundered to the brink of disaster by backing Alfred E. Smith against Franklin D. Roosevelt for the Democratic nomination for the Presidency. But there was an explanation for this mistake: sentiment. Hague had been an advocate of the Happy Warrior since 1924, and the grateful Smith had helped make Hague vice chairman of the Democratic National Committee. Nothing stirred Hague more deeply than the Irish clan spirit. Loyalty was one of the few words in the English language that made him choke up. Like the Tammany sachems across the river in New York, he refused to face the facts of the 1928 disaster—Al Smith was simply not presidential timber.

On June 24, 1932, Hague issued a blast against Roosevelt, declaring he could not "carry a single state east of the Mississippi and very few in the Far West. . . ." Since Roosevelt was governor of New York, this exaggeration struck more than a few politicians as ludicrous.

At the convention, Hague was the floor leader of the Smith forces and at an early stage in the struggle exuberantly declared, "We've got them licked." But no southern politician could be induced to try Smith a second time, and among northern Democrats Hague found himself totally out-generalled by a younger, smarter Irishman, James A. Farley of New York.

As Farley said of F. D. R.'s convention victory, "Everyone knew we had just nominated the next President of the United States." No one knew this better than Hague. Even before Al Smith made his peace with Roosevelt at the New York state Democratic convention, Hague had persuaded Farley to bring Roosevelt to Sea Girt, New Jersey, on August 27 with a promise that Hague "would provide the largest political rally ever held in the United States." Commandeering most of the rolling stock of the Jersey Central, plus squadrons of buses and cars, Hague assembled a total of 150,000 faithful. In the little resort town, sixty miles from Jersey City, they swarmed around the summer home of New Jersey's governor and cheered their lungs out for Roosevelt when he appeared on the platform to congratulate "my friend, Mayor Hague," for this overwhelming demonstration of Democratic muscle.

Fighting for his niche in the Democratic party, Hague slammed his Hudson County political dynamo to full throttle and produced an astonishing

UPI

One of Hague's most persistent critics, James F. Burkitt, still managed to get his message across after he was refused a speaker's permit on October 29, 1938.

184,000 votes for Roosevelt on Election Day. The performance swung New Jersey into the Democratic column, 806,000 to 775,000. The victory consolidated Hague's power in the county and the state on a hitherto unparalleled scale. Although Roosevelt piously declined to deal with Tammany Hall, all the federal patronage for New Jersey passed through Hague's City Hall. Some $47,000,000 in W.P.A. funds alone poured into Jersey City, enabling Hague to complete his medical center on a scale so large that the hospital's staff frequently outnumbered the patients.

The argument, fondly repeated by many students of American politics, that the New Deal and its welfare philosophy ruined the old-style political machines simply does not apply to Hague. Roosevelt stuck with him, even when the Mayor fought a tremendous war with the C.I.O. and the nation's liberal establishment in the late 1930's. Hague tried to bar the aggressively independent C.I.O. from his Hudson bailiwick, using the canard that the unionists were "Reds." Norman Thomas, Morris Ernst, and other liberals rushed into the fray. Although at one point a Jersey City police captain told a C.I.O. worker, "We're enforcing a Jersey City ordinance, not the Constitution," the U.S. Supreme Court eventually ruled

New Masses, JUNE 28, 1938

Testifying in defense of his city's laws in a 1938 federal court suit, Hague suggested that native-born radicals should be sent to "a camp in Alaska."

42

Hague considered his battle to keep the C.I.O. out of Jersey City an anti-Communist crusade; the liberal press, however, viewed him as an American Hitler.

that the C.I.O. had the right to distribute literature and give speeches inside Jersey City. In the course of the struggle, the liberals were outraged to discover that Hague's post-office spies were opening their mail. They howled for Hague's scalp, but once more F.D.R. stood by the Mayor. "We had a hell of a time getting Hague out of that one," a Cabinet-level official of the Roosevelt administration told me.

The reasons for Roosevelt's embrace of Hague were twofold. In the early years, there were not enough independent Democrats left in New Jersey to form an anti-Hague wing of the party. Later, Roosevelt needed Hague for his third-term and fourth-term pushes. With Ed Kelly, the boss of Chicago, in happy concert, the "Hague-Kelly axis" was the driving engine of Roosevelt's 1940 steamroller. After Roosevelt was nominated, practically by acclamation, a prominent Democrat ruefully declared: "Mayor Hague has more stuff on the ball than anyone else here in Chicago."

But Hague was to pay a bitter price for this more intimate relationship with Roosevelt. With an artful combination of cajolery and political arm-twisting, the President persuaded Hague to accept Charles Edison, a son of Thomas Edison, the inventor, as the Democratic nominee for governor in 1940. Edison was an independent Democrat who owed nothing to Hague, and he had plainly spent some time in the library reading Wilson biographies. With Hague sitting at his right hand and 150,000 Democratic faithful in the audience at Hague's by now traditional Sea Girt rally, Edison declared: "It is my happy privilege to stand here today and tell you that if you elect me, you will have elected a governor who has made no promises of preferment to any man or group. . . . I'll never be a yes man except to my conscience."

For senator that year Hague also had to accept, on White House orders, James H. R. Cromwell, a millionaire ex-playboy inflated for high office by a tour as minister to Canada. While Edison understandably excited no enthusiasm in Hague, Cromwell had precisely the opposite effect. Throughout the 1930's, while most of the country was in violent reaction against the rich, Hague had been courting their company and imitating their manners. He invited anyone and everyone from the ranks of the well-born to his magnificent Biscayne Bay mansion in Florida. Jersey City clubhouses whispered the story of the day that Deputy Mayor Johnny Malone, in Florida to confer with the Mayor, humbly asked if he could come to one of Hague's splendiferous parties, promising to stand obscurely in the corner and not open his mouth. "I'm sorry, Johnny," said the Mayor, "you just ain't got enough class."

Hague embraced Cromwell with an ardor that made no sense politically. Genial Jimmy had written many books and made scores of speeches in which he had alienated huge blocs of the electorate. He had nicknamed war veterans "the American Pillaging Force" and defined the Constitution as "a millstone around the necks of the American people." He had called for repeal of the National Labor Relations Act and come out in print for birth control. Yet Hague toured New Jersey beside Cromwell, obviously revelling in his company. He was almost delirious with pleasure when he and several select henchmen were invited to Boxwood Manor, an English-style castle in the center of a wooded estate, the property of Mrs. E. T. Stotesbury, widow of a Morgan partner, and Cromwell's mother.

Edison, preaching his independence of Hague, won the governorship handily. Roosevelt also carried the state, but Cromwell stumbled to defeat. As governor, Edison firmly practiced the independence he had preached during the campaign. This soon produced violent hostilities. The Governor, for instance, tried to solve the financial collapse of the state's railroads by forgiving them some $81,000,000 in back taxes. Almost half of this money belonged to Jersey City, and Hague began belaboring Edison for selling out to the interests.

It was like Old Home Week for

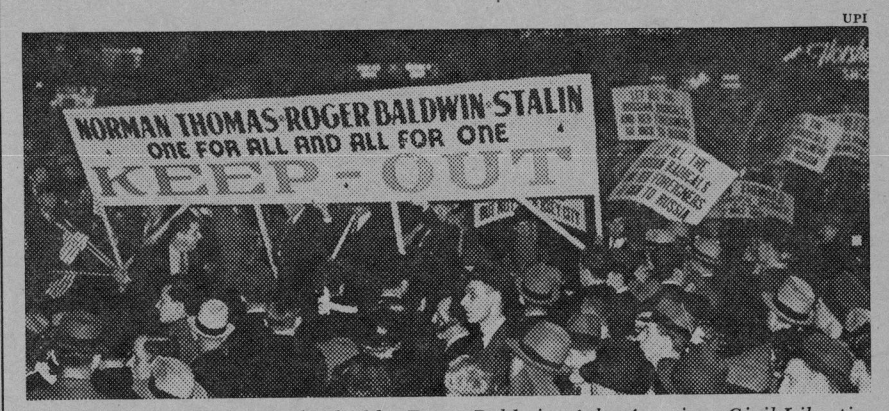

Socialist Norman Thomas, backed by Roger Baldwin of the American Civil Liberties Union, eventually won his right to speak in Jersey City, but not before Hague had turned their names into a pejorative slogan for his "Americanization" campaign.

Hague; it was the heady crusading days of 1920 all over again. The Edison script, which called for a Wilson-style confrontation, ended in political disaster for the Governor. When Edison went out of office, Hague was still state chairman of the Democratic party, vice chairman of the Democratic National

Committee, and as invulnerable as ever in Hudson County. One explanation is that earnest, honest Charles Edison was not Woodrow Wilson. Another, equally valid, is that the dimensions of Frank Hague's power far exceeded that of Wilson's old foe, Boss James Smith.

No one ever fought with Hague and emerged unscathed. When Walter Van Riper became attorney general of New Jersey in 1944, he launched a series of raids on Hague's sacrosanct "Horse Bourse." Within months Van Riper was indicted by a federal jury for kiting checks and for selling black-market gasoline through a service station he partially owned. He was acquitted on

Hague formally installed his nephew, Frank Hague Eggers, as mayor, in name if not in fact, at a massive rally in 1947.

both counts, and there is strong evidence that some of the witnesses committed perjury. But Van Riper, once considered a shoo-in as the next governor, was politically dead.

With "Hagueism" for a rallying cry, the GOP proceeded to elect two governors in a row, for the first time since Hague had come to power. This was a serious blow to Hague. From 1941 to 1949, counting Edison's term, he was voiceless in Trenton. Dozens of key appointments to the state's boards and commissions fell into Republican hands, as the terms of Hague Democrats expired. Deaths and resignations accounted for still more, in both the judicial and executive branches of the government. Worse, a new state constitution, with a provision which would force public officials to answer embarrassing questions, was proposed in 1944. A massive effort by the Hague organization, climaxed by an official denunci-

It's All Done With Mirrors
With Hague no longer on the ballot, his opponents began portraying Eggers as a respectable though impotent puppet.

ation of the document by Archbishop Walsh, defeated this threat temporarily. But it was still very much on the horizon; Republicans and Edison Democrats were beating drums for it with crusaders' fervor.

Within Hudson County, Hague suddenly began having almost as much trouble exerting his hitherto complete control. Insiders have always maintained that the trouble, which started in Bayonne, was Hague's own fault. By now, Hague was spending very little time in Jersey City. When he was not in Florida, he was sojourning in New York at the Plaza. Most of the city's political and economic business was conducted on the telephone, through Deputy Mayor Malone. For too many politicians in the organization, Hague had become a remote figure, no longer to be feared. When a public school was erected in Bayonne, Hague's leaders skimmed off all the gravy for themselves, ignoring the standard distribution that assured each politician a share, however small. Feuding promptly erupted inside the Bayonne organization, and a slate with a "Home rule, not Hague rule" slogan swept all five city commission seats in 1943. Similar revolts exploded in North Bergen and Hoboken during the next four years.

Perhaps, at seventy-one, Hague was weary at the thought of extinguishing these rebellions. They were ominous signs that a new generation of voters had come to maturity, and many of them were not inclined to accept Hague's leadership in the old unquestioning fashion. Jersey City, the heartland of Hague's power, had a similar corps of restive veterans home from the global wars and hungry for a slice of the political pie. Hague's next move seemed to be a major concession to a new era. He announced his resignation as mayor of Jersey City on June 4, 1947.

A magnificent ceremony was staged two weeks later in the auditorium of Dickinson High School, at which Hague handed over the official rule of the city to his nephew, Frank Hague Eggers, the commissioner of parks and public works. Moore and dozens of other politicians whom Hague had elevated to power appeared on the platform to gush forth hours of soggy oratory in praise of his accomplishments. Hague then rose and made it clear that he was *not* resigning as chairman of the Democratic party in the state and county. It suddenly dawned on a lot of people that the great change was really a great smokescreen. The choice of Eggers made Hague's sleight of hand even more transparent. Just to make sure he retained total control, he was ready to risk the hostility that such nepotism was certain to arouse.

The realization was discouraging to more than a few local Democrats, who yearned for relief from Hague's heavy hand. One of the most restless was John V. Kenny, leader of the second ward. Short, balding, and mild-mannered, Kenny was the son of Nat Kenny, the man who had given Hague his start in politics. Kenny was a good leader, who worked at his job in a ward that had been completely transformed since Hague's era; gone were the feuding, brawling Irish, replaced by Poles and Italians and Slovaks. They were intensely devoted to "the Little Guy," as many people called Kenny, for the same reason that Hague's Irish had been devoted to him.

In the light of these undeniable political realities, it was only natural for Kenny to think of himself as Hague's logical successor. But Kenny, a political realist, declined to challenge Hague personally. As a second warder, he was acutely aware of Hague's fondness for retaliating, not merely politically but physically. The Little Guy had no desire to get his head cracked. Better—or at least safer—to wait until the Big Guy was safely planted in Holy Name Cemetery, and then make his move. But the emergence of Eggers as the heir apparent forced Kenny to make a decision. If he wanted to inherit the crown, it was now or never. Quietly, Kenny began making secret trips to Newark to confer with leading Republicans. The only hope of beating Hague was a fusion ticket, fuelled by Republican money.

Hague knew about Kenny's dealing with the opposition almost immediately, thanks to his superb espionage system. He called a meeting of the Democratic county committee and announced that there was a double-crosser in their midst. With special ferocity, Hague read Kenny out of the Democratic party and deposed him as leader of the second ward.

Driven into a corner and made to look not a little like a martyr, Kenny fought back. Grimly he gathered together his ward supporters and a strong cadre of disgruntled young veterans from other parts of the city, and began building his fusion ticket. He made no attempt to surface during the November, 1948, elections. On this, the year of Harry Truman's come-from-behind victory, Hague cracked the whip furiously, and the organization had seldom looked better. Although Dewey carried the Garden State by 86,000 votes, every local Democratic candidate scored a crushing victory.

Earnest, hard-working Frank Eggers and the other commission candidates began making the rounds of the ward clubs and parish houses before Christmas, hitting the opposition of Kenny, who had yet to announce a ticket, and pounding home the achievements of the organization. To those on the outside, it was a very impressive show. But from all over the city, the word from the wards came: it was not working.

The Eggers team orated about the medical center, about the city's vice-free image and low crime rate. The Kenny opposition ignored achievements, issues, and political philosophy and blasted at only one target: Frank Hague. Their argument was simple. Hague was an evil dictator. Eggers was just a stooge. Endlessly they denounced the "Royal Family," condemned "King" Hague's wealth, sneered at his accomplishments, called him an absentee dictator, and proclaimed themselves the Freedom party. They published a Freedom newspaper which mocked the organization with biting humor and wry observation. They published photostats of Hague's bills at Sulka's, showing him spending $75 for a shirt and $25 for silk underwear. They persuaded supporters inside the telephone company to leak the astonishing amounts Hague ran up each month on long-distance calls from his Florida mansion to City Hall. They also shrewdly placed Polish and Italian candidates on their five-man ticket to oppose the organization's all-Irish slate.

More and more men and women of local prominence came out openly for John V. Kenny. Patrolmen in Journal Square directed traffic with their fingers raised in a V for a Kenny victory. Revolt was general among the younger men in the police and fire departments. City Hall itself seethed with malcontents and ambitious minor politicians who saw in a Kenny victory a chance for quick promotion.

Then came a voice from Florida. For months Hague had stayed in his Biscayne Bay mansion, letting Eggers and the other candidates make all the public statements. But now, as the battle roared toward a climax, he seemed to lose faith in the organization's ability to survive without him.

There was a hint of desperation in his announcement that, under his personal leadership, the organization was going to make a supreme effort—a tremendous rally in the heart of Kenny's second ward, the site of the old Horseshoe district. The Friday before the rally, Hague sent letters to over 7,000 voters in the second ward, recounting the story of his association with Kenny. He told how, out of gratitude to Kenny's father, saloonkeeper Nat Kenny of Horseshoe days, he had gotten the young man his first job and had helped him rise in politics. "If now he betrays me," Hague asked, "how can he be trusted not to betray you?"

While his victorious running mates all point to Jersey City, Mayor John V. Kenny pinpoints Florida, where Hague vacationed and where, as Hague's conqueror and the new Hudson sachem, Kenny himself spends much of his time.

Arriving at Eggers' funeral in 1954, a furious Hague pushes away the deputy sheriff who has surprised him with a subpoena in a $3 million "kickback" suit brought by the city employees.

On May 3, the ward clubs formed up outside City Hall at about 6:30 P.M. The orders had gone out to every job holder in the city to be on hand. But many stayed home, deciding that the loss of a job was a less formidable danger than a fractured skull. Hague, his lined, tanned face grimly set, escorted Eggers and the other candidates to the front rank of the parade. With long strides he led them up Grove Street into the second ward—and bedlam.

Six deep, the second warders lined the curbs, screaming contempt and de-

45

fiance at the Boss and his aging battalions. They pelted the marchers with eggs, tomatoes, stones, and chalk powder. Police had to fight to clear a space in front of the speaker's platform.

More than a few of the marchers retreated to the safety of Public School 37's auditorium immediately. The courageous formed up before a flag-draped platform outside the school; around them a mob of thousands surged, bellowing, screaming, sounding horns and cowbells, waving Kenny placards and streamers.

The police cordoned the platform, and Hague, Eggers, and the other candidates stepped out before the crowd. Eggs spattered them. The derision rose to an enormous crescendo. Eggers tried to speak. He went on for a few sentences, then stopped in despair. He could not even hear himself. With a shrug he motioned to the others to leave the platform.

The commission candidates filed off, but Frank Hague did not move. For a moment he stood alone, his face a mask of suppressed fury. Then he strode to the edge of the platform and glared down at the shrieking mob. For more than three decades Frank Hague had ruled them. He had fought those who opposed him with ballots and with clubs and fists. And he had won every time. Remembering, they suddenly shut their mouths.

For a long, hushed moment they stood facing each other. Then a small thin man in the first row sprang forward. A "Down with Hague" sign on a long pole swung toward the Boss, twisting and whirling like a crashing kite. Hague had to step back to avoid it, and in the same instant the man screamed:

"G'wan back to Florida!"

Hague almost choked with fury. Smashing aside the sign, he pointed down at the culprit.

"Arrest that man!"

He was speaking to the cordon of police around the platform. For too many years in Jersey City those words had been the signal for swinging clubs, the crunch of wood on bone.

The man fell back, cowering. The crowd held their breath. Then people realized that the police were not moving. Every policeman in the cordon was anti-Hague. Quite logically they had decided they had no obligation to obey orders from the *ex*-mayor of Jersey City.

The crowd exploded into a howl that dwarfed all their previous efforts. Hague stood staring at them. For a second something close to shock was on his face. Then he turned and stalked stoically off the platform.

Incredibly, the disaster in the second ward did not make Hague or Malone realize that the organization was in deep trouble throughout the city. They wrote off downtown and, with an irony that only those who understood Hague's history would appreciate, placed their hopes on the uptown wards where the middle class had looked down their noses at Hague and his Irish forty years ago. On Election Day, Kenny revealed how thoroughly he had studied Hague's tactics. His workers made the same heroic effort to get out their vote, matching the organization car for car, telephone call for telephone call. As many as forty-one watchers were on duty in each of the polling places, making it impossible for Hague to spring any of his old rough-and-tumble tactics.

Most important, the Kenny organization had unprecedented amounts of money to spend. The going rate in Jersey City had long been five dollars a vote. This was always dispensed freely, especially in the poorest sections of the city. Hague's ward leaders were soon deluged with frantic pleas for help from their district leaders. They simply could not match the Kenny prices, and the sums dispensed by City Hall to each ward for this purpose were soon exhausted. At 1 P.M., the leader of the sixth ward phoned Malone at City Hall. "Johnny," he said, "I've got to have ten thousand dollars right away. They're paying fifteen dollars a vote and they're murdering us."

"The hell with them," Malone rasped. "We're not goin' over five dollars a vote and that's final. It'll give them bad habits."

With a curse the ward leader slammed down the phone. Then he called the ward's chief bookmaker (and his best friend), George Ormsby. "Can you get me ten grand right away?"

"Come down and pick it up," Ormsby said.

Before the polls closed, the $10,000 was gone, plus several thousand dollars of the ward leader's own money, which he always kept in reserve on Election

Less than seven years separated the symbolic burial of Hague's rule in 1949 and the actual demise of Jersey City's longtime boss. Yet twelve years after he was rejected by the voters, his legacy continued—in such visible forms as the peeling painted legend (opposite) on a slum tenement near the Holland Tunnel, and, less tangibly, in the insular political attitudes that still set Hudson County apart from the rest of the state of New Jersey.

46

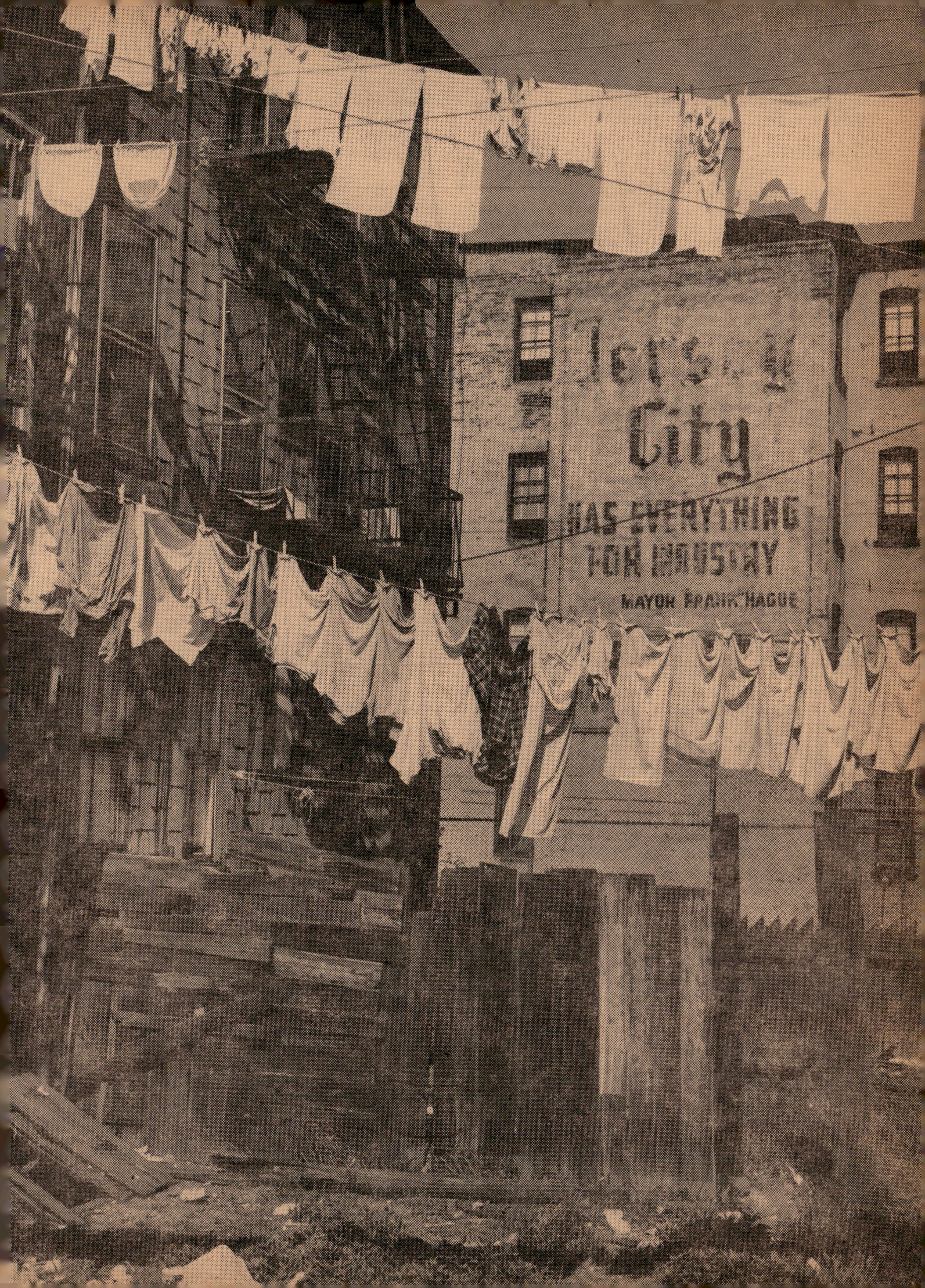
City
HAS EVERYTHING
FOR INDUSTRY
MAYOR FRANK HAGUE

Day. He should have saved it. At nine o'clock that night, the stunning news came over the radio. Kenny had won by 22,000 votes. He had carried every ward but one—the sixth.

A vast mob of Freedom ticket supporters snake-danced through the downtown streets carrying a coffin labelled "The Hague Machine." Kenny and several of his lieutenants stormed into City Hall, hoping to seize incriminating records. But the organization had known for hours that the election was lost, and there was nothing but charred scraps of paper in the furnace room. The vault in the mayor's office was empty. Earlier, according to several reliable witnesses, two police captains had helped lug suitcases filled with cash down to the vault of the First National Bank. The Kenny men did discover two thick ledgers, containing the names of more than 17,000 citizens who were politically unreliable, with careful comments written beside each name, based on reports from district leaders and other members of Hague's espionage system.

Kenny was in charge of City Hall, but Hague was still very much a factor on the political scene. His men controlled most of the county government. Moreover, there was a gubernatorial election coming up in November, 1949, and Hague had found his strongest candidate in years. He was Elmer Wene, a popular three-term congressman and millionaire chicken farmer from southern New Jersey. The combination of Hague and Wene seemed unbeatable.

With the irony that keeps recurring in Hague's story, Kenny found himself confronted with a situation similar to the one Hague had faced when he seized power in 1913. Then, Hague's chief rival, Wittpenn, was running for governor. Kenny knew that if Wene won he would immediately appoint a Hague prosecutor in Hudson County. With Hague already in control of the grand jury, it would be only a matter of months before most of Kenny's administration was in jail.

After a long strategic silence, Kenny announced that he was for Wene. But there was not an iota of enthusiasm in his endorsement. Meanwhile, Hague made an almost incredible blunder in

Mr. Fleming, a frequent contributor to our pages, is a native of Jersey City, where his father, the late Sheriff Thomas ("Teddy") Fleming, was the leader of the sixth ward.

his final pre-election speech. "We'll be back in the driver's seat in Trenton in January," he thundered. Instantly, the Republicans seized on their old "Beat Hague" battle cry, and Alfred Driscoll, fighting to be the first governor to succeed himself (as permitted by the new state constitution of 1947), made it the theme of his final campaign speech.

Wene lost by 70,000 votes. For the first time since 1920, Hudson County went Republican. Kenny had quietly reversed his political engine, just as Hague had done to Wittpenn in 1916. On election night, Hague resigned as state and county leader of the Democratic party. The long reign was over.

Hague clawed desultorily at Kenny for the next few years, until Kenny resigned as mayor and, eventually, sought refuge in the less visible role of Democratic county "leader," a position he still maintains. Neither temperamentally nor politically was Kenny capable of asserting Hague-size power. He has been content to remain an easygoing, behind-the-scenes leader in the Robert Davis tradition.

As for Hague, he shuttled between Florida and his Park Avenue apartment, an outcast from the state he had

PM, SEPTEMBER 2, 1941

once ruled. With the encouragement of the Kenny regime, job holders banded together and filed suit to recover the estimated $15,000,000 paid by three-per-centers over the decades. Hague had to stay out of New Jersey to avoid an always-waiting subpoena in this litigation, which never came to trial.

In some ways, his exile from Jersey City hurt Hague more than his loss of power. He had often said, "In the Horseshoe I was born, in the Horseshoe I will die." He had apparently envisioned a serene old age, surrounded by another generation of loyal Democrats to whom he could be the paterfamilias he never was in his years of action. A glimpse of this sense of loss comes from an old City Haller whom Hague used to call in the middle of the night during those last years. "Billy," he would say, "I can't sleep." He would then express anguished concern over a family whose father or brother he had ruined or maimed in earlier years. "Go down now and ask them if they're all right, if they want anything."

"My wife used to think I was crazy," says the storyteller, "but I'd get up, put on my clothes, and go down and see them, and tell them why I was there. Not once did any one of them ever ask for help. Sometimes they slammed the door in my face. Other times they'd just say, 'We don't want anything from him.'"

On January 1, 1956—the annual holiday on which he used to hold regal court in City Hall—Frank Hague died at his Park Avenue apartment of complications of pneumonia and arthritis. Only then did he return to Jersey City. At Lawrence Quinn's funeral home he lay in state for two days. Then eight professional pallbearers hefted the seven-hundred-pound hammered-copper casket and carried it out to a solemn high funeral mass at Saint Aedan's Church. There was only a small crowd in the street. One elderly woman stood holding an American flag and a crudely lettered sign: "God have mercy on his sinful, greedy soul."

A reporter asked a funeral-home aide why there were so few flowers. A true citizen of Jersey City, the aide shrugged. "When the Big Boy goes," he said, "it means he can no longer do anything for anybody."

The KEEPER of the KEY

"Granther" Sweeney worked on the railroad—and if duty demanded it, he'd rather fight than switch By MILTON SWEENEY COLWELL

My maternal grandparent, Patrick Sweeney, was indeed a giant among men. To me he was Thor, Atlas, Hercules, Paul Bunyan, and Saint Patrick, all rolled into one. When I knew him, back in the eighteen nineties, he was very old and nearing the end of his time. Still, he was straight as a rod, his lionlike head topped by a mass of rumpled hair, once red but by then a snowy hue. Steel-blue eagle eyes peered keenly from under heavy, frosty brows; a full white beard, worn long but with no mustache, framed his rugged face.

Standing six feet and seven inches, "Granther" had shoulders of yardstick span. Even then, approaching ninety years of age, he was amazingly strong, and I could well believe the stories I heard of his fantastic physical feats when he was younger. During the years 1846 to 1851, Patrick Sweeney had labored mightily in the building of the first railroad along the east-bank, water-level route of the Hudson River from New York to Albany, a distance of some hundred and forty-three miles. Thereafter, he became a railway switchman on the Hudson River Rail Road, as it was then known.

Thus it happened that on a sunny morning in April, 1862, Granther was on duty as a switchman at the little river town of Stuyvesant Landing, about twenty miles south of Albany. Despite the turmoil of the Civil War, this was a quiet job, permitting meditation and extracurricular interests. For as a rule there were but two trains north and two south during a twelve-hour stretch of duty, plus occasional wartime specials.

Granther often remarked that this particular April morning was extra fine and quiet. The old Hudson was unrippled, smooth and calm at high tide, reminding him of the River Shannon and the Lakes of Killarney, which he had known in his boyhood. So, Granther said, he just sat in the sun near his switch shanty, smoking his clay pipe and watching the river, especially where a big sturgeon had jumped and splash-landed in the east channel, starting a great, rippling circle on the surface of the water. Granther's sharp eyes had also spotted a fine stick of timber afloat in the stream. Why not, he thought, try for the sturgeon? The least he could do would be to salvage the drifting plank while he was at it.

But wait—duty came first! The southbound morning train from Albany would soon be along. Granther must switch it from its arrival track over to another, and send it on its way to New York. This waiting, he grumbled to himself, might make him miss his try for that gambolling sturgeon out there; he might even miss that fine piece of timber.

Was the train late? No, there it came, chuffing along toward the switch, its whistle tooting. A double set of rails led south from Albany; from Stuyvesant Landing to New York there was only a single track with occasional sidings to allow north- and southbound trains to pass each other. With more haste than usual, Granther opened the switch between the No. 2 track and the single line of rails.

After the train had gone, Granther closed and reset the switch in neutral, locking it tight and noting that the red-target danger signal was showing. Then, going to his train-sheet log, he entered therein the hour and minute of the day, and the engine number of the southbound train. Likewise, and most important as later events proved, he noted in his log that the train's engine carried no flags to indicate that any extra section or special train was following in its wake.

Now, his duty done for a while, Granther was free to give his attention to the river, its now ebbing tide prac-

Railroads were first used for large-scale transportation of soldiers and equipment in the Civil War. Above, a troop train is abou[t

tically lapping at his feet. First, he got out his heavy hook and line and baited it well with a thick slab of fat, raw bacon. Then, after knocking the hot dottle from his pipe and spitting on his hands in anticipation, he launched his flat-bottomed skiff and rowed rapidly out into the river, trailing behind him the fat bacon bait intended for the sturgeon.

Soon he was well out into the swiftly moving ebb tide of the east channel. Sure enough, there was his prized stick of timber drifting along to meet him. He made it fast to the skiff with a loop of rope, meanwhile looking about him for signs of the leaping sturgeon.

No fish was in sight—but suddenly his wandering gaze fastened with disbelief upon a plume of engine smoke approaching along the shore line from the north.

An extra train, southbound—and he not at his post! Grabbing the two oars, Granther put his powerful back and arms to work, making the skiff fairly leap from the water. Damn that southbound train that passed a while ago! It hadn't carried any flags for this following special. Now, unless he could beat the second train to the switch, he was indeed in trouble!

Rowing hard and watching, over his shoulder, the oncoming plume of smoke, Granther got within a hun-

50

depart from a loading station near a "volunteer refreshment saloon" maintained in Philadelphia for men going to the front.

dred yards of shore; he began to feel that he had won the race. At that precise moment the giant sturgeon chose to strike the trolling bacon bait.

Ordinarily, Granther would have drawn his boat hand-over-hand along the heavy troll line right up to the madly plunging fish and stunned it with a blow from a pick handle that he carried for the purpose. But time was fast running out. He thought of chopping the fish loose with his boat hatchet, and also cutting the line to the timber he had salvaged. But such wasteful action was against Granther's nature.

So, bending even more strongly to his oars, with the hooked and struggling sturgeon and the heavy plank acting as stubborn kedge anchors against his aching muscles, Granther finally managed to beach his boat. The unexpected special train was just screeching to a halt in front of the closed switch, sparks and flaming cinders belching from its cone-shaped stack, its brass bell clanging, its shrill whistle tooting peevishly. Heads appeared at the windows of all fifteen wooden cars. They were soldiers' heads, and Granther realized what this was all about: it was a special troop train taking recruits south for the Union armies.

The soldiers were shouting, whistling, singing, and

51

making other cheerful noises; but the officer in charge —a "big man with whiskers," Granther recalled—was not in a cheerful mood. He climbed out of the train and confronted Sweeney, who was now standing beside his switch like a large-sized Horatius at the bridge.

"What does this mean?" thundered the officer. "Don't you know that these are Federal troops, under orders from Washington to proceed to New York without delay? What do you mean by stopping this train?"

Clearly, thought Granther, the officer was unaware that only a single track led south from the switch—or that the regular northbound train was due to come up that track very shortly. He would make the matter plain. "The train ahead carried no signal for yez," he said. "And there bees an up train on its way."

The point did not register. "Unlock that switch instantly," commanded the officer; and he drew his sword. "Not a moment's delay, now! Unlock it!"

"I'll not," said Granther.

The officer swung a good kick at the switch padlock —but all it did was to break the high heel off one of his boots so that, as Granther told the story, "he limped around like his leg was shot, cursing a blue streak." Three soldiers, under orders from the swearing officer, started banging away at the lock with their musket butts; nothing happened. It was known later that a twenty-gallon keg of rum had been rolled aboard the train at Albany; Granther (who was himself a teetotaler) said that the men "smelt of likker to the breath" and aimed their blows haphazardly.

But now things took an ugly turn. The officer demanded the switch key, and when Granther refused it, four soldiers took to pummelling his ribs with their gun butts. Switchman Sweeney was having none of that: with each of his two long arms he rammed two heads together, and all four soldiers went down, their bayoneted guns clattering.

The odds were impossible, however. A dozen recruits now swarmed over Granther, pulling him down, and despite his flailing arms and legs they managed to pin him across the rails in front of the switch. Prodded by several bayonets, he got to his feet and was forced into his shanty, where the officer again demanded the key. Granther again refused, of course—but then, with bayonet points coming through his clothing and actually drawing blood, he submitted to a search. They found the switch key on a finely woven eel-skin thong around Granther's neck, buried in the thick mat of his red chest hair.

It looked as if the jig was up—and still Granther's straining ears did not hear the sound they eagerly waited for: the whistle of the oncoming northbound express. He made one last try. With a lurch of his huge shoulders he broke one arm free from his captors, ignoring the painful rip of a bayonet point across his belly as he moved. He grabbed the key from the soldier who was holding it, ripped it off the eel-skin thong, and flung it through an open window. With much satisfaction, amid the shouting, shoving soldiers, he watched it fall into the riprap of rubble lining the railroad right of way.

And just at that moment there came the high-pitched, whippoorwill whistle of the northbound express! The fracas came abruptly to a halt as everyone stared with sudden comprehension down the stretch of track leading south. There came the express around the bend, and it took little imagination to guess what would have happened if Granther had let the troop train through the switch and onto that single track a few minutes earlier.

Granther said that the commandant of the train, the "big man with whiskers," never apologized or said a word of any kind to him—"just gimped away in his high boots with his one heel." But some of the enlisted men were ashamed, apologizing and offering him drinks from their canteens—whether of rum or water he didn't know or care.

For in Granther's opinion, all of them were lunkheads—even the Irish among them! Why hadn't they smashed the switch lock with the big sledge hammer in his shanty? For that matter, why hadn't they found the spare key, only partly hidden in its cranny between two shanty boards? Farm boys is what they were! Farm boys and lunkheads—and lucky for them they were, or the northbound express would've made matchwood out of them!

Well, the ruckus was over, anyway. Granther took the spare key from the shanty, unlocked the switch, and set it for the waiting northbound train to proceed to Albany; he made the troop train wait until he was good and ready. Then he let it pull off the No. 2 track and head south on the single track, waving it past not in his regular manner, but with certain disdainful gestures peculiar to railroad men. He got a ragged cheer from the soldiers in return.

Feeling considerably scratched and bruised, Granther retrieved the key he had tossed out of the window, hung it around his neck, and considered what to do next. The river looked very cool and pleasant, and he had just time for a swim before the next train was due. He was up to his neck in the refreshing water before the thought hit him: the boat! His fine bit of a skiff, with that grand timber and sturgeon hanging onto it! The tide had carried it out; he'd lost the boat!

Striking out in a desperate flurry, he soon cleared a projecting point of land. Ah, there she was, his fine beauty of a skiff! She was riding high and handsome, not more than a quarter mile away, swinging lazily in an offshore eddy. In a few minutes, Granther was hauling himself over the side of the skiff, naked as the day he was born, but proud and pleased at having recovered his craft. Moreover, the big stick of flotsam timber still bobbed at its tether, and the great hooked sturgeon was moving only feebly at the end of the trolling line. Granther pulled the exhausted fish in and dispatched it with one quick blow of his fist.

Rowing back to shore with his trophies, he realized that he had missed his dinner. The Devil take those soldiers! They'd trampled his dinner pail when they tore up his switch shanty. Well, he'd soon be home and eating a good hot meal. Beaching the skiff and tying it well to a willow tree, Granther trimmed, skinned, and cleaned the big sturgeon, washing out the carcass and stretching it on the salvaged plank to drain. Then, dressed again in his red flannel shirt, pants, and boots, he filled his pipe and relaxed on the beach facing the river, puffing slowly and thinking about the events of the day.

The afternoon trains came and went without incident. Across the Hudson, the shadows gathered on the green, rolling hills of Greene County, reminding him as so often before of old County Donegal in Ireland. His night relief man turned up on time, and after half an hour spent telling the story of the troop train, the timber, and the sturgeon, Granther headed for home. On one shoulder he carried fifty pounds or more of salvaged plank, with the big sturgeon on top of that.

On the way home, of course, he must stop here and there to retell in graphic detail the day's happenings, meanwhile slicing off big chunks of sturgeon for awe-struck friends and neighbors. So he got home at midnight, to a cold supper—with a bare plank, all the sturgeon gone.

But that wasn't really the end of Granther's big day. Apparently, on the way to New York, the officer in charge of the troop train had time to think the whole thing over. He reported the episode truthfully to the stationmaster in New York, and the story soon got around. One day, a few weeks later, Patrick Sweeney, switchman, received from Samuel Sloan, president of the Hudson River Rail Road, a bank draft for $1,000. Closely following this stunning award—for it was a very large amount in those days—came a day when Mr. Sloan's private car rolled up to Granther's switch shanty. The two big men shook hands, had dinner in the private car, and discussed the troop-train matter in detail. Granther even told about the the sturgeon and the timber. Before they parted, Mr. Sloan asked for the old brass switch key—in fact, he took it with him, promising to return it later. Grandfather Sweeney lived for a long time after that, and in mighty good health, too. Still on duty as a switchman in his mid-eighties, he was a kind of living legend in his part of the country, "able to endure [said a newspaper account in 1890] more hard work and more fatigue than any railroader on the line, without reference to age or physique."

When he finally died in 1898 at the age of ninety-four, the whole town of Stuyvesant Landing turned out for the funeral, and people came from many miles away to pay their last respects. There was a wake—the kind Granther would have liked, with plenty of food and drink, cigars, and a great bowl of loose tobacco for men to fill their pipes from. It went on all night, and many a story was told and retold—including, you may be sure, the story of Granther and the troop train. And when he was laid to rest in his big oaken casket in the cemetery, he had around his neck the finely woven eel-skin thong with the switch key on it, just as he had worn it for forty years. It had long since come back, gold plated, from Mr. Sloan; and on it there had been engraved these words: "To Patrick Sweeney, Switchman, HRRR, 1862, A Brave Man, Keeper of the Key, in Honor, Loyalty, and Devotion to Duty."

"Granther" Sweeney, looking hearty in 1890, when he was well over eighty years of age

---

Mr. Colwell, formerly a mechanical engineer, died in 1967. In preparing this narrative about his maternal grandfather he was assisted by his brother, Robert Emmett Colwell, a retired army officer who lives in Stuyvesant, New York.

During World War I Childe Hassam painted New York in all its patriotic glory

THE BANNER YEARS

By DAVID G. LOWE

The First World War was a battle of banners, a conflict in which the French Tricolor, the British Union Jack, the red, white, and blue Russian ensign, the black, red, and gold imperial German standard, and America's own Old Glory seemed, in the eyes of all they summoned, to emblazon their nation's righteousness.

In this whirlwind of patriotism the artists of the world were not about to be left standing in the trenches. If the Duchess of Portland could pack parcels for Queen Alexandra's Field Force Fund and the Countess Manon von Dumreicher give 5,000 cork legs for maimed soldiers in the Austrian military hospitals, the artists certainly must do something. Very early in the war the governments of Great Britain, Canada, France, and Australia began sending famous painters to the front to cover all phases of the conflict; the list included John Singer Sargent, Sir William Orpen, Sir John Lavery, Wyndham Lewis, and Muirhead Bone.

America was late in getting into the fight; but when it did go "over there," it went with a bellicose enthusiasm that matched that of any enemy or friend. New York City had long been a center of sympathy for the Allied cause; one of the first acts of Mayor John Purroy Mitchel in the spring of 1917 was to proclaim Fifth Avenue "The Avenue of the Allies" and to suggest that appropriate flags be displayed. The response was immediate; the next day the *New York Times* had no less than eight advertisements for flags. "Show your colors," one suggested, but there was another one which would have shocked Americans of an earlier generation; it offered "Union Jacks by the yard." For as it developed, the Mayor's proclamation quickly led to the designation of various blocks to honor the different Allies. It is no exaggeration to say that the appearance of this international rainbow symbolized the entry of America into the great world; this massive fluttering of the banners of a dozen nations on the main street of our largest city forecast the death of American isolationism.

The artists of America were no less anxious than others to make their contribution to the war effort. In May, 1917, a huge exhibition of paintings was held in New York: they were contributed by artists and were to be sold for war relief. One of the canvases was given by Childe Hassam. It was an unmartial New England scene; but before the war was over, the conflict would provide Hassam with the finest subject of his career. It was a subject far from the bloody trenches of France, for the United States, unlike the other Allies, did not send painters to cover the war. Hassam's theme was New York, particularly Fifth Avenue, panoplied like a dreadnaught prepared for an admiral's review.

Childe Hassam's New York flag paintings represent one of those fortunate meetings of talent, subject, and conviction. Born in 1859 near Boston, the painter grew up with a

TEXT CONTINUED ON PAGE 58

Above: The first of Hassam's flag series, Just Off the Avenue, Fifty-third Street, *May, 1916. The church is Saint Thomas' Episcopal; the brownstones are the site of the Museum of Modern Art. Right:* Allies Day, May, 1917, *looking north on Fifth Avenue, with Saint Thomas' and the Gotham Hotel on the left.*

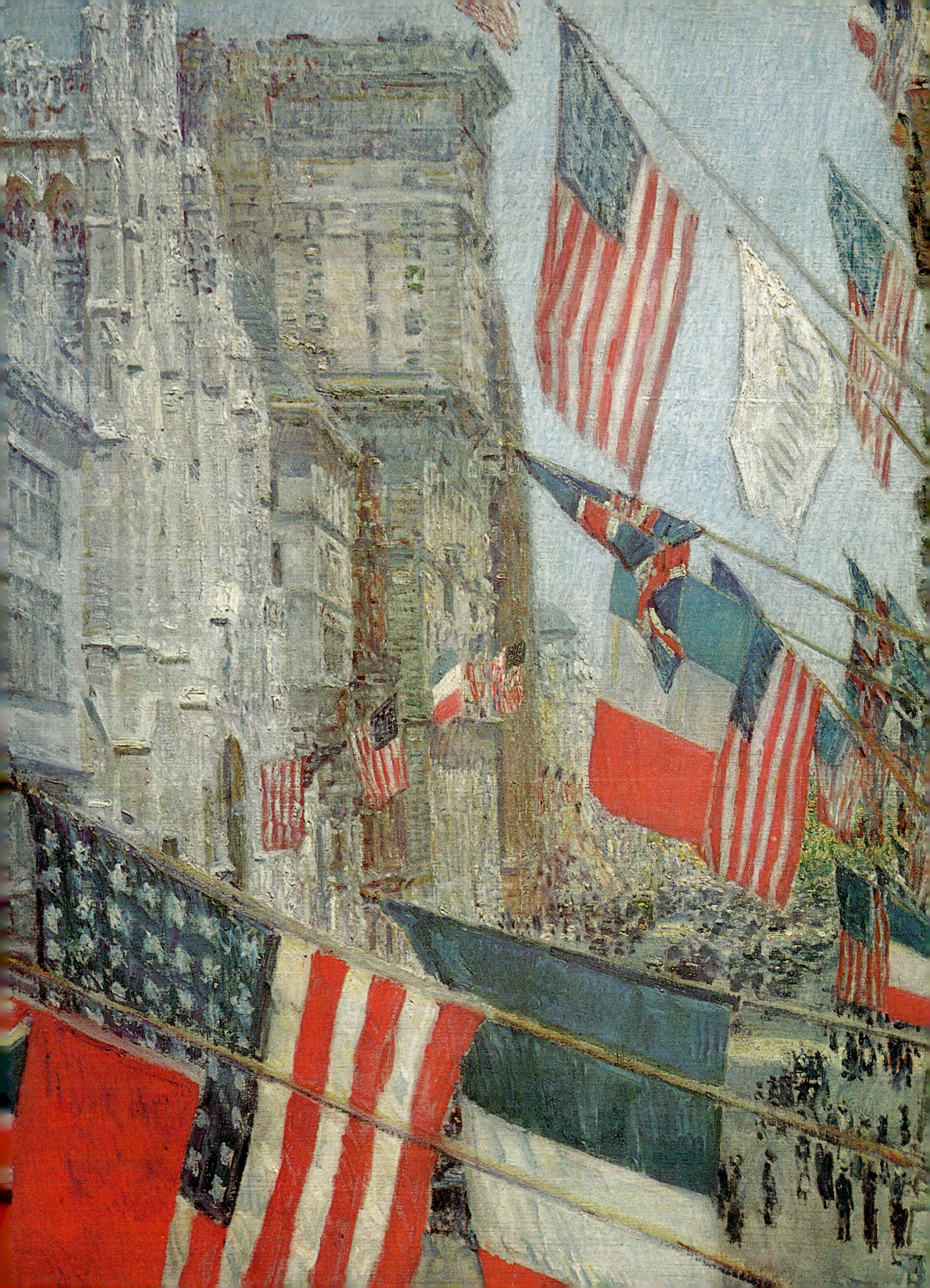

COLLECTION OF MR. AND MRS. IRVING MITCHELL FELT

In Allied Flags, Union League Club, 1917 *Hassam painted a stronghold of pro-Allied feeling in New York. During the great Fifth Avenue "preparedness parade" of May 13, 1916, this Republican citadel at Fifth Avenue and Thirty-ninth Street was festooned with flags and displayed a large electric sign proclaiming "Absolute and Unqualified Loyalty to Our Country." The pa-*

rade, which featured a patriotic women's division, two hundred brass bands, and sixty-three marching groups, marked the beginning of the flag mania on the avenue. Almost every window along the route of march showed an American flag; a reporter estimated their number at half a million. The man with a portfolio just below the British and French flags is Hassam himself.

Above: Union Jack, April Morn, 1918 *commemorated the first anniversary of the United States entry into the war. Left:* The French Block, 1918, *a show of Franco-American solidarity. Below:* Italian Day, May, 1918. *Opposite:* Victory Day, May, 1919, *a colorful welcome for returning U.S. troops.*

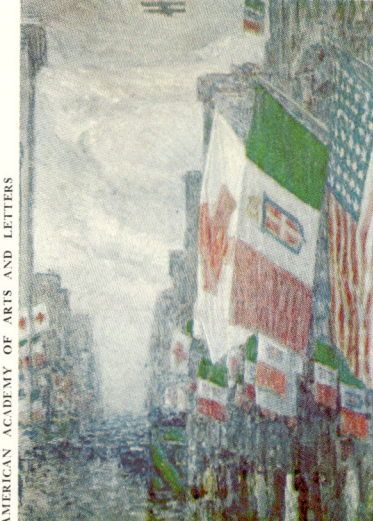

strong feeling for his native land. This patriotic pride he expressed in a letter to Robert Louis Stevenson: ". . . my ancestors fought in every war . . . for human liberty. Stephen Hassam . . . was a powder boy at Bunker Hill, and lived to bury a son who was killed at Malvern Hill in our Civil War. They lie side by side in the old town of Charleston, New Hampshire; John Hassam, age 21, Stephen Hassam, age 100."

After his marriage Hassam went, in 1886, to Paris, where he studied for three years and came under the influence of Monet and the French impressionists. In 1889 he returned to America and settled in New York, where the lively brush strokes and bright clear colors of city scenes such as *Washington Arch in Spring* and *Fifth Avenue in Winter* earned him the title of "the American Impressionist."

It is not surprising that the movement of multicolored flags against static buildings should have attracted a painter of a school that had an almost scientific interest in the components of color and the effects of changing light. As early as 1890, in a picture titled *The Country Fair: New England,* Hassam had painted an American flag against a severe white church front. And in *July 14, Rue Daunou,* a Bastille Day scene in Paris painted in 1910, he had depicted waving flags in a crowded urban setting. Thus it was natural that the Avenue of the Allies, with its brilliant decorations for Liberty Loan drives, Home Defense parades, the Red Cross, and visiting Allied dignitaries like Marshal Joffre and Arthur Balfour, should have become Hassam's supreme theme.

On November 15, 1918, four days after the armistice, New York's Durand-Ruel Galleries, one of the major dealers in impressionist art, held an exhibition of Hassam's flag paintings. They numbered twenty-three, though he painted one more in 1919. In 1922 at the Corcoran Gallery in Washington nineteen of the paintings were shown, and at that time several critics expressed the hope that the series would be kept together and exhibited as a memorial of the Great War. But nothing was done, and by the time of Hassam's death in 1935 almost half of the flag paintings had been sold and scattered. He bequeathed the remaining fourteen —along with a large collection of his other work—to the American Academy of Arts and Letters, with the stipulation that they be sold and the income used to buy the works of young American and Canadian artists for presentation to museums in the United States and Canada. Since that time the academy has disposed of all but two of the flag paintings.

In the fall of 1968, to commemorate the fiftieth anniversary of the armistice, the Bernard Danenberg Galleries of New York exhibited eleven of the flag paintings. There once again could be seen these colorful reminders of a time when flag burnings were unthinkable, an era when the French ambassador to Russia, Maurice Paléologue, watching the Union Jack hoisted up beside the French Tricolor and the Russian imperial standard after the British had joined the war against Germany, could write in his diary: ". . . the flags of the three nations blend eloquently. Composed of the same colors, blue, white and red, they are a picturesque and striking expression of the coalition." Fortunately, when the time came, Old Glory blended beautifully into the color scheme. It was indeed a war of banners.

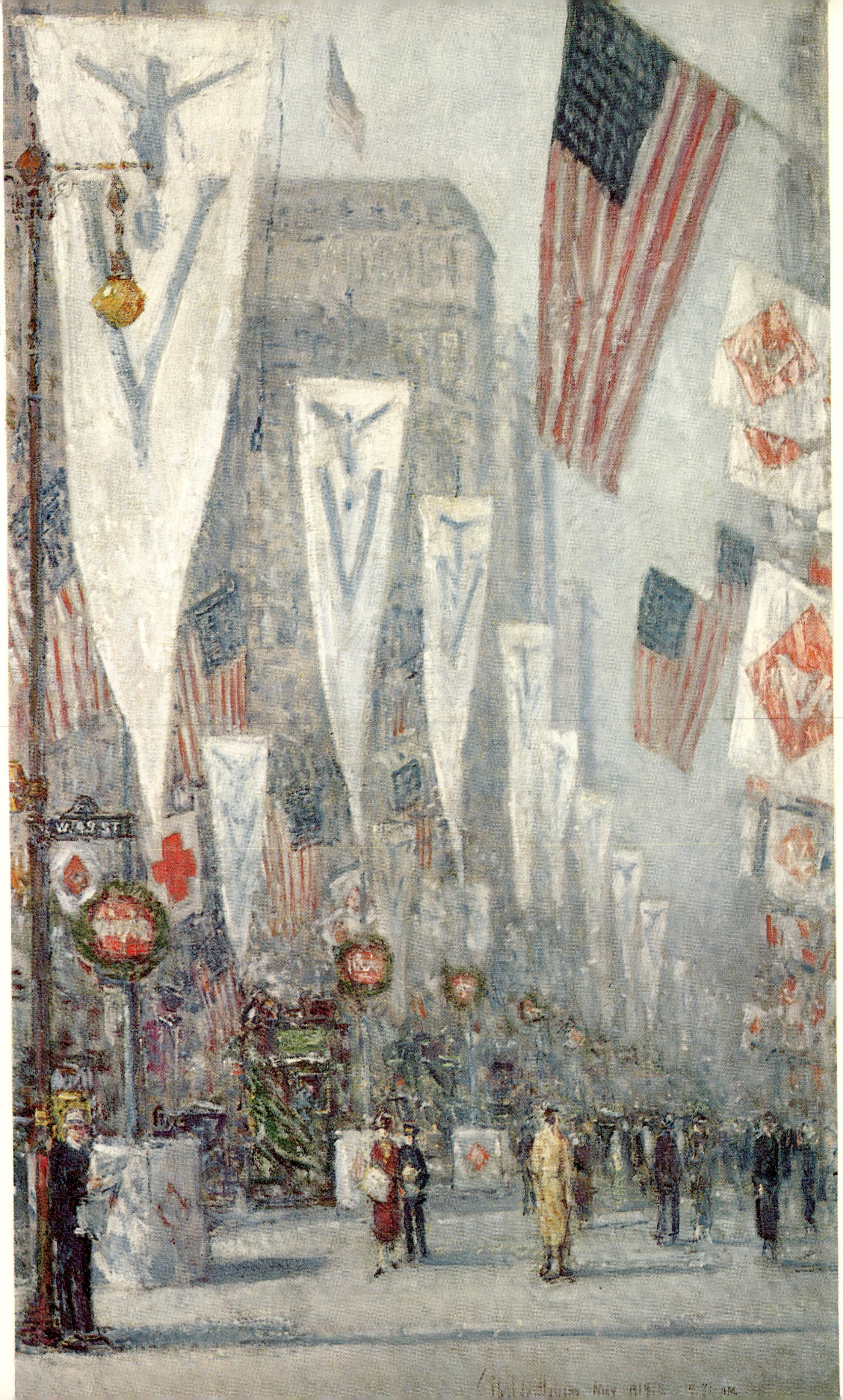

What became of the prehistoric race that built the elaborate ceremonial mounds found in the Ohio and Mississippi valleys? Nineteenth-century America had a romantic but self-serving answer

By ROBERT SILVERBERG

To the early European settlers of North America, this land had one serious shortcoming: it lacked visible signs of a past. Egypt had her pyramids, England her Stonehenge, Greece her Acropolis; but those who came to this green New World failed to find those traces of awesome antiquity on which romantic myths could be founded. It was not cheering to feel that one was entering an empty land peopled only by naked, wandering savages. Mexico and South America had yielded stone temples and golden cities, but here in the north was, seemingly, a continent only of woods and plains, inhabited by simple huntsmen and equally simple sedentary farmers. Were there no grand, imagination-stirring symbols of vanished greatness? In all this mighty domain, was there nothing to compare with the antiquities of the Old World?

"... and the mound-builders

Men in search of a myth will usually find one, if they work at it. In the Thirteen Colonies the mythmakers had little raw material for their fantasies; but as the colonists gradually spread westward and southward they came upon mysterious and tantalizing earthen mounds. It was obvious that they were manmade relics of an earlier time. How were they to be interpreted?

The mounds lacked beauty and elegance, perhaps. They were mere heaps of earth. Some were of colossal size, like the Cahokia mound in Illinois, standing one hundred feet high and covering sixteen acres; others were mere blisters rising from the ground. Some stood in solitary grandeur above broad plains, while others sprouted in thick groups. All were overgrown with trees and shrubs, so that their outlines could barely be distinguished. Once cleared, the mounds revealed

traditions about the mounds; when questioned, they shrugged and spoke vaguely about ancient tribes.

The mounds naturally came under close scrutiny. By the early nineteenth century hundreds if not thousands of them had been examined, measured, and partly excavated. These early studies revealed a great variety of shape. Near the Great Lakes they tended to be gigantic effigies, in low relief, of birds, reptiles, beasts, or men—apparently of some sacred significance. These effigy mounds are most common in Wisconsin, although the best known is the Great Serpent mound in Ohio, an earthern snake twenty feet wide and a yard high that wriggles along for some 1,330 feet. In the Ohio Valley, the customary shape of a mound was conical, up to eighty or ninety feet in height; these usually contained tombs. Elsewhere, notably in the

vanished from the earth"

a regularity and symmetry of form. Within them were found evidences of former civilization: human bones, weapons, tools, jewelry.

The greatest concentration of mounds lay in the heart of the continent—in Ohio, Illinois, Indiana, and Missouri. There were subsidiary mound areas in western Tennessee and Kentucky, and nearly every major waterway of the Midwest was rimmed by clusters of them; there were also outlying mound zones from western New York to Nebraska. In the South, mounds lined the Gulf of Mexico from Florida to eastern Texas, and reached up through the Carolinas and across to Oklahoma. There were so many of them—ten thousand in the valley of the Ohio River alone—that they seemed surely to be the work of a vanished race which with incredible persistence had erected them in the course of hundreds or perhaps thousands of years, and then had disappeared from our land.

Why a vanished race?

Because the Indians of the Midwest, as the settlers found them, were sparse in number and limited in ambition; they were seminomadic savages who seemed incapable of the sustained effort needed to quarry and shape tons of earth. Nor did they have any

Opposite: A striking relic of the Mound Builders, here seen from the air, is the Great Serpent mound near Locust Grove, in southern Ohio. Built about 2,500 years ago by the Adenas, it was a ceremonial effigy rather than a tomb.

South, there were immense flat-topped mounds, truncated pyramids of earth, some terraced or having graded roadways leading to their summits. Mounds of this sort appeared to have been platforms for temples.

In addition to effigy mounds, burial mounds, and temple mounds, two types of embankments were seen, mainly in the Ohio-Indiana-Illinois-Missouri zone. On hilltops, huge "forts" covering many acres had been erected with formidable dirt walls. In lowland sites were found striking geometrical enclosures—octagons, circles, squares, ellipses—with walls five to thirty feet high surrounding plots of as much as two hundred acres. Running out from the enclosures often were parallel walls many miles long, forming great avenues.

From the beginning, antiquarians worked hard to explain the mounds. Scholars ransacked history for evidence of ancient mound-building cultures and found it in Herodotus, in Homer, in the annals of Rome, in the Viking sagas; even in the Old Testament, which described how the Canaanites and Israelites had worshipped their deities in "high places"—surely, said the scholars, artificial mounds. The discovery of the American mounds opened the floodgates of speculation. If the Israelites had built mounds in the Holy Land, why not in Ohio? Learned men suggested that our land had been visited in antiquity by Hebrews, Greeks, Persians, Romans, Vikings, Hindus, Phoenicians—anyone, in short, who had ever built a mound in the Old World.

In this way was born a legend that dominated the American imagination throughout the nineteenth century. It was the myth of the Mound Builders, a lost race of diligent and gifted artisans who had passed across the scene in shadowed prehistory, ultimately to be exterminated by the treacherous, ignorant red-skinned savages who even now were causing so much trouble for the Christian settlers of the New World. The myth took root, flourished, grew mightily; men spun tales of lost kings and demolished cities; a new religion even sprang from the legends. What was the truth behind all this supposition?

Deserted and overgrown earthworks were found by the settlers who began to enter the Ohio Valley in the seventeen fifties, and within two decades sporadic and tentative descriptions of them were appearing. In 1787 a contingent of New Englanders arrived in Ohio and founded a village they called Marietta. Shortly, accounts of the extensive Marietta earthworks were exciting eastern scholars. Ezra Stiles, the president of Yale, argued that they proved the descent of the Indians from Canaanites expelled from Palestine by Joshua. Benjamin Franklin, however, asserted that the Ohio mounds might have been constructed by Hernando de Soto in his wanderings. This contention was echoed by Noah Webster, although the lexicographer later abandoned the idea and credited the mounds to aborigines.

General Rufus Putnam, one of Marietta's founders, made a careful map of the earthworks there. One feature was an irregular square enclosure covering about forty acres and containing four truncated pyramids, the largest of them 188 feet by 132 feet at the base, and ten feet high. Other mounds lay nearby, and at right angles to the enclosure was an avenue 680 feet long, 150 feet wide, bordered by embankments eight to ten feet high. "This passage," wrote the archaeologist Ephraim George Squier in 1847, "may have been the grand avenue leading to the sacred plain above, through which assemblies and processions passed, in

BY I. J. EGAN; CITY ART MUSEUM OF ST. LOUIS

the solemn observances of a mysterious worship."

The founding fathers of Marietta ordered the most impressive of these mounds preserved as public parks, and they remain to this day. A clever Mariettan, the Reverend Manasseh Cutler, attempted in 1788 to compute the age of the mounds by counting the growth rings in the stumps of trees found on them; he calculated that the mounds had been erected no more recently than the early fourteenth century, and might well be over a thousand years old.

As the westward migration accelerated, interest in the mounds and their builders became intense—and theories of their origin multiplied. Benjamin Smith Barton, a Philadelphia naturalist, suggested in 1787 that they were Viking tombs; for it had been noticed that Norsemen had interred their lords in burial mounds not much different from those in Ohio. Barton went on to suggest that after their sojourn in Ohio the Vikings had moved along to Mexico, whose stone pyramids seemed to many like improved versions of the earthworks in the United States. Barton's fanciful notions contrasted with the more conservative ideas of another Philadelphian, the famed botanist William Bartram, who had taken a solitary jaunt through the mound country of the Southeast in 1773–77. Bartram examined dozens of mounds, such as the Ocmulgee group opposite the present city of Macon, Georgia, and Mount Royal on the St. Johns River in Florida. It seemed to him likely that some of the mounds were the work of the Creek and Cherokee Indians who still occupied the regions, and that others, the grandest, had been constructed by unknown predecessors. Yet when he queried the Cherokees he reported that they "are as ignorant as we are, by what people or for what purpose those artificial hills were raised." Still, at no point did Bartram postulate Vikings or other non-Indian transients as their builders; to his sober way of thinking, the mounds were probably the relics of some vanished Indian civilization. Thomas Jefferson, who not surprisingly was intensely interested in the mounds, was even more open-minded. "It is too early to form theories on those antiquities," he wrote in 1787. "We must wait with patience till more facts are collected."

Jefferson himself, a lifelong student of Indian lore, excavated a Virginia mound sometime prior to 1781 and published an account of his findings in his monograph *Notes on the State of Virginia* (1785). His archaeological technique was strikingly modern, giving careful attention to stratification and the position of artifacts; but he offered no imaginative explanations of the mound's purpose or origin.

Others were less hesitant, especially after the founding of such towns as Cincinnati, Manchester, Chillicothe, and Portsmouth brought a deluge of new data about the Ohio mounds. The English astronomer Francis Baily, accompanying a party of settlers down the Ohio in 1796, stopped to examine a group of mounds on what is today the West Virginia side of the river, and made the first recorded notice of the striking Grave Creek tumulus, which unknown pioneers had already discovered and partly excavated. The mounds, Baily wrote, must have been "built by a race of people more enlightened than the present Indians, and at some period of time very far distant." This viewpoint

CONTINUED ON PAGE 90

In the middle of the nineteenth century, thousands of American mounds were excavated by eager antiquarians and archaeologists. This painting, part of a 348-foot muslin scroll called Panorama of the Monumental Grandeur of the Mississippi Valley, *shows a somewhat schematized cross-section of a typical burial mound in Louisiana. Skeletons lie in various positions at various layers, and pottery and miscellaneous artifacts are visible in the vault underneath.*

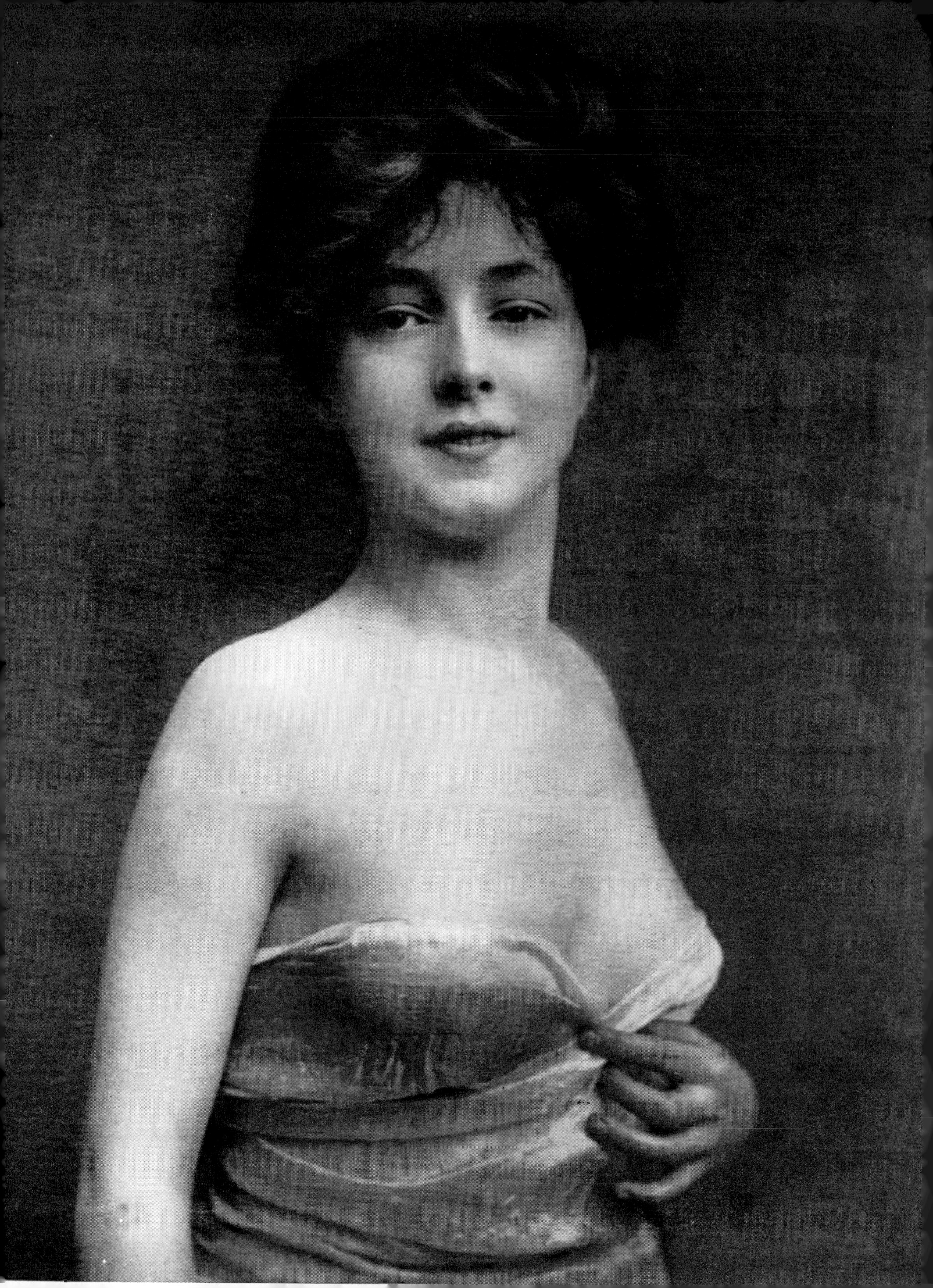

FACES FROM THE PAST—XXIII

A number of people who attended the opening of *Mamzelle Champagne* at the roof theatre of Madison Square Garden noted the arrival of Mr. and Mrs. Harry Kendall Thaw and their two male guests. Young Mrs. Thaw, the former show girl Evelyn Nesbit, was well known as one of the beauties of New York, and her husband, the thirty-five-year-old heir to a Pittsburgh rail and coke fortune, had achieved notoriety as an irresponsible playboy who was continually in the news: he once drove an automobile through a display window; he tried to ride a horse into an exclusive club that had blackballed him from membership; he reportedly gave an elaborate dinner in Paris at which the only guests were women of questionable reputation and the favors were pieces of jewelry; at another of his parties music had been provided by John Philip Sousa's entire band.

On that opening night—June 25, 1906—*Mamzelle Champagne* dragged badly (Mrs. Thaw described it as "putrid"), but no one seems to have observed Thaw leaving his table. When a member of the cast began singing "I Could Love a Million Girls," three pistol shots suddenly cracked, and the audience whirled around to see a man slump in his chair and slide to the floor, silver and glassware crashing about him. Standing beside him, Harry Thaw held a pistol in the air as if to signal the end of the deadly business; then he walked back and joined his wife and friends.

"Good God, Harry!" she cried, "What have you done?"

"It's all right, dear," he replied, kissing her. "I have probably saved your life."

At that, a fireman on duty at the Garden disarmed Thaw and a policeman led him to the elevator. Behind them the panicky crowd and the girls from the chorus clustered around the fallen man. Lying dead in a pool of blood, his face blackened beyond recognition by powder burns, was Stanford White, fifty-two-year-old man about town (a "voluptuary," some called him) and America's most famous architect, whose proudest achievement was Madison Square Garden.

Six months later the most sensational trial in the country's history began, a trial that revealed to plain people everywhere the hypocrisy of Victorian morality. Although Thaw was on trial for his life, the high moment of drama came when Evelyn Nesbit Thaw was called to testify. Ten thousand jammed the streets to see her—a twenty-two-year-old girl who looked sixteen ("the most exquisitely lovely human being I ever looked at," wrote Irvin S. Cobb)—and a shocked nation began to witness what one commentator called "the vivisection of a woman's soul."

Evelyn, it was clear, had come a long way from Tarentum, Pennsylvania, where she was born. Detail by lurid detail, the prosecution took her through the story of how she had become an artist's model at fourteen, then a show girl with the hit musical *Florodora*. Along with other prominent New York men, Stanford White had arranged to meet her, and in his apartment one night, she said, he gave her drugged champagne and ravished her. After she became his mistress, White delighted in setting her naked on a red velvet swing and pushing her so high her feet touched a Japanese parasol that hung from the ceiling. In 1903 she left White for Thaw and went on the first of two premarital trips to Europe with him. She returned home alone, took up with White again, and revealed to him the sadistic brutality she had suffered at Thaw's hands after he learned of her relationship with White. Then—despite all she had discovered about the unbalanced Thaw—she left for Europe with him again. As most reporters perceived, it was Evelyn, not her husband, who was on trial: the prosecutor stated in his summation that she was a "tigress between two men, egging them on. To Thaw she said White had wronged her. To White she said Thaw had beaten her with a whip." Since White was married and could not give her respectability, she had decided in 1905 to marry Thaw. A year later her husband, who went into paroxysms of rage at the mention of White's name, could stand his jealous doubts no longer and killed the architect.

Three and a half months after the trial began it ended with a hung jury; so nine months later the whole sordid tale was recited before another jury, which concluded that the defendant was not guilty, on grounds of insanity. But the judge, declaring Thaw a manic-depressive and dangerous to the public safety, committed him to the Matteawan State Hospital for the Criminal Insane. Much of the next fifteen years he spent in asylums; in 1924 he was released and lived in semiseclusion, except for occasional colorful encounters with police and press, until his death in 1947.

For Evelyn, the years that followed the trial were all downhill: squabbles with Thaw and his family over money, affairs with other men, divorce, suicide attempts, night-club acts that took her into ever tawdrier cabarets, run-ins with the curious and the police. Through it all she made a living recalling her vicissitudes and the sensational trial in different versions of her "own true story." In 1934 she told it again in a book, *Prodigal Days*, and in 1955 she was hired as "technical consultant" for a motion picture, *The Girl in the Red Velvet Swing*, which purported to be her life story. Finally, at eighty-two, she died in a convalescent home, all too aware that for the lovely young girl life had ended that night sixty years ago at the roof garden. "Stanny White was killed," she said, "but my fate was worse. I lived."

—*Richard M. Ketchum*

"The scene of slaughter was exceedingly picturesque"

Lagoon whaling just before the Civil War, when the slaughter of the grays was at its peak

Trapped in its Baja California breeding lagoons, the gray whale was almost harpooned out of existence. Today the growing herd is faced with a different threat that is perhaps just as dangerous

By WESLEY MARX

In the late summer of 1857, Charles Melville Scammon, captain of the 181-ton brig *Boston*, presented his crew with a dangerous proposition. Their voyage, he reminded them, had thus far failed to yield a single barrel of oil or a single sealskin. If the ship returned empty to its home port of San Francisco, there would be no bonus money for the men. Their eight-month contracts were about to expire; what Scammon wanted them to do was to extend their tours and follow the migrating gray whales to a hitherto undiscovered breeding lagoon on the coast of Baja California, in Mexico.

The crew of the *Boston* agreed, but not without hesitation. Hunting the slow-moving grays in the confines of a shallow lagoon might appear tame compared with the hazards of open-sea whaling, but it was not without hazards of its own: many a tombstone in the cemeteries of New England whaling ports bore the inscription "Killed While Lagoon Whaling."

Scammon was well aware of the perils, but he was also on the verge of devising a new method of whaling that would reduce "gray fishing" to grim efficiency. In the process he would touch off one of the bloodiest eras in whaling history. Yet Scammon was no ordinary whaling captain. He took a scientist's interest in the animals he hunted; before he was through, he would assemble a pioneer scientific treatise which would establish him as one of the foremost mammalogists of his age—and which would constitute a useful beginning for modern scientists seeking to prevent the total extinction of the majestic gray whale. In whaling's heyday the gray, named for the spots that dapple its immense black body, was not a commercially prized species. Its blubber yielded no more than forty barrels of oil—half the yield of a sperm or a bowhead; and its baleen (the tufted gums that filter the animal's diet of plankton) was too coarse to be used commercially as whalebone for corsets and buggy whips.

But hunting the gray had its advantages. Most large whale species, in retreating from the plankton pastures of the polar seas in late fall, steer clear of coastal waters and head instead for off-island breeding grounds in the open ocean: the Azores, Madagascar, or Micronesia. As a result, the New England whalers were forced to pursue creatures faster and larger than their own ships through gales, dead calms, and uncharted seas. But the gray whale breeds in a much more convenient locale; from the Arctic it swims six thousand miles due south to the warm and placid coastal lagoons of Baja California. Here, hemmed in by constricting shores, the grays could be harpooned in large numbers and their blubber flensed and tried out under a pleasant desert sun. This colossal opportunity had only to be effectively exploited.

In the winter of 1846, a New England whaling ship, waiting for the summer sun and the return of the whales to northern waters, had anchored in Magdalena Bay on the Baja California coast. Spacious lagoons indented the bay's shore line, and the astonished crew saw countless whale spouts rising above the calm blue surface of the water. The whaler, herself in hibernation, had stumbled across a major breeding ground of the gray whale. A killing spree promptly ensued.

At first lagoon whaling, soon dubbed "the mudhole season," was merely a diversion for the off-season. But such a patronizing description in no way obscured the dangers involved; for if the gray whale was particularly vulnerable to a harpoon in the confined space of his breeding ground, the harpooners themselves were just as vulnerable to the survival tactics of a tormented whale. At sea, a harpooned whale tended to run and "sound," that is, dive for the bottom, in the hope of shaking loose the whaleboat at the end of the harpoon line. Shallow lagoons thwarted this tactic and forced the gray whale to meet its adversaries head on. Since the grays could maneuver much more quickly than the whaleboats, the pursuers could suddenly find themselves the object of pursuit. Sometimes a wounded gray would corner its tormentors and ram their wooden craft. At other times, a whale's mighty flukes would clear the water and come crashing down on the luckless crew in a devastating tactic called "lobtailing." Other species of whales resorted to these direct tactics only occasionally; the grays had to rely on them constantly and soon acquired considerable cunning. Sometimes the harpoon line would suddenly go slack. The perplexed crew would look over the side of the boat to see where the whale was, but the waters would be murky with mud and sand churned up by their quarry. Then, in a frightful flash, the men would feel their boat being lifted clear of the water and a moment later find themselves hurtling through the air. The whale, playing possum, had waited for the lagoon current to bring the boat overhead and then had lashed upward with its flukes in a kind of reverse lobtail.

The gray's ferocity began destroying the reputations of many bonus mates, boatheaders who received extra pay in recognition of their skill in hunting whales. After a luckless encounter with a gray, one mate returned forlornly to his ship and reported to the cap-

Captain Scammon

tain, a well-known New Bedford skipper named Simmons, that there "ain't enough left of the whaling boat to kindle the cook's fire." Simmons reminded his mate in no uncertain terms that he was being paid to "turn up" whales, not to reduce the ship's valuable complement of whaleboats. "I shipped to go a-whaling," complained the frustrated mate. "I'd no idea of bein' required to go into a duck pond to whale after spotted hyenas. Why, Cap'n, these here critters ain't whales." Then what were they? Simmons inquired. "I have a strong notion that they are a cross 'tween a sea-serpent and an alligator," declared the disgruntled bonus mate.

Mistaking a calf for an adult whale frequently resulted in loss of life as well as reputation. After interviewing Captain J. L. Eddy, a veteran of lagoon whaling, a correspondent of the Wilmington, Delaware, *Journal* reported: "Woe to the boats if they kill the young one first. The mother rushes at them with the utmost fury and stoves them in with her flukes. Such is the female devil; and Captain Eddy says as many men are lost in catching them as in all the other whaling grounds put together."

This bad press acted to the gray's temporary advantage, for whaling captains were loath to pit their men and boats against the "devilfish" or the "hardhead." The more fearless—or reckless—among them who did hunt during the mudhole season sought to discourage possible competitors by embellishing tales of the gray's known ferocity. One captain invariably sailed into Honolulu with a stove boat prominently displayed on his main deck. Once ashore, with a few tots of rum under his belt, the captain would recount how one of his novice harpooners had darted a calf by mistake. The mother promptly charged, and the nervous occupants of the boat, including the captain, barely managed to beach the craft on the lagoon shore. But still they were not safe. The distraught harpoonist shouted, "Cap'n, the old whale is after us still," and ran into the desert. "I then told all hands," declared the grinning captain, "to climb trees."

For a decade after its inital discovery, then, lagoon whaling remained a limited diversion. But the supply of bowheads and sperms was not unlimited, and by 1855 the industrious New England whaling fleet was under increasing pressure to confront the devilfish and to locate more of the lagoons where it bred.

"Being on the coast of California in 1852, when the 'gold fever' raged," Scammon later explained, "the force of circumstances compelled me to take command of a brig, bound on a sealing, sea-elephant and whaling voyage, or abandon sea life, at least temporarily." Only twenty-seven at the time, Scammon was already an alert, experienced, and knowledgeable man of the sea. Born in Maine into the family of a Methodist preacher who doubled as treasurer of the township, he had been raised in comfortable surroundings in which a love of learning was encouraged. One of his brothers, Eliakim, became a Union general who numbered James Garfield and William McKinley among his subordinates during the Civil War. Another brother, Jonathan, became a Chicago railroad financier and a prime mover in the city's public school system. Charles's avocations were reading, sketching, and writing poetry for his invalid sister, but he decided to make his living on the sea. As in the case of another New Englander, Herman Melville, this dual temperament eventually enabled Scammon to recognize that whales had much more than commercial significance.

Scammon's nautical career began in the coastal trade, transporting turpentine, peanuts, and resin up and down the eastern seaboard. It was not gold that brought him to California, but rather the opportunities for promotion to merchant master. A scarcity of

ALL WHALING SCENES FROM CAPTAIN SCAMMON'S *Marine Mammals* (1874); UNIVERSITY OF CALIFORNIA LIBRARY

The gray whale's 6,000-mile migration southward to the lagoons starts in the Arctic Ocean.

berths, however, forced him into whaling, and he soon became the chief whaling captain for A. L. Tubbs and Company, the San Francisco branch of a Boston wholesale house. Scammon's wife and son came to San Francisco to settle; occasionally they accompanied the head of the family on a whaling expedition.

They were not aboard the *Boston*, however, on her epic voyage in 1857 when Scammon talked his crew into trying lagoon whaling. No one had any illusions about the dangers ahead, least of all Scammon himself: in Magdalena Bay the season before, he had lost two boats altogether; the others were stove a total of fifteen times. Six of his crew were badly injured: one had both legs broken. But the experience did not discourage Scammon; rather, it inspired him. Now, having secured the agreement of the *Boston*'s crew, he reprovisioned at Santa Catalina Island, rendezvoused with a small schooner sent down from San Francisco by Mr. Tubbs, and began to trail the migrating grays southward along the seven-hundred-mile Baja coastline. About halfway down, a desert headland extends into the Pacific to form the immense and open Sebastián Vizcaíno Bay. Here the observant Scammon previously had seen gray whales, their blows ascending into the air like fountains, disappear—apparently into the desert. The schooner was dispatched to follow the coastline and search for an entrance to the lagoon. Two days later, a messenger from the schooner reported the existence of an entrance large enough to accommodate the brig. The *Boston* got under sail and, helped through the narrow and shallow entrance by a providential breeze, soon found herself gliding on a large, placid lagoon some thirty-five miles long and up to eleven miles wide; it had no name. Fish, porpoises, green turtles, and waterfowl were in abundance, but there were only a few whales. Undaunted, Scammon decided that he had simply gotten there ahead of the main body of migrating grays.

While he waited he was not idle. He dispatched the *Boston*'s four whaling boats to collect driftwood on the ocean side of the lagoon. This errand almost doomed the voyage. To protect the boats from the surf, the sailors tied them together and left them just inside the lagoon entrance in the care of a boatkeeper. After basking in the warm sun for a while, the sentry decided to pull the plug in one boat and cool off in an impromptu bathtub. The "bathtub" promptly became waterlogged and capsized, and the floundering boatkeeper abandoned the boats and swam for the safety of the shore. Soon the astonished driftwood collectors saw their sole means of pursuing whales drifting through the lagoon entrance into the Pacific on the outgoing tide. A few of them, strong-swimming Kanakas from Hawaii, desperately paddled through the surf on makeshift surfboards of planking. The ship's carpenter, also a strong swimmer, joined the chase, which soon turned into a losing contest with the surf. The exhausted Kanakas managed to return to shore, but the carpenter was never seen again. The tragedy seemed complete until the tide changed and washed three of the boats back to shore. This sight, according to Scammon, evoked "a spontaneous cheer from the men."

The boats were recovered just in time, for whales now began to appear in large numbers. Scammon was jubilant. "Two large cows were captured without difficulty, which gave all hands confidence in our ultimate success," he noted in the ship's log. This confidence crumbled the next day. Before a single whale could be harpooned, two of the three whaleboats were stove in by a succession of flashing flukes. The *Boston*'s remaining boat and the schooner's lone boat undertook to rescue men trying to keep afloat in the lagoon with fractured legs and twisted arms. Amidst this human carnage, a gray whale would casually emerge to blow and then slip back beneath the blue cover of the lagoon. "When the first boat arrived with her freight of crippled passengers, it could only be compared to a floating ambulance crowded with men —the uninjured supporting the helpless," observed Scammon, who now found himself in command not of a whaling ship but of a hospital ship, and a crowded one at that. "No whaling was attempted," he wrote, "as nearly half the crew were unfit for duty and a large portion of the rest were demoralized by fright."

To make matters worse, Scammon had two badly damaged boats and no carpenter to repair them. After several days, he did manage to outfit the schooner's boat for whale pursuit, but when the boat approached a slumbering whale the crew, with the exception of the boatheader and the boatsteerer, jumped overboard. One of the men, a bulky army deserter who had boasted of his exploits in the Second Seminole War, landed on the flukes of the whale. The unmasked braggart escaped unharmed as the whale simply settled gently under the water, "thereby ridding itself of the human parasite," Scammon sarcastically remarked.

"Our situation was both singular and trying," the Captain later wrote. "The vessel lay in perfect security in smooth water; and the objects of pursuit, which had been so anxiously sought, were now in countless numbers about us." The *Boston* was floating on a treasure trove that defied exploitation. What was clearly needed was a technique for catching the devilfish without endangering either whaleboats or men.

Scammon was equal to the occasion. A few days later, he launched his remaining boat on a special mission that transformed whale hunting into carefree slaughter.

The crew carefully hugged the shallow shore line, out of reach of the whales, and finally anchored inshore where the lagoon narrowed into a neck of deep water. When a whale surfaced to spout in this narrow passage, a man in the boat stood up and aimed a stubby bomb-lance gun that fired a projectile designed to pierce the whale's blubber and timed to detonate inside its lungs. The second time the whale emerged, the man took careful aim and fired; the color of the whale's spout turned from white to crimson. The gunner followed up with direct hits on two more passing whales.

Such marksmanship would have been regarded as futile at sea. A "bombed" whale would have to be quickly made fast to the boat; otherwise, it would sink or eventually float to the surface out of sight. But Scammon was confident that the enclosed lagoon would contain the bombed whales. One of the whales was secured instantly. The following day, a lookout climbed the schooner's rigging and spied the other two carcasses floating near the head of the lagoon, buoyed up by gases generated through the decomposition of their blubbery hulls. Scammon was no longer pursuing whales; he was ambushing them.

Thus, in one stroke Scammon had discovered a prime breeding ground of the gray whale and had devised a way of rendering the ferocious mammal defenseless. The ensuing carnage kept the *Boston*'s try-pots bubbling, smoking, and stinking through the night. All the oil barrels were soon filled, and dead whales still ringed the ship. An aftercabin was converted into a bread locker, freeing bread casks for use as oil barrels. When these were filled, deck pots, coolers, and mincing tubs were pressed into service and finally the try-pots themselves were filled and capped. Scammon and a delighted crew, some of whose limbs were still mending, sailed back to San Francisco "with the vessel so deeply laden that her scuppers were washed by the rippling tide."

The low waterline of the *Boston* soon became the talk of the Pacific whaling fleet, and Scammon, anticipating that other whaling captains would want to share in the source of his "greasy" luck, signed his crew on for another voyage to keep them from disclosing the lagoon's location. But when Scammon, now in command of the *Ocean Bird,* left San Francisco to rendezvous with the grays the following season, a fleet of nine vessels, capable of lowering thirty boats, dropped into his wake. The men on these vessels, naturally enough, named the lagoon after the man who had discovered and exploited it. It is called Scammon Lagoon to this day.

Mass whaling transformed the lagoon into a frantic marine slaughterhouse. To Scammon, "the scene of slaughter was exceedingly picturesque and unusually exciting." Bomb-lance guns crackled "like musketry" and the foamy thrashing of bombed whales resembled an "aquatic battle scene." Bustling boat crews knitted shut the giant lips of dead whales and towed the bloated corpses to their ships and the try-pots, whose stinking smoke spiralled into the desert sky.

The influx of whalers resulted in further refinements of lagoon-whaling techniques. Whale calves, until then dangerous nuisances, became deadly lures. At low tide, a boat would chase a stray calf into shallow water; soon the anxious mother would appear to retrieve her calf, only to become stranded. Once the mother had become exhausted by frantic efforts to extricate herself, the whaling boat returned for the kill. Sometimes the harpooner would step out of the boat, wade over to his giant quarry, and plunge the harpoon home.

Lagoon whaling made for an uncommon sociality in a business that was, and still is, marked by isolation. Rival crews engaged in daily gams; as the sailors conversed in a babble of Portuguese, Kanaka, and English, wives of whaling captains exchanged social visits whenever a boat was free to transport them. But the close quarters that made this pleasant intimacy possible often led to frayed tempers when it came to catching whales. Some whalers persisted in chasing the grays and making them fast. This open-sea technique soon became a comedy in the lagoon, for struck whales ran off in all directions, crossing lines and colliding with boats and even with one another. Amidst curses in all languages, tangled lines had to be cut, and competing boat crews continually exchanged threats. From the deck of the *Ocean Bird,* Scammon watched one boat, bearing down on its harpooned whale, threatening to cross the line of another.

"That won't do! I struck my whale first," cried out an anxious voice in the second boat. "Cut that line or I'll put a bomb through you."

The mate in the first boat responded heartily, "Shoot and be damned! I won't let go this line till we get t'other side of Jordan."

The industrious slaughter often continued through the night. In the darkness, white water flashed as whales writhed under the pricks of countless harpoons. Disembodied voices sounded sharp commands across the night. In one instance, Scammon heard a worried captain issue a cut-loose order to his bonus mate. "I've killed the bloody greek seven times but he won't turn up," a baffled voice responded. "He's got more lives than a Kilkenny cat." A burst of cheers moments later indicated to the anchored whale fleet that the stubborn whale had finally turned up.

Due mainly to Scammon's new hunting techniques and his profitable use of them, gray whaling was soon prosecuted just as intensively in other lagoons, small and large, along the Baja California coastline. In addition, eleven whaling stations along the California coastline bushwacked grays en route to their breeding grounds. The deserts that flanked the lagoons effectively discouraged desertion among the crews, a serious problem in whaling waters off inviting tropical islands. The turtles, fish, and waterfowl that thrived in the lagoons provided a varied diet. Drinking water was a problem at first, but a running spring was soon discovered on the offshore island of Cedros. Whaling, ordinarily dangerous and lonely, had been reduced to a fairly safe and sociable occupation. Each January and February, billowing sails decorated with large crosses, cannonballs, stars, or crescents turned the Baja coastline into a maritime carnival of color and confusion.

Such commercial aggression could have but one result. By 1861, four years after Scammon first sailed into his lagoon and almost lost his whaling boats, gray whaling was no longer economical. There were too few grays left. During these bloody years Scammon Lagoon alone yielded an estimated 22,250 barrels of oil. Altogether, lagoon whaling accounted for an estimated 10,800 whales, not including the calves who endlessly circled the ships where they had last seen their mothers until starvation or killer whales made an end of them. Lagoon whaling ended with the collapse of the New England whaling industry. During the Civil War, the fleet was decimated by Confederate raiders, one of which, the cruiser *Shenandoah*, actually destroyed the entire Arctic fleet after hostilities had officially ended (see "Last of the Rebel Raiders" in the December, 1958, AMERICAN HERITAGE). The whaling industry might have recovered from the war had it not been for the discovery in 1859 of a thick black liquid oozing out of the ground in Pennsylvania. Petroleum soon took over the chore of lighting the world.

Most whalers forgot about the gray whales. But not Charles Scammon. Even as his adventurous instincts had delighted in recording the color and excitement of lagoon whaling, the reflective side of his nature had been fascinated with the whales themselves. At the same time he had been ordering his harpooners to bomb the whales and his flensers to strip the blubber, Scammon was also measuring the girth of dead whales, inspecting the contents of their stomachs, and executing precise drawings of their conformations. The Captain jotted down his detailed observations alongside log entries that recorded the number of whales struck and barrels filled.

By the time lagoon whaling was obsolete, Scammon was contemplating a project no whaler or scientist in America had ever attempted—a comprehensive natural history of whales. That he was a self-educated mammalogist and writer dealing with a subject that had only limited appeal to prospective publishers did not discourage Scammon, but he did have to find a means of supporting his family while he pursued his

Whaling stations, like this one near Carmel, ambushed grays en route to the lagoons.

writing. Granted a commission as a captain in the U.S. Revenue Marine Service (forerunner of the Coast Guard), the ex-whaling captain began chasing smugglers and rescuing ships in distress. His off-duty hours he spent collating his own observations and statistics on whales, as well as the information he gleaned from extensive correspondence with whaling captains in the United States and around the world. Several years after he had first followed the grays, a map-charting mission took him back to the Baja coast, where he gazed with a mixture of pity and pride at Scammon Lagoon. "The decayed carcasses and bleaching bones strewed along the shores," he wrote, "give evidence of the havoc made by the most enterprising and energetic class of seamen that sailed under our national flag."

Scammon first published his scientific observations

CONTINUED ON PAGE 106

71

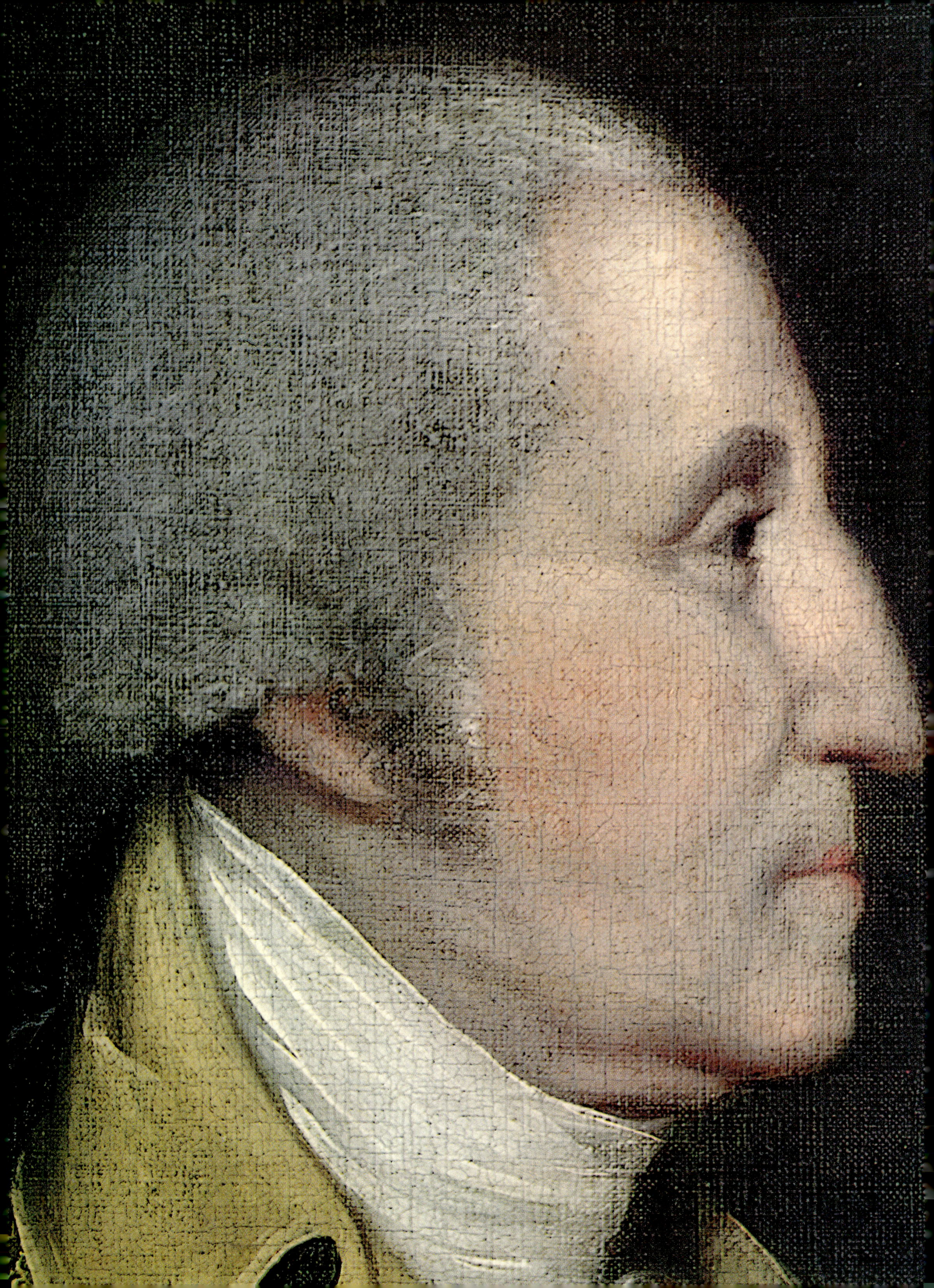

WASHINGTON AFTER THE REVOLUTION: III

The President's Progress

Washington's journey to his inauguration resembled a triumphal procession of royalty, but he felt like "a culprit who is going to the place of his execution"

By JAMES THOMAS FLEXNER

Never was the election of a President so much a foregone conclusion and yet so tortuous in consummation. The Electoral College met on February 4, 1789, but its unanimous vote for Washington could not be official until the president of the Senate, temporarily elected for the purpose, opened the ballots in the presence of both houses. Congress was due to convene in New York on March 4. On the fifth, only eight senators and seventeen representatives —pitifully less than a quorum—had appeared.

As the most unpleasant season of the farming year moved slowly by, Washington waited at Mount Vernon in a frustration that was increased by the nonarrival of some promised grain seed, which prevented him from carrying out that year's stage in his long-range plan for the rotation of crops. "£500 would be no compensation," he wrote, "for this disappointment."

The continuing word was that legislators were dribbling into New York—now a senator, then a representative—but a quorum was still unachieved on March 30 when Knox notified Washington that the delay had already cost the new government the spring imposts, estimated at £300,000. Washington replied that he was sorry about the imposts but was more worried over "the stupor, or listlessness" being displayed by the men on whom the success of the Constitution would depend. The high-spirited anticipation he had so recently savored faded rapidly into such gloom that he wrote as darkly as he had ever written during the blackest hours of the Revolution:

My movements to the chair of Government will be accompanied by feelings not unlike those of a culprit who is going to the place of his execution: so unwilling am I, in the evening of a life nearly consumed in public cares, to quit a peaceful abode for an Ocean of difficulties, without that competency of political skill, abilities and inclination which is necessary to manage the helm. . . . Integrity and firmness is all I can promise; these, be the voyage long or short, never shall forsake me although I may be deserted by all men. For of the consolations which are to be derived from these (under any circumstances) the world cannot deprive me.

Washington was not cheered when he faced up to the fact that, if he were not to leave debts behind him in Virginia, he would have "to do what I never expected to be reduced to the necessity of doing," what, indeed, he regarded as the most disastrous of all steps for a farmer: borrowing money at interest. After he had finally steeled himself thus to raise more than a thousand pounds, he discovered to his dismay that his credit was not considered good enough. Businessmen were not willing to lend. Finally, he tried a personal connection, appealing to "the most monied man I was acquainted with." But Charles Carroll of Car-

Opposite: George Washington was fifty-seven when he was inaugurated as President in 1789. He doubted he had the political skills the position demanded. "Integrity and firmness," he wrote, "is all I can promise." Both are evident in this enlarged detail from a portrait of 1790 by Joseph Wright.

rollton also refused, explaining that he could not collect interest on the money he already had out on loan.

A wealthy inhabitant of Alexandria, Richard Conway, finally accommodated Washington to the extent of £500—at six per cent interest. The money in hand, Washington paid the most pressing of his debts and found there was nothing left. He had to beg from Conway another hundred pounds so that he could pay his expenses to New York and the Presidency.

The government of the United States being still unorganized, no way existed to supply a presidential residence. Governor George Clinton of New York, an old friend but a conspicuous Antifederalist, asked Washington to stay with him. Washington replied that it would be wrong "to impose such a burden on any private family"; he also put off Clinton's request to be kept informed on when to expect Washington's arrival. "No reception," Washington explained, "can be so congenial to my feelings as a quiet entry devoid of ceremony."

Applying to Madison, Washington wrote that if lodgings could not be hired which were "tolerably convenient (I am not very nice) I would take rooms in the most decent Tavern." His mind surely running on his financial situation, he specified, "I am not desirous of being placed *early* in a situation for entertaining." He was, however, eager "to conform to the public desire and expectation with respect to the style proper for the chief magistrate to live in," and hoped that Madison would advise him concerning what the public wanted.

Washington made a quick trip to Fredericksburg to visit his eighty-two-year-old mother, who was now dying slowly and painfully of cancer of the breast. Then he returned to his waiting at Mount Vernon.

Martha made no secret of her bitterness at the impending destruction of her domestic life. She blamed fate, it is true, rather than her husband. She was willing to admit that he had to follow what his conscience told him was his duty. Washington did not push her any harder than was absolutely necessary. She would, of course, in the end have to apply her superlative social gifts to the role of First Lady; and Washington himself intended to set an example of promptness by starting out as quickly as possible after he had been notified that the government had certified his election. Martha, however, with Nelly and little Washington, could follow at their leisure.

On April 14, at about noon, Charles Thomson, who had been the secretary of the Continental Congress, stood at Mount Vernon's door. After Washington had greeted his old friend, they walked together into the high-ceilinged banquet hall that was the most formal room available. The two men stood there, facing each other, in the quiet of a Virginia afternoon. Thomson made a little speech and then proffered a letter from John Langdon, president pro tempore of the Senate. Washington learned that he had been unanimously elected President of the United States: "Suffer me, Sir, to indulge the hope, that so auspicious a mark of public confidence will meet your approbation."

Washington now read the brief contents of a paper he had prepared: "Whatever may have been my private feelings and sentiments," he could not "give a greater evidence of my sensibility of the honor" done him by his "fellow-citizens . . . than by accepting the appointment." He was conscious of his inability but would seek to do as much as could be "done by an honest zeal." In order to keep no one waiting longer than was absolutely necessary, "I shall therefore be in readiness to set out the day after tomorrow."

Concerning April 16, Washington wrote in his diary:

About ten o'clock, I bade adieu to Mount Vernon, to private life, and to domestic felicity, and with a mind oppressed with more anxious and painful sensations than I have words to express, set out for New York in company with Mr. Thomson and Colo. Humphreys, with the best disposition to render service to my country in obedience to its calls, but with less hope of answering its expectations.

Since he believed that the future of the government depended tremendously on its acceptance by the people, Washington was much concerned about how his progress through the states to the capital would be received. But his first stop, Alexandria, was not so much a test for the future as a parting from the past.

His neighbors entertained him at a dinner studded with congratulatory toasts and affectionate speeches. He finally rose and made a brief acknowledgment, which ended:

All that now remains for me is to commit myself and you to the protection of that benificent Being, who, on a former occasion has happily brought us together, after a long and distressing separation. Perhaps the same gracious Providence will again indulge us with the same heartfelt felicity. But words, my fellow-citizens, fail me: Unutterable sensations must then be left to more expressive silence; while, from an aching heart, I bid you all, my affectionate friends and kind neighbours, farewell!

As Washington advanced beyond home ground, the explosion of enthusiastic strangers into his presence seemed all that the most ardent Federalist could have desired. There was a perpetual bowing and clanking beside his carriage. Delegations of local dignitaries awaited him at each town, and relays of horsemen, relieving each other every dozen miles or so, formed a continuous guard of honor. Washington could hardly see the countryside, so thick were the clouds of dust thrown up by the many hooves. As an observer noticed, the dust settling on Washington's clothes made it impossible to distinguish the true color of his coat or trousers.

In Baltimore, Washington was kept up late by an

At Trenton, New Jersey, on the way to his inauguration, Washington was greeted near an arch of evergreens by a bevy of flower girls. Here, a dozen years before, his little army had known brief triumph and then near disaster; the memories—and the reception—touched the President-elect deeply. A primitive artist painted this picture a century later from descriptions furnished him by descendants of citizens who had seen the General pass and had never forgotten it.

endless succession of toasts and speeches at a dinner. He was off at 5:30 the next morning, but that was not too early to be piped out of town by a roar of cannon and accompanied by another group of leading citizens on horseback. After seven miles, he alighted and managed to persuade this escort to go home. Then for two days, as he advanced through sparsely settled country, there were gaps in the chain of ceremony, and he could distinguish, in the smaller crowds that awaited him in towns, the emotional faces of soldiers he had last seen years before in bloody campaigns. But things warmed up again at Wilmington: another dinner, and horsemen who accompanied him to the Pennsylvania line where Pennsylvania horsemen were waiting, headed by the suavely smiling General Thomas Mifflin.

At Chester, some fifteen miles from Philadelphia, Washington alighted from his carriage and mounted a white horse. A parade of other horsemen gathered behind him. As he advanced along the familiar road toward the Schuylkill River, he saw awaiting him at every crossroads a new detachment of riders. He would stop, the whole procession coming to a halt, for another round of ceremonial greetings. Then the newcomers fell in at the end of the ever lengthening line.

Finally there came into Washington's view the pontoon bridge across the Schuylkill at Gray's Ferry. It now resembled a grove of laurel and cedar growing out of the water. Green boughs hid all the woodwork, and, at either end, tall arches of laurel rose gaudy with banners and devices. Washington might have guessed (had he not been told) that this was the work of that indefatigably ingenious painter Charles Willson Peale. However, as he admired the effect, which according to one spectator "even the pencil of a Raphael could not delineate," he could not guess all that Peale had in store for him.

Riding under the first arch, he saw peering at him from the shrubbery a handsome fifteen-year-old girl, whom he perhaps recognized as Peale's daughter Angelica. She seemed to be encrusted with laurel. He had started to bow to the young lady when she set in motion what the *Pennsylvania Packet* called "certain machinery." Something separated from the arch above and, before Washington could duck, landed on his head. Raising a startled hand, he found that he was now crowned with laurel. (The idea was that the hero, in his modesty, would have refused the wreath if offered in a more conventional manner.) According to a Peale family legend, Washington pushed off the wreath but kissed Angelica.

Between the bridge and the city, 20,000 citizens—so the *Packet* estimated—"lined every fence, field, and avenue. The aged sire, the venerable matron, the blooming virgin, and the ruddy youth were all emulous in their plaudits." At the city limits, more infantry wheeled and more artillery set matches to their cannon. Then these new units fell into the line behind Washington, as did squads of citizens at every block until (according to the newspaper) "the column was swelled beyond credibility itself." The parade finally reached the City Tavern, where Washington was tendered "a very grand and beautiful banquet." The evening was topped off with fireworks.

When the next morning dawned rainy, Washington grasped the opportunity of requesting the city troop of horsemen not to accompany him out of town: "He could not think of travelling under cover while others get wet." Whatever may have been Washington's secret relief at being able to leave quietly, his act sent the editor of the *Packet* into a panegyric on the modesty of an elected leader as contrasted with the pride of European kings.

As Washington crossed the Delaware opposite Trenton, his mind ran on his "situation" there during the darkest days of the Revolution, when he had struck out in utter despair: an icy river—sleet and wind—half-naked, starving men—cannon and musket fire—bloody stumps staining new-fallen snow—an incredible victory that had helped turn the tide.

On reaching the New Jersey shore, Washington was supplied with a fine horse. He led a noisy procession toward the bridge across Assunpink Creek, behind which his army had taken refuge from a superior enemy before he set off on the wild and dangerous circuitous march to Princeton. When Washington saw that the bridge across which his artillery had once so desperately fired was now surmounted with a triumphal arch of evergreens, his first thought may well have been, "What, again?" But this was to be even more affecting. "A numerous train of white robed ladies leading their daughters" stood where Washington had seen men die. Above them, on the top of the arch, a dome of flowers bore, pricked out in blossoms, the two bloody dates "December 26, 1776–January 2, 1777," and also a legend: "THE DEFENDER OF THE MOTHERS WILL BE THE PROTECTOR OF THE DAUGHTERS."

The procession stopped, and Washington advanced alone. Thirteen young ladies stepped out to meet him. They were dressed in white, decked with wreaths and chaplets of flowers, and held in their hands baskets filled with more blooms. They sang:

> *Virgins fair, and Matrons grave,*
> *Those thy conquering arms did save,*
> *Build for thee triumphant bowers*
> *Strew, ye fair, his way with flowers—*
> *Strew your Hero's way with flowers.*

They threw their flowers under his horse's feet.

Writing formally in the third person, Washington later thanked the ladies

for the exquisite sensation he experienced in that affecting moment. The astonishing contrast between his former and actual situation at the same spot, the elegant taste with which it was adorned for the present occasion, and the innocent appearance of the *white-robed Choir* . . . have made such impressions on his remembrance, as . . . will never be effaced.

No knight of ancient legend ever felt more chivalrous toward the fair sex. In wartime, Washington had done everything in his power—even to the detriment of the cause—to prevent women from becoming involved. The memory of the mothers and daughters on the bridge near Trenton would remain with him as an emotional high point till his dying day.

The contrast with this hushed, almost sacred occasion made Washington more and more unpleasantly conscious of the hysterical notes in the plaudits which hour after hour beat continually around him. Did the rantings of the orators, the passionate handshakes, the throat-tearing cheers signify an affectionate welcome and reasoned approval of the government about to be established? Or was it all the senseless frenzy of the mob giving way to uncontrolled emotions? There was nothing Washington could do but roll on in his carriage, bow out the window, emerge to shake hands whenever there was a delegation, change to horseback whenever there was a parade to lead.

Finally he was across New Jersey and at Elizabeth, where he was to embark for the fifteen-mile trip by water that would take him past Staten Island, out into the Upper Bay, and then through the inner harbor to the tip of Manhattan Island.

He found awaiting him a sumptuous barge that had been built especially for the occasion at the expense of forty-six leading citizens. It was forty-seven feet long at the keel, and over the elegantly appointed deck stretched an awning festooned with red curtains. There was a mast and a sail, but the main reliance was to be on the oars, thirteen on each side, which were manned by a picked group of New York harbor pilots, all dressed in white smocks and black-fringed caps.

Onto the deck there trooped, after Washington, representatives from the state and city governments, from the Senate and the House of Representatives. The vessel had hardly started to move before a naval parade began to form behind it. Among the first to fall in were the New Haven and Rhode Island packets. Washington was pleased to see, in another boat, two familiar faces: John Jay and Henry Knox. For the rest, there were more vessels and mostly strange faces.

As Washington's barge came opposite a battery on Staten Island, cannon began firing a thirteen-gun salute. At this signal, all the boats broke out, like so many suddenly opening flowers, into a splurge of banners. Then, from closer to Manhattan, there spoke out a tremendous voice. A Spanish warship was echoing the salute with larger guns than any the infant republic possessed. And the stranger from Europe also had more flags: her rigging bloomed, to applause, with the ensigns of twenty-seven—or was it twenty-eight?—different nations.

As the pilots rowed with perfect rhythm down the bay, a sloop under full sail slipped gracefully along-

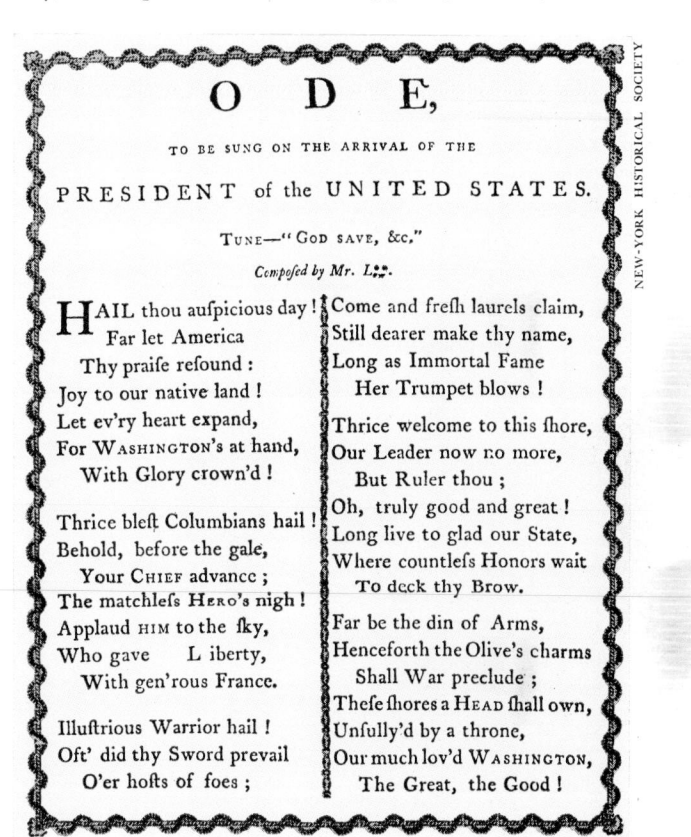

> ### ODE,
> TO BE SUNG ON THE ARRIVAL OF THE
> ### PRESIDENT of the UNITED STATES.
> TUNE—"GOD SAVE, &c."
> *Compoſed by Mr. L:;:.*
>
> HAIL thou auſpicious day!
> Far let America
> Thy praiſe reſound :
> Joy to our native land !
> Let ev'ry heart expand,
> For WASHINGTON'S at hand,
> With Glory crown'd !
>
> Thrice bleſt Columbians hail !
> Behold, before the gale,
> Your CHIEF advance ;
> The matchleſs HERO'S nigh !
> Applaud HIM to the ſky,
> Who gave Liberty,
> With gen'rous France.
>
> Illuſtrious Warrior hail !
> Oft' did thy Sword prevail
> O'er hoſts of foes ;
>
> Come and freſh laurels claim,
> Still dearer make thy name,
> Long as Immortal Fame
> Her Trumpet blows !
>
> Thrice welcome to this ſhore,
> Our Leader now no more,
> But Ruler thou ;
> Oh, truly good and great !
> Long live to glad our State,
> Where countleſs Honors wait
> To deck thy Brow.
>
> Far be the din of Arms,
> Henceforth the Olive's charms
> Shall War preclude ;
> Theſe ſhores a HEAD ſhall own,
> Unſully'd by a throne,
> Our much lov'd WASHINGTON,
> The Great, the Good !

NEW-YORK HISTORICAL SOCIETY

side. Two gentlemen and two ladies stood facing Washington and, as the water scudded between, they sang new words to "God Save the King." (The verses were printed on broadsides like the one above.)

Washington had hardly taken off his hat and bowed to acknowledge the compliment when another musical boat appeared directly alongside the first. The singers leaned over the water to exchange music, and then all rendered an ode in elaborate parts. "Our worthy President," one witness exulted, "was greatly affected by those tokens of profound respect."

As if Nature herself wished to join in the adulation, a number of porpoises frolicked briefly in front of Washington's barge. Then Washington's eyes were suddenly caught by an even more remarkable sight. The

TEXT CONTINUED ON PAGE 107
ILLUSTRATION OVERLEAF

BY L. M. COOKE; NATIONAL GALLERY OF ART, GIFT OF EDGAR WILLIAM AND BERNICE CHRYSLER GARBISCH

78

Washington covered the last fifteen miles to New York on April 23, 1789, in an elaborate, gaily decorated barge manned by thirteen harbor pilots. As he neared the tip of Manhattan, flags fluttered briskly and the cheers and noisy salutes of the harbor shipping rang in his ears. A local newspaper called the event "animated and moving beyond description."

Oliver Ellsworth succeeded Jay and while Chief Justice negotiated with Napoleon to prevent a Franco-American war.

Chief Justice John Marshall advised Adams on naming the "midnight judges." One, Marbury, came back to haunt him.

Chief Justice Roger B. Taney, named by Jackson, continued advising Old Hickory, especially on banking legislation.

Justice John Catron injudiciously leaked word of the Court's forthcoming Dred Scott ruling to President Buchanan.

Justice David Davis did not step down from the Court while seeking a third-party nomination for the Presidency in 1872.

Justice Joseph P. Bradley, as one of fifteen electoral commissioners, helped swing the election of 1876 to Hayes.

Justice Louis Brandeis advised Woodrow Wilson on labor, shipping, and government organization problems in World War I.

Chief Justice (and ex-President) **William H. Taft** counselled Wilson's three Republican successors in the White House.

As Justice Fortas found out, nobody feels comfortable when the constitutional wall between the Executive and the Judiciary is breached. But the precedents are many: they began with the birth of the Court

Justice Owen J. Roberts headed F. D. R.'s commission to determine why the Japanese caught us unprepared at Pearl Harbor.

Justice Robert H. Jackson prosecuted Nazis at Nuremberg. The Chief Justice deplored the idea —and Jackson's absence.

Justice Felix Frankfurter backed F. D. R.'s court-packing before appointment, afterward continued "Dear Frank" letters.

Chief Justice Earl Warren headed Lyndon B. Johnson's commission to investigate the assassination of John F. Kennedy.

THE JAY PAPERS III:
The Trials of Chief Justice Jay

Edited and Annotated by RICHARD B. MORRIS

In the public mind there has always clung to the person and the office of a justice of the United States Supreme Court an aura as close to priestliness as our secular political system admits of. It seems fitting, somehow, that the white marble building in which the Court deliberates strongly resembles a classical temple.

Given the fact that judges are human beings who in many cases have risen to the bench from the pragmatic world of politics, this aura is of course a fantasy. Still, it always comes as a shock when controversy surrounds a member of the Court, as it did last year when President Johnson's nomination of his friend and appointee Justice Abe Fortas to be Chief Justice ran into so much opposition in the Senate Judiciary Committee that Mr. Fortas asked the President to withdraw his name.

The event was by no means without precedent. A century ago Ulysses S. Grant had not one but two candidates for Chief Justice turned down: first Attorney General George H. Williams, because it was felt he lacked the necessary legal expertise, and then Caleb Cushing, because he had allegedly been proslavery during the Civil War. The extended hearings on Justice Fortas raised two quite different and more sensitive questions: May a justice of the Supreme Court rightfully engage in extrajudicial activities while he is on the bench? and, May those activities include giving confidential political advice to the President who nominated him?

For certain kinds of extrajudicial service, even controversial service, the Court has known ample precedent. One thinks immediately of the most recent example, Chief Justice Earl Warren's presiding over President Johnson's commission to ascertain the facts about the assassination of President Kennedy; the wrangling over what quickly became known as "the Warren Report" still has not died. And many will recall the service of Justice Robert H. Jackson as a prosecutor at Nuremberg; the Chief Justice at that time, Harlan Fiske Stone, publicly questioned the propriety of such activity on Jackson's part and complained to President Truman that Jackson's prolonged absence placed an extra burden on the other justices. Controversial or not, such public assignments to members of the court have usually been carried out with considerable distinction.

JOHN JAY

Less well known are the activities of various justices as confidential advisers to Presidents. But of this, too, as Mr. Fortas pointed out to the Judiciary Committee, history furnishes many examples; some of them are described in the pictures and captions on the opposite page. It seems only natural for a President to continue to seek counsel of a man he has elevated to the high court when long and intimate association with such a man appears to make his counsel worth seeking.

Indeed, the issues dramatized by the Fortas case are as old as the Supreme Court itself, for the very first Chief Justice, John Jay, established a precedent by engaging in both public and private extrajudicial activities that got him into considerable difficulties and caused his friend and patron President Washington no little embarrassment. This fascinating historical parallel is documented in the article beginning on the next page, the last of three devoted to Jay's career and based on his unpublished papers at Columbia University.

—The Editors

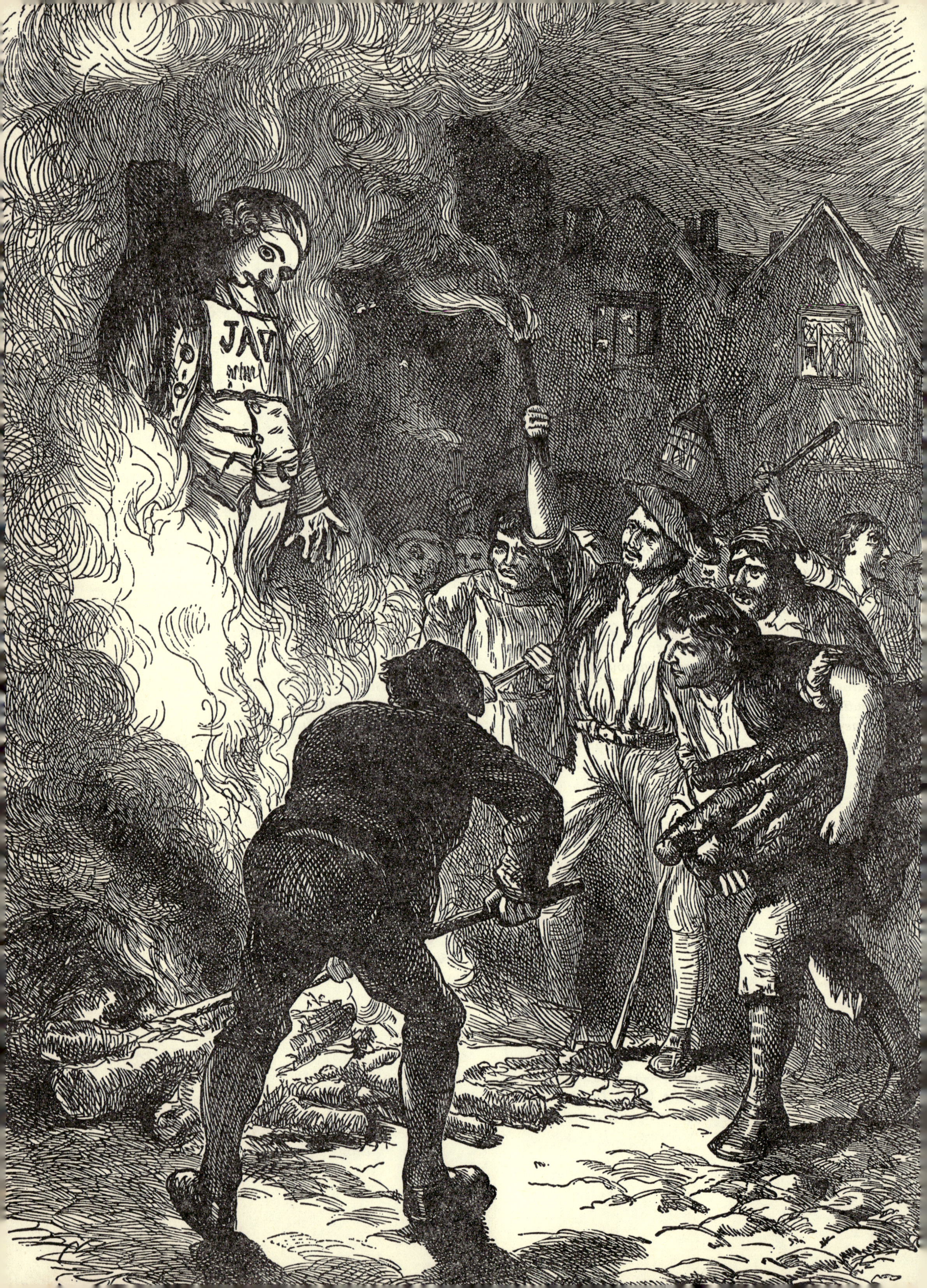
JAY

President Washington named John Jay to be the first head of the Supreme Court because the New Yorker had been one of the most eloquent and persuasive partisans of the Constitution and its ratification. During the years of the Confederation, strong bonds of mutual esteem and affection had been forged between the two men, who shared an identity of views on the need to build a national character, to strengthen the machinery of the central government, and to bring about conformity to treaty obligations.

Jay was only forty-three when he became Chief Justice, and his legal and judicial experience had been relatively limited. He had not practiced law since 1774, though he had served a very brief term thereafter as chief justice of New York during the Revolutionary years. When Washington notified him of his appointment, Jay was in fact still holding over as Secretary of State, now ad interim for Thomas Jefferson, who did not assume the post until March of 1790. For almost six months Jay wore two very different hats.

It has been the fashion among historians of the Supreme Court to minimize the significance of the Jay Court because of its comparative inactivity, and to treat the Chief Justice as something of a cipher. The facts do not support such an appraisal. On the bench Jay proved himself to be both a creative statesman and an activist Chief Justice whose concepts of the broad purpose and powers of the new nation under the Constitution were to be upheld and spelled out with boldness and vigor by John Marshall. What other Chief Justice, one might ask, not only stumped the country on foreign-policy issues, but went abroad while yet in office to negotiate a highly controversial treaty with a major power? What other Chief Justice ran for governor of his home state not once but twice, not resigning from the Court until he was notified that he had won the second election? What other Chief Justice enjoyed the notoriety of being threatened with prosecution for criminal libel on account of his extrajudicial activities?

As Chief Justice, Jay distinguished between his personal role and that of the Court. He held strict views of the Court's functions and denied the right of the other two branches of the government to assign it "any duties but such as are properly judicial and performed in a judicial manner." He also declined, in his official capacity, to render advisory opinions to the executive branch of the government. But Jay's concept of what was proper for the Court did not keep him from political activism as an individual. In his private capacity he did not hestitate to counsel President Washington, heads of departments, and even the Senate. But it should be pointed out that from the start the President had given him a blanket invitation to do so. In November of 1790 and again in the following September, Washington solicited Jay's ideas, hoping that they would "not be confined to matters merely Judicial, but extended to all other topics which have, or may occur to you as fit subjects for general, or private Communications."

That Jay freely took the President at his word is demonstrated by the record. In 1790, American neutrality was threatened by a potential collision between British and Spanish subjects at Nootka Sound off southwestern British Columbia. Washington asked his heads of departments—and Chief Justice Jay as well—for advice in the event that Britain should attempt to march troops from Canada across American territory. Knowing that the United States was unable to assume the risks of war, Jay was inclined to be dovish; if Britain politely asked for permission, he told the President, it might be better to try to cultivate her good will by extending it. In the event that the redcoats simply marched into American territory without leave, however, Jay was prepared to don the wings of a hawk. "Such a Measure would then be so . . . flagrant and wanton a Violation of the Rights of Sovereignty," he wrote, ". . . that their March (if after Prohibition persisted in) should I think be opposed and prevented at every Risque and Hazard." Fortunately for American neutrality, Spain, lacking robust support from revolutionary France, conceded most of the British demands, and war in North America was avoided.

In 1792, when the first rumblings of discontent against the whiskey tax had come out of western Pennsylvania, Secretary of the Treasury Alexander Hamilton prodded Jay to join him in getting the President to outlaw the demonstrations. Jay answered as follows:

N York 8 Septr. 1792

Dear Sir

I have conferred with Mr. King [Federalist Senator Rufus King of New York] on the Subject of your Letter of the 3rd Inst. We concur in opinion that neither a Proclamation nor a *particular* charge by the court to the G[rand] Jury, would be adviseable at present. To us it appears more prudent that this Business be opened by the Presidts. Speech at the ensuing Session of congress—their address will manifest the

Left: The treaty Jay negotiated with Britain in 1794, while still Chief Justice, was so unpopular at home that he was hanged or burned in effigy in several cities. He had, it was said, sold out his country for gold.

sense of the House, and both together operate more effectually than a Proclamation.

No strong Declarations shd. be made unless there be ability and Disposition to follow them with strong measures—admitting both these Requisites, it is questionable whether such operations at this moment would not furnish the antis with materials for decieving the uninformed part of the Community, and in some measure render the operations of administration odious. Let all the Branches of Govt. move together, and let the chiefs be committed publickly on one or the other Side of the Question. I percieve Symptoms of the crisis you mention—if managed with Prudence and Firmness it will weaken its authors. If matters can pass on *Sub Silentio* untill the meeting of Congress, I think all will be well. The public will become informed, and the Sense of the Nation become manifest. Opposition to that Sense will be clogged with apprehensions, and strong measures if necessary will be approved and be supported.

If in the mean Time such outrages shd. be committed as to force the attention of Govt. to its Dignity, nothing will remain but to obey that necessity in a way, that will leave nothing to Hazard. Success on such occasions shd. be certain—whether this shd. be done under the President's personal Direction must I think depend on circumstances at the Time, or in other words on the Degree of Importance which those Circumstances combined may evince.

JOHN JAY

Thus far Jay had remained behind the arras, but events soon thrust him to the forefront and into a more explosive role. What triggered the Chief Justice's public intervention in nonjudicial affairs was France's declaration of war against Great Britain in February, 1793, which converted the French Revolution into a war on the high seas and a land war of continental dimensions. When the news reached Philadelphia in April, Washington hastened thither from Mount Vernon to discuss it with his Cabinet. Jay, at Hamilton's suggestion, drafted a neutrality proclamation for possible use by the President. Excerpts follow.

[April 11, 1793]

Whereas every Nation has a right to change and modify their constitution and Government, in such Manner as they may think most conducive to their welfare and Happiness. And whereas they who actually administer the Government of any Nation, are by foreign Nations to be regarded as its *lawful Rulers,* so long as they continue to be recognized and obeyed *as such,* by the great Body of their people.

And whereas Monarchy has been in fact abolished in France, and a Government, recognized and obeyed by the great Body of the *nation,* does there *actually* exist and operate; it is proper as well as necessary that the political Intercourse between that Nation *and this* should be conducted thro the Medium of that Government where it shall so continue to be recognized and obeyed.

Altho the Misfortunes (to whatever Cause they may be imputed) which the late King of France and others have suffered in the Course of that Revolution or which that nation may yet experience are to be regretted by the Friends of Humanity, and particularly by the People of America, to whom both that king and that Nation have done essential Services; yet it is no less the Duty than the Interest of the United States, strictly to observe that Conduct towards all Nations, which the Laws of nations prescribe.

And whereas war actually exists between France on the one side and Austria, Prussia, Great Britain and the United Netherlands, on the other; and to avoid being involved in that Calamity, it is necessary that the United States should by a Conduct perfectly inoffensive cultivate and preserve the Peace they now enjoy; with a firm Determination nevertheless, always to prefer War to Injustice and Disgrace.

I do therefore most earnestly advise and require the Citizens of the United States to be circumspect in their Conduct towards all nations and particularly towards those now at war . . . I do also recommend to my fellow Citizens in general, that [they abstain from] such public Discussions of certain questions foreign to us, as must tend not only to cause Divisions and Parties among ourselves, and thereby impair that union on which our Strength depends, but also give unnecessary Cause of offence, and Irritation to foreign powers. And I cannot forbear expressing a wish, that our Printers [i.e., newspaper publishers] may study to be impartial in the Representation of Facts, and observe much Prudence relative to such Strictures and Animadversions as may render the Dispositions of foreign Governments and Rulers, unfriendly to the People of the United States. . . .

I do also enjoin all Magistrates and others in authority to be watchful and diligent in preventing aggressions against foreign nations and their people; and to cause all offenders to be prosecuted and punished in an Exemplary manner.

A crisper proclamation, drafted by Attorney General Edmund Randolph, was eventually issued by President Washington, but Jay's version is interesting for two reasons: in the first place, it raised an issue then novel to international law—using as a test for the recognition of new, revolutionary governments the extent to which they rested upon a popular mandate. Jay's concept anticipated Woodrow Wilson by 125 years. In the second place, Jay's stated intention to curb public debate foreshadowed some of the High Federalist restraints that were to be embodied a few years later in the Alien and Sedition Acts.

Jay was to experience difficulty walking the fine, straight line he had drawn between the freedom to express his personal opinions in the high councils of government and the restrictions which his position as Chief Justice placed upon him. A severe test came with the Genêt affair, which seriously jeopardized the neutral stance of the Washington administration.

Enthusiasm of American Jacobins for intervening on France's side in the expanding European war had reached a high pitch and soon became a fever when, just at the time Jay was drafting the neutrality proclamation, there arrived at Charleston, South Caro-

The first meeting of the Supreme Court took place in the Royal Exchange at the foot of Broad Street in New York on February 1, 1790. As the minutes (below) indicate, it was not an earth-shaking session. No important case came before the Court until Chisholm v. Georgia *in August of 1792.*

lina, France's newly appointed youngish minister to the United States, Edmond Charles Genêt. The instant he landed, Genêt began to whip up pro-French propaganda and to mobilize public sentiment against the neutral course that was being charted by President Washington. More important, he insisted both in public and in private discussions with American political leaders that the United States fulfill its obligations under the Franco-American treaties of 1778 by providing bases from which French privateers might operate against the British.

Almost singlehandedly, Chief Justice Jay sought to stem the rising pro-French tide. In the first place, he exploited the opportunities provided by the Judiciary Act of 1789, which required the judges of the Supreme Court to sit in the United States circuit courts.*

On May 22, in a charge to the grand jury of the circuit court of Richmond, Virginia, he strongly condemned American debtors who sought to avoid paying debts due British creditors—debts that had been guaranteed by the Treaty of 1783, which Jay himself had drafted. In addition, he charged the grand jury to observe the laws of neutrality.

... When two or more [nations] are at war about objects in which other nations are not interested, the latter are not to interfere except as mediators and friends to peace; but, on the contrary, ought to observe a strict impartiality towards both....

If in this district you should find any [American citizens] engaged in fitting out privateers or enlisting men to serve against either of the belligerent powers, and in other respects violating the laws of neutrality, you will present them....

But the belligerent powers owe duties to us as well as we to them. They may violate our neutrality and commit offenses. If you find any foreigners in this district committing seditious practices, endeavouring to seduce our citizens into acts of hostility, or attempting to withdraw them from the allegiance of the United States, present them. Such men are guilty of high misdemeanour....

The nation must either move together or lose its force. Until war is constitutionally declared, the nation and all its members must observe and preserve peace, and do the duties incident to a state of peace....

The Jay court handed down decisions that outraged the Francophile faction in America. Over and above this, however, the Chief Justice felt it incumbent on himself personally to try to reverse the current of public opinion about Citizen Genêt and his unneutral behavior. This was to lead Jay into trouble.

Even a confirmed Francophile like Thomas Jefferson soon found that Genêt's indiscretions were proving a political liability. Independent of the President and the Secretary of State, Genêt proceeded to refit an English brig, the *Little Sarah,* which a French frigate had captured and brought into the port of Philadelphia. It was renamed *La Petite Démocrate,* and Genêt, in defiance of Jefferson, arranged for the brig to slip out of port to do battle with the British. In an effort to restrain Genêt from thus compromising America's neutrality, the governor of Pennsylvania, Thomas Mifflin, had dispatched his secretary of state, Alexander J. Dallas, to intercede with the French minister.

---

*Jay and his associates were to find this extra burden an extremely tedious task and were loud in their protests, but, though temporarily relieved of circuit-riding duties by an act passed in 1801, the Supreme Court justices were back on circuit as a result of a repeal of that act by the Jeffersonians the following year. It was not until 1891, when a long-delayed judicial reform established a new circuit system, that Supreme Court judges were relieved by law of circuit duties.—R.B.M.

According to Mifflin's reputed account as related to him by Dallas, the Frenchman "flew into a great passion," expressed his contempt for Washington, and threatened, if necessary, to "appeal from the President to the People."

It is at this point that John Jay comes into the story. Dallas reported the interview to Governor Mifflin, who in turn told the tale to Hamilton and Secretary of War Henry Knox. Before they left Philadelphia for New York, Jay and Senator King heard the story from Hamilton, a statesman hardly renowned for his discretion. Thus, fourth-hand, the story made the rounds of New York City, at the very moment Genêt arrived on a propaganda visit. A huge mass meeting in front of Trinity Church sponsored by the Federalists adopted resolutions praising President Washington for his Neutrality Proclamation. Then the Federalists brought up their big guns.

Appearing under the names of Jay and King in the New York *Diary or Loudon's Register,* the following "card" publicized Genêt's alleged threat.

New York, August 12, 1793
Messrs. Printers:
Certain late publications render it proper for us to authorize you to inform the public, that a report having reached this City from Philadelphia that Mr. Genêt, the French Minister, said that he would appeal to the people from certain decisions of the President; we were asked on our return to that place, whether he had made such a declaration; we answered that he had—and we also mentioned it to others, authorising them to say that we had so informed them.
JOHN JAY
RUFUS KING

Widely reprinted in the Federalist press, Genêt's alleged remarks unleashed a storm of denunciations of the French minister. Countering, the Francophiles cast doubt on the veracity of the account and denounced Jay as the "prince of the Jesuits." Genêt himself immediately appealed to President Washington for a testimonial that the Frenchman had "never intimated to you an intention of appealing to the people"; replying for the President, Jefferson informed Genêt that Washington declined "interfering in the case."

Having irreparably damaged his standing even with his own partisans in America, poor Genêt now sought redress from the very government he had treated so shabbily. Turning to Secretary of State Jefferson and Attorney General Randolph, he had the effrontery to demand that Chief Justice Jay and Senator King, the authors of the "libel," be "prosecuted at the Federal Court."

Faced with the threat of a libel suit, Jay and King felt obliged to call upon Hamilton and Knox to substantiate their story. Hamilton, who had intimated that if possible the source of the story should not be disclosed, now had no alternative but to corroborate their account, which he and Knox did in a statement in the New York *Daily Advertiser:*

Philadelphia, Nov. 29, 1793.
We, the subscribers, certify that we did severally communicate to the above mentioned John Jay and Rufus King, the particulars contained in the foregoing statement. That such of them as are therein mentioned to have been reported to Governor Mifflin by Mr. Dallas were communicated by the Governor to each of us as having been received by him from Mr. Dallas. That such of them as respect Mr. Jefferson, including the information to him from Mr. Dallas of Mr. Genêt's having said *"that he would appeal from the President to the People,"* were communicated to us by Mr. Jefferson.
ALEXANDER HAMILTON
H. KNOX

Dallas, from whom Jay and King had also expected some support, now equivocated, finally admitting—in a signed newspaper article—that his memory of his conversation with Genêt was hazy, and that if pushed to recall it exactly, he would have to say that the expression that "he would appeal from the President to the People" was not a direct quote from Genêt but rather Dallas' own paraphrase of the conversation.

Genêt's audacious move raised all sorts of embarrassing issues. The prosecution of the Chief Justice and a leading Federalist senator for criticizing the conduct of a foreign diplomat was without precedent, and it left President Washington in an awkward position. Any action he took might seriously jeopardize relations among the three separate branches of the government and inflict dangerous wounds on the doctrine of separation of powers. The projected suit was also calculated to bring the Supreme Court into contempt.

Still, Washington felt he had to take official cognizance of Genêt's request. Through Jefferson he called on Randolph to take prompt action "as it concerns a public character [Genêt] particularly entitled to the protection of the laws." Jefferson, now sick and tired of Genêt, recognized that prosecuting so high a figure in the government as the Chief Justice could easily boomerang. Yet his advice to Randolph was ambiguous. The President, he advised the Attorney General, felt that Genêt's charges had to be dealt with; on the other hand, he felt that "our citizens ought not to be vexed with groundless prosecutions." Randolph refused to bring Genêt's suit; the Frenchman could, said the Attorney General, hire his own lawyer to handle it. Genêt did so, engaging Edward Livingston, a political foe of Jay's.

Meanwhile, President Washington was terribly embarrassed by the indiscreet conduct of the Chief Justice

Secretary of State Jefferson, at left, failed to dissuade the French minister, Genêt, from trying to drag the United States into the Anglo-French war. Chief Justice Jay's intervention in the affair was a grave embarrassment to President Washington.

of the United States, and presently he called Jay on the carpet. Our only record of their conversations is contained in a memorandum in Rufus King's handwriting.

February, 1794

... In December [1793] Mr. Jay and I addressed a letter to the President ... explanatory of our conduct, complaining of the letters which by his direction had been written by the Attorney General and the Secretary of State relative to this affair, and [asking the President] to direct the Secretary of State to furnish us with a certified copy of his Report to the President, of the interview between Mr. Dallas and him, and that he would permit us to publish the same in order to place before the public the evidence relative to Mr. Genêt's Declaration. ...

The President sent for Mr. Jay—they conversed freely upon the subject—the President justified his own conduct and expressed his opinion that nothing incorrect or unfriendly had been intended by Jefferson or Randolph and complained of the severity of our Letter—spoke of the difficulty of his situation and of the necessity of his conducting with great caution. Mr. Jay explained our situation, the purity of our views, the anxiety for the public peace wh. had stimulated our conduct, and the wounds inflicted upon us in consequence of the Part we had acted; that under such circumstances we were entitled to the full Force and disclosure of those Truths which would justify us in the presence of our fellow citizens. ...

Much conversation passed at this interview; the President

PICTURE CREDITS FOR PAGE 80: LEFT TO RIGHT, ROW 1, INDEPENDENCE NATIONAL HISTORICAL PARK; WASHINGTON AND LEE UNIVERSITY; U.S. SUPREME COURT; TENNESSEE STATE LIBRARY AND ARCHIVES; ROW 2, NATIONAL PORTRAIT GALLERY; U.S. SUPREME COURT; UPI; ROW 3, U.S. SUPREME COURT; TAFT MUSEUM; ROW 4, U.S. SUPREME COURT; U.S. SUPREME COURT; HARVARD LAW SCHOOL; NATIONAL GALLERY OF ART.

expressed his friendship for Mr. Jay, and his respect and regards for me, etc., etc. ...

This arrangement was agreed on—Mr. Jay sent the Draft [of the Jay-King letter] to me immediately on his return to New York and I delivered it to the President, wh. together with the [President's copy of the] Letter, and a paper in the President's handwriting justifying his conduct and which he gave to me to read, he, in my presence, put into the fire. ...

As in all good fairy tales, the villain was given his comeuppance and the righteous were rewarded. Amidst preparations by the Democratic-Republicans of New York City for a dinner in Genêt's honor came word of his recall. His successor, Jean Antoine Joseph Fauchet, forced Genêt to drop his libel suit against Jay and King, but a forbearing American government allowed the ex-minister to remain here, realizing that had he been returned to France, he would most assuredly have been liquidated. Genêt settled down into relative rustic seclusion, married a daughter of Governor George Clinton of New York, and became an American citizen. He lived in peaceful retirement in upstate New York until his death in 1834.

If there was any breach between the President and the Chief Justice as a result of the notoriety that Jay had gained in the Genêt affair, it was soon healed, for in April, 1794, Washington named Jay to go to Great Britain to negotiate a treaty settling outstanding grievances between the two nations, grievances intensified of late by British interference with neutral shipping and by impressment of American seamen, actions spurred by her involvement in the European war against France. The nomination had rough sledding in the Senate. For three days hostile senators debated the propriety of a Chief Justice doubling in a diplomatic post and objected to Jay's well-known British predilections, but at last Jay was confirmed, eighteen to eight.

So much has been written about the shortcomings of Jay's Treaty that little more need be said. On the positive side, the British agreed to withdraw from the forts in the American Northwest which they had continued to occupy in violation of the Treaty of 1783. The new treaty also provided for the referral to joint commissions of the issues of the pre-Revolutionary debts, the disputed northeast boundary between the United States and Canada, and the matter of compensation for illegal maritime seizures. The treaty placed British trade with the United States on a most-favored-nation basis, admitted U.S. vessels to British East Indian ports on a nondiscriminatory basis, and opened the West Indies trade to U.S. vessels not exceeding seventy tons' burden, provided they did not take as cargo cotton, sugar, or molasses. But the treaty contained no reference to the hot issue of impressment, to control of the

Indians, or to settlement of American claims for slaves removed by the departing British as the Revolution ended or of British counterclaims for the return of Loyalist property seized in America. Its meager concessions in the West Indies drew the ire of all sections of the country.

It is now known that the American negotiator was, without his knowledge, deprived of his ace-in-the-hole when Hamilton, in conversation with George Hammond, the British minister, gratuitously disclosed that the United States had no intention of going to war to enforce its demands on Great Britain. What is less evident, perhaps, is that Jay's reluctance to take a tough stand in the negotiations stemmed in no small part from his legal and juristic training. Jay was a stickler for the letter of the law, and he believed that although the failure of the British to evacuate the frontier posts was a violation of the Treaty of Paris, it was not unprovoked. Americans had brought it on themselves by refusing to return Loyalist property confiscated during the war, and by not paying the prewar debts they owed to British merchants. In a hitherto unpublished memorandum which he drafted in London, he carefully set forth the sequence of treaty violations as he saw them.

Jay's coat of arms

August 5, 1794

The Provisional Articles were signed at Paris November 30th 1782. They were to constitute the treaty of Peace *to be concluded* between Great Britain and the United States, but that Treaty was not to be concluded till terms of peace with France were settled. Even these Articles were not ratified in America till the 15th April 1783, several months before that Treaty was signed, and when even the Provisional Articles were not mutually ratified.

The Treaty of Peace was in fact not signed till September 3rd, 1783. It was not ratified in America till the 14th of January 1784; and that Ratification was not exchanged in Europe till the end of May 1784, nor received in London till the 28th of that Month.

Till that period, no order for evacuating the Forts could with propriety be sent from hence. . . . But in the intermediate time measures had been taken in America which are incontestible infractions of the Treaty; measures not merely resulting from the continuance of a Status Quo, agreeably to reason and to the practice of all Nations, during the suspension of hostilities, and till the final exchange of ratifications; but new Legislative Acts, adopted after the knowledge of the terms agreed upon, avowedly intended to defeat the execution of those terms when the treaty should be concluded and ratified, and in their operation necessarily producing that effect.

On the bare statement of these dates, there can be no doubt from which side the first violation of the Treaty proceeded, if that discussion were now necessary or useful.

While Jay's legalistic quibbling inhibited his operations as a diplomat, his legal background was reflected in the articles of the Jay Treaty providing for mixed commissions to settle both the debt issue and the northeast boundary. The latter commission established a precedent for boundary disputes to which the United States was a party. In turning over to a mixed commission the settlement of the debts due British creditors, the Chief Justice was castigated for damaging the prestige and authority of his own court by depriving it of jurisdiction over such crucial matters, which would then be turned over to an extrajudicial body conceivably controlled by a foreign power. It must be remembered, however, that not long before this the Chief Justice, with the concurrence of a majority of the associate justices, had upheld the right of an individual to sue a state without the state's consent (*Chisholm v. Georgia*). A wave of states' rights indignation thereupon swept the country, and eventually the Eleventh Amendment was adopted to bar all such actions. Hence it can be argued that, in keeping so emotionally charged a political issue as the debts out of the Court, Jay demonstrated both prudence and common sense. He made certain that the running sore of the debt issue would not weaken the Court's authority as the issue of state sovereignty had done. If Jay in this instance used his treaty to dilute federal jurisdiction, he more than made amends by his strong decisions as Chief Justice upholding the sovereignty of the United States over violations of international law.

Jay's defense of his treaty is contained in a private letter he sent to President Washington at the close of his mission.

London, 6th March 1795

Dear Sir:

. . . After considering all that I have heard and seen on the subject, it is my opinion that the common and popular (not Official) language and conduct of America relative to Great Britain, manifested such a disposition, as to create serious apprehensions in this country, that we should join with the French in the war. . . . Various circumstances, however, induce me to believe, that the [British] Cabinet ultimately determined to give Conciliation a fair experiment, by doing us substantial justice, and by consenting to such Arrangements favorable to us, as the national interests, and habitual prejudices would admit. To relax the navigation Act, was to alarm these prejudices; and therefore was a measure which required caution and circumspection, especially in the first instance. To break the Ice, was the difficulty; to enlarge the Aperture afterwards would be more easy; and it will probably be done, if we should be reasonably temperate and prudent. To admit us into their East and West India dominion and into all their continental American territories, under any modifications, were decided deviations from their former policy, and tended to shock ancient prejudices. Yet these things have been done. None but a strong Administration would have ventured it. These are Offerings to conciliation, and conclude [*i.e.,* prove] though not confessedly, satisfaction to our claims of justice.

... Whatever the American opinion of [the treaty] may prove to be; the Administration here think it very friendly to us; and that it could not in the present moment have been made more so, without exciting great discontent and uneasiness in this country.

The present situation of Great Britain may to us and others appear to be perilous, but the Ministry seem to have no such fears. They have been uniformly bent on prosecuting the war with vigour, and since my arrival I have observed no change in that resolution . . . I will mention a striking anecdote.

You have doubtless heard, that the merchants concerned in the American Trade gave me a dinner. The principal Cabinet Ministers were present, and about 200 merchants. Many Toasts were given. When the "President of the United States" was given, it was proposed to be with three Cheers, but they were prolonged (as if by preconcert, but evidently not so) to six. Several other toasts passed with great acclamation, particularly "The wooden walls of Old England." Almost every Toast referable to America, and manifesting a desire of conciliation and cordiality, met with General and strong marks of Approbation. Towards the conclusion of the feast, I was asked for a Toast. I gave a *neutral* one, vizt. "a safe and honorable peace to all the belligerent powers." You cannot conceive how coldly it was received, and though civility induced them to give it three Cheers, yet they were so faint and single, as most decidedly to show that peace was not the thing they wished; these were *Merchants.* . . .

Except an inconsiderable number, the men of Rank and Property, and all whom they can influence, thoroughout the Kingdom, think the war is indispensible to their safety. . . .

I have great reason to believe that the King [George III] the Cabinet and Nation, were never more unanimous in any system than in that of conciliation with us . . . If it should not succeed; they will naturally pass like a Pendulum to the other extreme.

This system rests principally on their Confidence in the Uprightness Independence and wisdom of your Conduct. No other man whatever enjoys so completely the Esteem and Confidence of this Nation as you do; nor except the King is any one so popular. The idea which every where prevails is, that the Quarrel between Britain and America was a family Quarrel, and that it is time it should be made up; for my part I am making it up, and for cherishing this disposition on their part; by Justice, Benevolence and Good manners on ours. To cast ourselves into the Arms of this, or of any other nation, would be degrading, injurious and puerile; nor in my Opinion ought we to have any political Connection with any foreign power. . . .

The Tranquillity of the present session of Congress is a pleasing Circumstance; but I suspect it has proceeded more from their having had nothing to differ about, than from a spirit of forbearance or a desire of unanimity. The result of my negociations will doubtless produce fresh difficulties; and give occasion to much declamation, for I have no idea that the Treaty will meet with antifoederal approbation. Besides, men are more apt to think of what they wish to have, than of what is in their power to obtain. . . .

Jay returned to New York on May 28, 1795, to be saluted by a cannonade from the Battery and the ringing of church bells, and to be greeted by a welcoming delegation of citizens who notified him that he had recently been a candidate for the governorship of New York state and that on the basis of early returns it seemed as though he had been elected. Three years before, Jay had run for the governorship, only to be counted out by George Clinton's Antifederalist machine. While he did not actively canvass votes at that time, neither did he seem to feel that he should resign from the Court in order to stand for elective office. If Jay established a precedent for judicial politicking, it has not survived into our modern era: Associate Justice Charles Evans Hughes resigned from the high court in 1916 when he ran for the Presidency, and similar action would be expected of any high judicial officer today.

His election to the governorship in 1795 could not have been a complete surprise to Jay. As early as December, 1793, Federalist political managers had held conversations with the Chief Justice about running for governor again. He expressed his preference for the Supreme Court, but, as his friend Egbert Benson reported to Rufus King, "he would not desert them." King and Hamilton had expected Jay to return from England before the elections of April, 1795. When he did not return, various Federalist caucuses proceeded to nominate him in absentia, and the Republican factions closed ranks behind Abraham Yates, who happened to be the chief justice of the New York supreme court. The battle of chief justices was fought in Jay's absence, with Jay, considered the man who would bring peace back from England, narrowly victorious by a vote of 13,481 to 11,892. His election confirmed, Jay sent a letter of resignation to the President on June 29 and two days later was sworn in as governor.

On that very day the newspapers carried the first summaries of the treaty he had concluded in London. The "declamation" Jay had foreseen now began—with a vengeance. A stunned nation denounced the treaty for making so few concessions to the United States.

Professor Morris, Gouverneur Morris Professor of History at Columbia, is editing the university's collection of Jay's unpublished papers. They will be brought out in two volumes sometime next year by Harper & Row.

Jeffersonian Democrats got out their scalping knives and their tar and feathers. John Jay was traduced as a rogue and a traitor; he was burned in effigy in New York and Savannah, and hanged in effigy in Charleston. On the fence of a prominent Boston Federalist was chalked in large letters: DAMN JOHN JAY! DAMN EVERY ONE THAT WON'T DAMN JOHN JAY!! DAMN EVERY ONE THAT WON'T PUT LIGHTS IN HIS WINDOWS AND SIT UP ALL NIGHT DAMNING JOHN JAY!! Fortunately for the Supreme Court, it was spared the public odium which would have been heaped upon it had not the voters of New York separated John Jay from his judicial duties.

With the backing of the President and Hamilton, the Jay Treaty was eventually ratified, though over the stiffest opposition. As for the former Chief Justice, he served two terms as governor, and lived in respected retirement until 1829, retrieving that reputation as a fine public servant that he had so fairly earned.

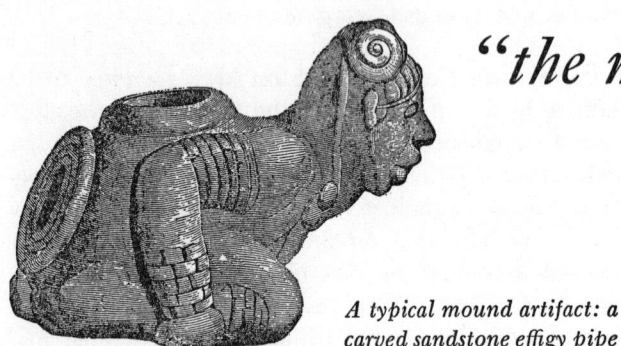

"*the mound-builders vanished*"
CONTINUED FROM PAGE 63

A typical mound artifact: a carved sandstone effigy pipe

was to be prevalent in the controversy that raged over the mounds for the next hundred years.

Identifying the vanished race became a popular scholarly pastime. The Ten Lost Tribes of Israel, of whom nothing had been heard since the conquest of Jerusalem by the Assyrians in 722 B.C., were a favorite choice. Many accounts appeared of the Hebrew migration to the Americas, listing dates of arrival, routes taken by specific tribes, and the mounds erected by each. There was no shortage of other ideas, however. Caleb Atwater, an Ohio postmaster who was the first to carry out an extensive archaeological study of the mounds, cited the presence of Old World mounds from Wales to Russia, and brought the Mound Builders to America via Asia, the Bering Strait, and Alaska. Writing in 1820, Atwater provided parallels between the cultures of India and ancient Ohio to prove his point: "The temples, altars, and sacred places of the Hindoos were always situated on the bank of some stream of water. The same observation applies to the temples, altars, and sacred places of those who erected our tumuli." The migration had occurred long ago, he says—"as early as the days of Abraham and Lot," maybe—judging by "the rude state of many of the arts among them." After building the humble earthen heaps in Ohio, though, the Mound Builders had begun gradually to move south, gaining in skill all the while, until they reached Mexico. This can be seen in the line of mounds that, Atwater says, "continue all the way into Mexico, increasing indeed in size, number, and grandeur, but preserving the same forms."

In comparison with some of his contemporaries, Atwater was a model of controlled, judicious thought. Among the fantasists was William Henry Harrison, who had first seen the mound country as a young officer fighting against the Ohio Indians in 1791. Some thirty years later, as a retired United States senator not yet thinking of the White House, Harrison produced a romantic analysis of the Mound Builders, imagining stirring battles, sweeping migrations of tribes, mighty hosts of enlightened beings streaming through the heartland of what one day would be the United States. He wrote:

We learn first, from the extensive country covered by their remains, that they were a numerous people. Secondly, that they were congregated in considerable cities. . . . Thirdly, that they were essentially an agricultural people; because, collected as they were in great numbers, they could have depended on the chase but for a small portion of their subsistence.

He imagined "that they were compelled to fly from a more numerous or a more gallant people," abandoning their great settlements. As for the hilltop fortifications, "it was here that a feeble band was collected . . . to make a last effort for the country of their birth, the ashes of their ancestors, and the altars of their gods. . . ."

Such vivid depictions caught the public fancy, and other "historians" were soon profiting from the fad. In 1833 a journalist named Josiah Priest published an elaborate explanation of the mounds in a jumbled volume, *American Antiquities*. It was a best seller: some 22,000 copies were bought in thirty months.

The speculative ferment over the mounds naturally had its impact on the imaginations of poets and novelists. The first domestic treatment of the subject in verse seems to have been "The Genius of Oblivion," published in 1823 by the New Hampshire poet Sarah J. Hale. Her thesis was that the Mound Builders were refugees from the Phoenician city of Tyre, who fled to America. In "Thanatopsis," the poem that established his reputation in 1817 when he was only twenty-three, William Cullen Bryant spoke of the ancient race of men interred in "one mighty sepulchre" among "the hills rock-ribbed and ancient as the sun." Fifteen years later, in "The Prairies," he was moved by a visit to the mound country to evoke "the dead of other days" and "the mighty mounds that overlook the river."

> ... *A race, that long has passed away,*
> *Built them;—a disciplined and populous race*
> *Heaped, with long toil, the earth. ...*
> ... *The red man came—*
> *The roaming hunter tribes, warlike and fierce,*
> *And the mound-builders vanished from the earth. ...*
> ... *The gopher mines the ground*
> *Where stood the swarming cities. All is gone;*
> *All—save the piles of earth that hold their bones,*
> *The platforms where they worshipped unknown*
> *gods. ...*

Novelists, too, heeded the appeal of the mounds, and for a while the genre of Mound Builder fiction was an active subbranch of American popular literature. A typical specimen is Cornelius Matthews' *Behemoth: A Legend of the Mound-Builders* (1839), which described the efforts of the Mound Builders to cope with a mammoth of supernatural size and strength that rampaged through their cities until slain by a hero named Bokulla.

Such fictions were avidly consumed by a New York farm boy named Joseph Smith, who was to found a major religion with tenets based on the Mound Builder tales. (See "The Farm Boy and the Angel" in the October, 1962, AMERICAN HERITAGE.) Born in 1805, Smith as a boy was given to experiencing religious visions, and also to speculating on the origin of the mounds. His mother later recalled:

He would describe the ancient inhabitants of this continent, their dress, mode of travelling, and the animals upon which they rode; their cities, their buildings, with every particular; their mode of warfare; and also their religious worship. This he would do with as much ease, seemingly, as if he had spent his whole life with them.

In 1823, Smith declared, an angel named Moroni came to him at night and showed him a book written on golden plates, which he could find buried in a hillside near Palmyra, New York. Four years later he began, with divine aid, to translate the plates, and by 1830 he produced the 588-page Book of Mormon.

The Book of Mormon, which inspired a religious movement that endured vicious persecution, the martyrdom of its leaders, and the official opposition of the United States government, reveals that Joseph Smith had carefully studied the Mound Builder legends. Owing much in style to the King James Bible, and deriving many of its themes from the Old Testament, it tells how, about 600 B.C., a party of Israelites escapes from Jerusalem just prior to its destruction by Nebuchadnezzar. Through God's guidance they cross the ocean to America, where they prosper and multiply, building mighty cities and great mounds and surrounding them with huge fortifications. But they split into two factions, the Nephites and the Lamanites. The Nephites till the land and become rich, but the Lamanites are ungodly, and sink into savagery. To punish them, God turns their skins red. They are, in fact, the ancestors of the American Indians. The Nephites, too, grow corrupt, backsliding into idolatry, and God, angered by their sins, sends the Lamanites to destroy them. In a climactic battle in A.D. 401 the last of the Nephites are engulfed by the red-skinned barbarians; one priest survives to compile the record on golden plates, which he buries and which remain hidden until discovered and translated by Smith.

By some two million Americans today The Book of Mormon is regarded in the same light as the Gospels or the Five Books of Moses. To their critics, however, Mormon beliefs are merely amusing fantasies, and the sacred Book of Mormon itself is just another literary expression of the Mound Builder mythology.

This conical mound, with its protective moat, was built about 2,500 years ago in what is now northeastern Kentucky.

In the middle years of the nineteenth century came a reaction against the more extravagant expressions of the lost-race myth. New archaeological research helped to foster this cooler attitude. Abelard Tomlinson, a member of the family that owned the property on which the vast Grave Creek mound stands in what is now West Virginia, excavated it in 1838. Sinking a seventy-seven-foot shaft, he found a stone-covered log-walled chamber that enclosed a skeleton decorated with a profusion of copper rings, shell beads, and mica plates. The Grave Creek artifacts were examined by Henry Rowe Schoolcraft, one of the great early figures of American anthropology, who pondered the problem of the mounds and in 1851 concluded:

There is little to sustain a belief that these ancient works are due to tribes of more fixed and exalted traits of civilization, far less to a people of an expatriated type of civilization, of either an ASIATIC or EUROPEAN origin, as several popular writers very vaguely, and with little severity of investigation, imagined.... There is nothing, indeed, in the magnitude and structure of our western mounds which a semi-hunter and semi-agricultural population, like that which may be ascribed to the ancestors of Indian predecessors of the existing race, could not have executed.

Schoolcraft was a generation ahead of his time. Americans, scholarly and otherwise, ignored his strictures and continued to relish the fantasies of a departed civilization.

Ephraim Squier produced his era's definitive study of the Mound Builders in 1847: *Ancient Monuments of the Mississippi Valley,* a ponderous folio written in collaboration with an Ohio physician, Edwin H. Davis, and published by the newly founded Smithsonian Institution. Their book instantly established itself as a work of commanding importance in American archaeology. As a summary of the knowledge of its particular field at that time, it was remarkable; as a model for later workers, it was invaluable; as a detailed record of the Ohio mounds as they appeared about 1847, it was unique. Squier and Davis described, classified, and analyzed hundreds of mounds, suggested varying purposes for them, and provided detailed charts so accurate and attractive that blowups of them are posted today at many of the surviving Ohio earthworks. Yet Squier and Davis adhered to the lost-race theory. Any visitor to the mounds, they wrote, must surely come away impressed by the "judgment, skill, and industry of their builders.... a degree of knowledge much superior to that known to have been possessed by the hunter tribes of North America previous to their discovery by Columbus, or indeed subsequent to that event." The handsome tools, weapons, and pottery excavated from mounds, the vigorous pipes carved in animal forms, and other finely wrought Mound Builder relics called forth from them the judgment that "as works of art they are immeasurably beyond anything which the North American Indians are known to produce, even at this day, with all the suggestions of European art and the advantages afforded by steel instruments." It was an accurate observation, but it led the scholars to mistaken inferences.

Carved figures of birds are among the most frequently found relics of the Mound Builders' civilization. Some of them are elaborately decorated: this hawk—or eagle—originally had eyes fashioned of small pearls.

The modern era in archaeology was now beginning. The cities of Egypt and Assyria were being exhumed; the Neanderthal skull had been found, transforming man's view of his past; Heinrich Schliemann was planning his excavation of Troy. In the United States some archaeologists continued to revolve the Israelite, Viking, and Mexican theories of the Mound Builders' origin; others introduced the exciting theory that they were survivors of the lost island Atlantis; and still others began to search for a more rational explanation of the earthen monuments. To most, the existence of the Mound Builders as a distinct, ancient, and vanished race still looked like the most probable alternative, especially after certain pipes in the form of elephant effigies turned up near Davenport, Iowa. It was generally agreed that the mammoths and other American elephants had died out thousands of years ago; and if elephant effigies were being uncovered in mounds, did that not prove the great antiquity of the Mound Builders? The voices of those who ascribed the mounds to the ancestors of recent Indian tribesmen were drowned out.

But then a new voice was heard through the land: that of John Wesley Powell, the one-armed Civil War veteran best known for his 1869 journey down the turbulent Colorado River. He had become, ten years later, the founder of the Smithsonian Institution's Bureau of Ethnology. With great eloquence and passion Powell had called for such a department to study the North American Indians. He did not at first intend that his department should do any archaeological work; he planned only to survey the languages, arts, institutions, and mythologies of extant tribes. But in 1881 a group of archaeologists quietly lobbied behind Powell's back and got Congress to tack an extra five thousand dollars to the Bureau of Ethnology's budget for "continuing archaeological investigation relating to mound-builders and prehistoric mounds."

Powell was not pleased, for he did not have funds enough even to do the ethnological work as he thought proper; but he obeyed Congress's behest, and set up a division within the bureau to investigate the mounds. He himself had done some mound digging in the Midwest from 1858 to 1860, and had found glass, iron, and copper artifacts in them that seemed plainly to have been acquired from white men. This led him to the conclusion that some of the mounds "were constructed subsequent to the advent of the white man on this continent." Since Congress had mandated a mound examination, Powell decided to use the opportunity to check his own theories. Late in 1881 he picked Cyrus Thomas, an Illinois-born entomologist, botanist, and archaeologist, to take charge of the bureau's mound explorations. When Thomas came to the Bureau of

92

Ethnology he was, he said, a "pronounced believer in the existence of a race of Mound Builders, distinct from the American Indians." Powell gave him one clerical assistant and three field assistants and told them to draw up a plan for a mound survey. The slayer of the myth was at hand, whether he himself knew it or not.

As Thomas laid his plans, another Bureau of Ethnology staff member, Henry W. Henshaw, fired the opening salvo of the campaign in the bureau's second annual report, published in 1883. Henshaw took out after Squier and Davis, though paying homage to their "skill and zeal" and to "the ability and fidelity which mark the presentation of their results to the public." He punctured certain erroneous zoological conclusions that they had drawn from animal-effigy pipes, which to them seemed to indicate Mound Builder commerce with South America and Africa. Then he turned on the famous elephant effigies "found" in Iowa, pronouncing them clumsy fakes. This drew outraged cries from the Davenport Academy of Natural Sciences in Iowa, which had sponsored the discovery of the elephant pipes and resented the "intemperate zeal" of the Bureau of Ethnology, which from its "commanding position . . . in the world of science" had chosen to deliver "an attack of no ordinary severity . . . upon the Davenport Academy of Natural Sciences."

While Henshaw battled with the Iowans over the authenticity of the elephant pipes, Thomas and his assistants roamed the Midwest and Southeast, collecting thousands of artifacts from mounds, including a good many of European manufacture, such as silver bracelets and crosses and specimens of machine-worked copper. All this served to reinforce Powell's original conviction that

> . . . a few, at least, of the important mounds of the valley of the Mississippi had been constructed and used subsequent to the occupation of the continent by Europeans, and that some, at least, of the mound builders were therefore none other than known Indian tribes.

Thomas' first formal theoretical statement on the mounds occupied more than a hundred pages of the Bureau of Ethnology's fifth annual report, released in 1887. Though he stated again and again that his conclusions were preliminary, Thomas' agreement with the Powell position was evident on every page. He opposed the "lost race" theory, and said:

> . . . whether the "Indian theory" proves to be correct or not, I wish to obtain for it at least a fair consideration. I believe the latter theory to be the correct one, as the facts so far ascertained appear to point in that direction, but I am not wedded to it; on the contrary, I am willing to follow the facts wherever they lead.

Thomas conceded that the picture of a mighty nation occupying the great valley of the Mississippi, with a chief ruler, a system of government, a vast central city, was "fascinating and attractive." He saw the romance in the image of the disappearance of this nation "before the inroads of savage hordes, leaving behind it no evidence of its existence, its glory, power, and extent save these silent forest-covered remains." But he warned that this theory, when once it has taken possession of the mind, "warps and biases all its conclusions."

After publishing several subsequent shorter reports, Thomas settled down to the production of his magnum opus: the massive essay, covering 730 quarto pages of small type, that fills the whole of the Bureau of Ethnology's twelfth annual report (1894). Here the Mound Builder myth was interred at last beneath a monument of facts. The heart of the report, covering nearly 500 pages, was simply a digest of field research,

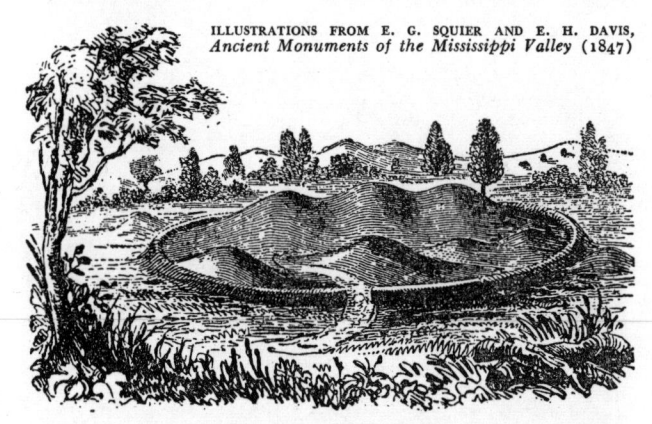

ILLUSTRATIONS FROM E. G. SQUIER AND E. H. DAVIS, *Ancient Monuments of the Mississippi Valley* (1847)

Many of the Ohio mounds were used as places of religious ceremony, to judge from the altars and other paraphernalia found inside them. This connected group of seven mounds in Ohio's Scioto Valley was opened early in the 1800's.

interspersed only occasionally with quotations from early explorers or with Thomas' interpretative conjectures. This was followed by an essay of some eighty pages on the types and distribution of mounds, showing with considerable force and skill the implausibility of assigning all the earthworks to a single "race." Lastly, Thomas reviewed the entire mound problem as it had unfolded since the eighteenth century, dealing in turn with each of the theories he was overthrowing. He deflated the lost-race fantasy with vigor and conviction. His basic conclusion, vital to any comprehension of American prehistory, was cool and rational:

> The mound-builders were divided into different tribes and peoples, which, though occupying much the same position in the culture scale, and hence resembling each other in many of their habits, customs, and modes of life, were as widely separated in regard to their ethnic relations and

languages as the Indian tribes when first encountered by the white race.

That statement needed refining—for actually the various mound-building groups did not occupy "much the same position in the culture scale." But it went to the essential truth of the situation: the archaeologists, as they sought to unravel the mystery of the mounds, had to be prepared to deal with diversity, not unity. Thomas' great report marked the end of an era. No longer could one speak of "the Mound Builders" in quite the same way, with the old implications of a single empire. But Thomas had raised as many questions as he had answered. It remained for archaeologists to examine the contents of the mounds more closely, to analyze the cultural traits of their builders, to study relationships—in short, to develop a coherent picture of the ancient American past.

That picture has largely come clear today, though all the problems are far from solved. In place of a

The "great mound" that is the big tourist attraction of Moundsville, West Virginia—about twelve miles from Wheeling—was probably the tomb of a chieftain and his family. This view shows it in the mid-nineteenth century.

monolithic race of Mound Builders, archaeologists have identified a succession of mound-building cultures spanning several thousand years. Careful excavation, comparison of artifacts and structural techniques, and use of such modern archaeological methods as carbon-14 dating have served to replace the old myth with reasonably certain scientific conclusions. Skeletal and cultural evidence shows clear kinship between the builders of the mounds and their less advanced neighbors and successors.

The pioneers of the earthworks were the Adena people, named from the estate near Chillicothe, Ohio, where their characteristic artifacts were first identified. The Adena culture, it appears, took form about 1000 B.C., and was typified by the burial of the dead in log-walled tombs beneath conical earthen mounds.

One archaeological faction holds that the Adenas were migrants from Mexico, carrying with them cultural traits superior to those of the Ohio valley where they settled; a more recent thesis makes them indigenous to the Northeast and the lower Great Lakes area. The Grave Creek mound in West Virginia, the largest conical mound in the United States, is Adena work, as is Ohio's Great Serpent mound.

About 400 B.C., apparently, a new group of Indians entered Adena territory: the Hopewells, named for a site in Ross County, Ohio, considered typical of their culture. These people were long-headed, unlike the round-headed Adenas, and they brought with them to Ohio an elaborate way of life that flowered wonderfully after the collision, peaceful or otherwise, with the Adenas. The Hopewell folk were, in effect, the Mound Builders of whom the nineteenth-century mythmakers dreamed. Although neither Phoenician nor Hindu nor Viking but merely American Indians out of the eastern woodlands, they did fill many of the qualifications of that phantom race of superior beings to whom the Ohio mounds had so often been attributed. They extended their influence out of southern Ohio into Indiana and Illinois and southeastern Iowa, northward to Wisconsin and Michigan, southward down the Mississippi past St. Louis. They evolved a complex funereal ritual including the erection of groups of conical mounds to house their dead notables; and they buried in the mounds a wealth of fine goods manufactured from exotic raw materials obtained through trade from such distant points as the Gulf coast and the Southwest.

Most of the mounds and earthworks that can be seen in Ohio today were made by the Hopewells. The most awesome, perhaps, is the great enclosure at Newark, which once covered four square miles. Only fragments remain: a joined circle and octagon, another circular enclosure, and some parallel walls. Though these structures are in part incorporated in a municipal golf course, they retain their majesty and splendor. From Hopewell mounds have come jewelry of bone, shell, and stone, breastplates and headdresses of copper, and ornaments cut from sheets of glittering mica. The abundance and high artistic quality of these burial goods mark the vitality and imagination of this remarkable culture. A strong Mexican influence is present in much Hopewell art, leading even the most conservative archaeologists to trace a flow of ideas out of Mexico and up the Mississippi to Ohio.

The end of the Hopewells came about A.D. 550, perhaps even earlier. They ceased to build their great ceremonial centers, and in another two centuries their distinctive way of life had disappeared, their territory was depopulated, and the people themselves had been absorbed into humbler tribes. We do not know why. "Cultural fatigue" has been suggested; a change of climate, perhaps; civil war; even that old standby, invasion by savages. There are indeed indications that toward the end the Hopewells took to the hills and tried to hold out behind high earthen walls. It was in vain; the forest closed over their mounds, and simpler folk took possession of their domain. Within a few generations, the newcomers had forgotten whatever they knew about the Hopewells. So mythical Mound Builders of non-Indian blood had to be invented by the white man, and fabulous tales woven about them, while outraged Hopewell spectres glowered in silent fury.

Long after the Hopewell collapse, the mound idea burst forth again in the Southeast, in a quite different form. Once again great ceremonial centers were erected; once more an elaborate social system came into being; there were developments in art and technology that rivalled and often exceeded Hopewell at its finest. The new mounds, however, were flat-topped platforms on which wooden temples, not burial structures, rose. These earthen pyramids, eighty to one hundred feet high and covering acres of ground, appeared first in Alabama, Georgia, and the rest of the Gulf coast states, and spread as far west as Texas and as far north as Illinois. By A.D. 900 most Indian tribes living along the Mississippi and its major tributaries knew something about the gospel of the platform-mound religion, and within another three centuries a chain of major ceremonial centers stretched across the continent from Oklahoma to Alabama. The Temple Mound people were agriculturalists, apparently far more skillful farmers than the Hopewells; we have found their hoes, made of stone, shell, or the shoulder blades of animals, and even the traces of their fields. They made excellent jewelry and pottery which shows obvious influence from the arts and crafts of Mexico, and their giant mounds, too, seem earthen imitations of Mexico's truncated pyramids.

Their culture flourished and expanded for hundreds of years, reaching a strange climax about 1500 with the development of the so-called Southern Cult, a religious movement typified by grotesque decorative styles employing figures of buzzards and snakes, flying horned serpents, weeping eyes, skulls, and eerie faces. The appearance of this cult has been explained as a shock reaction springing from the bloody and disastrous invasion of de Soto and his Spaniards in 1539–43, but recent research has shown that it antedates de Soto, and may have been an expression of vitality rather than terror, its symbols representing harvest and renewal rather than death and nightmare.

But by the end of the sixteenth century the Temple Mound culture was in decay, and its important centers —Cahokia in Illinois, Etowah in Georgia, Spiro in Oklahoma, Moundville in Alabama, and others—were abandoned. They were already in decline when the white man appeared, and they withered at his touch. The ancient customs lingered, reduced and diluted; about the huge mounds of revered ancestors the familiar rituals and festivals continued, but in a mechanical, ever less meaningful way, until their inner nature was forgotten and their practitioners could no longer remember that it was their own great-great-grandfathers who had built the mounds. The Creek, Chickasaw, and Choctaw Indians who occupied the Southeast when the Europeans came were in all likelihood the unknowing descendants of the Temple Mound folk. But only the Natchez Indians maintained their old ways into the eighteenth century, when the French destroyed their culture.

Archaeologists today, having disposed of the Mound Builder legend, busily search for detailed knowledge of the development, decline, and possible relationships of the Adena, Hopewell, and Temple Mound people, reducing romance to a complex series of phases, aspects, and cultural traditions. They smile at the fancies of yesteryear. Some of the mounds remain, celebrated locally as tourist attractions; and it is difficult now to comprehend the intensity of interest they provoked a century and more ago, or to grasp the deeper motives that led so many to believe that they were the work of superior beings hidden in the mists of time. Yet there is magic in the mounds now, despite the labors of those who have shown us why we must not talk of a nation of Mound Builders. Looking at these mysterious grassy monuments, one succumbs easily to fantasy, and feels the presence of the ghosts of departed grandeur; and then, in warm understanding, one reaches out across the decades to the makers of the Mound Builder myth.

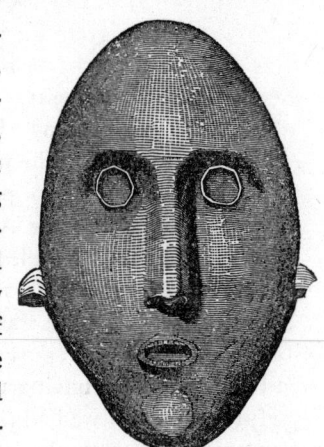

Some of the carved masks collected in midwestern mounds are, like this one, strongly reminiscent of the Aztec masks of Mexico.

Mr. Silverberg, who lives in New York City, has written widely on archaeological subjects, including Lost Cities and Vanished Civilizations *and* The Great Wall of China. *His recent* Mound Builders of Ancient America *(New York Graphic Society, 1968) is suggested for further reading.*

Return of the Exiles

CONTINUED FROM PAGE 24

already had with race riots during my regime as attorney general had been in Los Angeles—what we euphemistically called a "civil disturbance"—in the late summer of 1943. Mexican-American young men, called variously "pachucos" or "zoot-suiters," were picked on by mobs led primarily by servicemen from the Navy or Fort MacArthur. I think the original fight was over the available young ladies of the neighborhood, but "zoot-suiters" were something like the hippies of today. They wore strangely cut clothes and they had kind of duck-tailed hair-dos, and this, as you know, seems to enrage some people. At any rate, it enraged the young servicemen and some local patriots. It was really terrible. The kids were chased—I remember one Mexican boy was chased right onto the stage of the Orpheum Theater in downtown Los Angeles, and his clothes were ripped from him. There were thirty-five people killed in those riots! At the time, I was in San Francisco; I went immediately to Sacramento and talked with Governor Warren. He shared my alarm. I came down to Los Angeles and talked to the newspapers. We were able to persuade them to stop printing provocative stories about the riots, and the Army and Navy co-operated by declaring Los Angeles off-limits for servicemen. Within two or three days the trouble was over.

But we'd had a good scare, and I was able to get the state to subsidize a report on the nature of race riots and how to avoid having them. That report was very useful to us when we had the problem of the returning Japanese because the basic assumptions in it were the foundation of what I used to call our prophylactic approach to law enforcement.

Actually we had first used this approach in another connection. When we passed a law outlawing slot machines, there were a number of sheriffs who just couldn't seem to address themselves to it. So we'd call and say, "We hear you're having trouble. If you would like us to come down and help you get rid of the gamblers and the slot machines, we'll be glad to. Just let us know." This "we-boys" technique put me on the side of the sheriff instead of against him, and it worked very well.

Basically, the assumption now—in 1943—was that the police could prevent a race riot, and that it was to their advantage to do so. The most important means for doing this was taking an unequivocal stand against this sort of lawlessness when it began. We had a long check list of steps that could be taken in any local police department—ways to pick up warning signals well ahead of time, ways to build better relationships between minority groups and the police, how to stop the circulation of rumors, reduce other kinds of tension. But the big push, of course, was for education—a training course for peace officers in the problems of minority group relations. It was part of the final report—the little blue book, as we called it.

We got copies of the blue book into the hands of every peace officer in the state. Actually it was circulated all over the country. They were having race riots in Harlem and Detroit and many other places in 1943, and there was lots of interest in our material.

One of the first things we did, now that we knew the Japanese were coming back, was to get out an updated edition of the blue book and see that it got around, to ease the path of the returning Japanese and to curb the professional patriots.

What were the professional patriots doing?

All sorts of weird and shocking things. You may recall that up in Hood River, Oregon, the American Legion post had voted to remove the names of Nisei servicemen from its honor roll. Well, the city fathers in Gardena, California, did the same thing.

And there were more serious things—vandalism, dynamitings, fires. Oil lanterns were thrown at the windows of an old Buddhist temple in San Francisco where a group of returning Japanese were being sheltered. There was vandalism in a Japanese cemetery in Salinas. They were announcing up in Placer County that there would be no relief for indigent Japanese.

The illustrations on these pages are from Citizen 13660, *a book by Miné Okubo, a young woman who was among the thousands of Japanese-Americans interned early in World War II. Surprisingly detached in its pictures and their captions, the book is a pictorial record of Miss Okubo's life at the Tanforan Racetrack assembly center in San Bruno, California, and later at the camp at Topaz, Utah. Miss Okubo is now an artist in New York City.*

Barrack rooms at Topaz were bare rectangles whose masonite floors were hard to keep clean.

Miss Okubo wrote that the blocks of barracks all looked alike; "people were lost all the time."

And there were scare shootings. I remember seeing Nisei homes where bullets had gone right through the thin walls and passed within inches of sleeping children. One of the worst was an incident in Placer County, where it was perfectly well known who had shot up the house of a recently returned couple, but the local jury simply tapped them on the wrist and the judge suspended sentence.

Then there was that really dreadful incident in a little town called Loomis. A family of Japanese returned, mother, father, and three daughters, and found their home burned to the ground. That time the vigilantes overreached themselves. The War Relocation people let it be known that this family had four sons in the armed services, one of them already dead overseas, and three of the four decorated for bravery. The town conscience was touched. Money was collected, and I believe one of the churches undertook to see to it that a new house was built.

But there's no question that there was a real attempt, with organizational backing, to drive these people out of California. The motives were interesting. We conducted quite an investigation around Fresno, where there was a great deal of anti-Japanese sentiment, and we found that much of it was generated by a village banker who had been a great friend of the Japanese when they were being evacuated—when there had been no time to make arrangements. What happened in this little town must have been fairly typical. Our friendly banker said, "I'll take care of your property for you while you're gone." But now the Japanese, whom he had probably never expected to see again, were returning, and they would be asking for an accounting. We had pretty good evidence against this "worthy steward"; unfortunately, before we could proceed he had a heart attack and died. If we had been able to develop it, it might have gone a long way to explain the economic motives of patriotism in that corner of California.

Did your "we-boys" approach get co-operation from most of the sheriffs?

There were only two instances of outright defiance. One was the sheriff in Nevada County. He said, "The Japanese shouldn't have come back and they're not entitled to any protection and they aren't going to get any from me." He actually tried to stop the Southern Pacific from using Japanese section hands on the right of way!

I'd sent one of my prophylaxis task forces up there to see if they couldn't cool him off, but I finally had to call Governor Warren. I asked him if he didn't think we ought to call out the state Guard. Warren, who wasn't as impetuous as I, said, "Let me call the sheriff." I don't know what he said to him. I know what I would have said in his place. "Look here, this crazy Kenny is on my neck, and I'm going to have to call out the Guard. . . ." At any rate, whatever he said worked.

Then there was the sheriff of Orange County. He took the position that it was just unreasonable of me to ask him to get in wrong politically by defending the Constitution in the matter of these returning citizens. I believe Warren talked to him on the phone, too. Warren really knew how to handle these law enforcement people because he'd been one of them. But he was ready to back me up, and they knew it.

The following year there were only two sheriffs defeated for re-election in California. One was the sheriff of Nevada County, and the other was the sheriff of Orange County.

You mentioned a prophylaxis task force.

The man who headed up that aspect of the work was Charles Johnson. He'd been an appointee of Warren's; I found him there when I took office in 1943.

Well, he was very interested in this prophylactic technique method, and he got in touch with the War Relocation people, and they would let him know when a group of Nisei were about to return to a given area. Charley and another agent would go down to wherever it was and drop in on a whole roster of citizens: the sheriff, the police chief, the mayor, the board of supervisors or the city council, the editors of the newspapers, and the commanders of the American Legion and the

The lack of privacy and faulty partitioning made "a single symphony of loves, hates, and joys."

Solitude came only to those who, in Miss Okubo's words, ventured "out into the wide open spaces."

The clothing issued to internees came from Sears, Roebuck, and the fit was often approximate.

V.F.W. Charley would say, "Now you're going to get these Japanese-American citizens back, and of course we expect their return to be peaceful and orderly, and what can we do to help you?" Just that "Big Brother is watching you" hint was usually enough.

One of the greatest weapons we had, though, was the 442nd Regimental Combat Team—the magnificent all-Nisei regiment that made such a heroic showing on the Italian front and later in the Battle of the Bulge. The 442nd was based in Hawaii, but it included a number of California Nisei. And the War Relocation people had some forty or fifty of these decorated heroes—we used to call them rag-rug boys because of all their ribbons—and they were taken around the state as missionaries of good will. It was a brilliant public relations campaign, and it probably did more good than any other single action.

Another prophylactic technique we used was the posting of a reward. I got some wealthy private citizen in San Francisco to put up $5,000 for information leading to the arrest, and so on, of anyone causing—or even making threats about causing—physical harm to a returning Japanese. I've always believed that since the people you're after are rats, the best way to proceed against them is to offer an inducement to their fellow rats to turn them in. I believe we only had to pay the reward once, but that's not the point. The object of prophylaxis is to prevent. The knowledge that the reward is there for whoever can claim it deters a certain percentage of incipient criminal behavior.

Did the sentiment against the returnees slack off after V-J Day?

No. We still had a problem. At the time only about 12,000 had come back to California. We were expecting another 35,000 or 40,000, and in increasingly large groups. There was no reason to assume the hatemongers would give up just because the Emperor had.

All in all—when they all had returned—how many incidents of violence were there? Serious incidents?

Perhaps a hundred in all. Serious ones? Well, there weren't any killings. Not even any serious injuries. That was to a certain extent luck. Also, now, in the post-V-J Day stages, we finally got something going in the way of prophylactic education for police officers.

You recall we had made a plea for that sort of thing back in 1943, with our little blue book, but we hadn't got many takers. Individuals may have read the material—I'm sure they did—but there were no formal programs, classes, or anything of that nature.

At this time—1945—there was another remarkable man on my staff, another Warren discovery. Bob Powers had been police chief of Bakersfield for a number of years. He was a sort of white blackbird, as the French put it. An unformally educated intellectual. Powers could talk cop talk with cops and sociology with sociologists. When we got our chance to set up the first program of special education in race relations for policemen, Powers bridged the gap. He was what was called in those days a "discussion leader," a natural.

In September of 1945 the city manager of Richmond felt there was a real threat of "civil disturbance" in his area and called our office for help. Maybe he'd been reading his copy of our little blue pamphlet.

It was decided to run a sort of pilot project in training police officers in race relations. You must keep in mind that nothing like this had yet taken place in California—probably not anywhere in the country at this time. There was no precedent to follow. At my suggestion Powers got hold of the regional representative of the American Council on Race Relations, Davis McIntire. He had the kind of expertise we needed.

Powers and McIntire were delegated by the city manager to plan and carry out a course for a selected group of about fifteen policemen. What they finally decided to do was to go to the root of the problem, try to change the basic attitudes of these policemen, attack their prejudices head-on, and let the problem of tactics take care of itself. What they were after was an encounter group. Open-end, round-table, no holds barred.

They made a few phone calls and turned up some consultants, representatives of various minorities. One was Walter Gordon, who was later a federal judge in

Some Japanese-Americans preferred tub baths to showers— and tub could mean anything.

Gardens sprang up haphazardly in the camp; precious cardboard was used to deflect dust storms.

Mosquitoes were a constant bane at Topaz; the hard, alkaline soil made a perfect breeding ground.

the Virgin Islands. He was, in those days, a rarity—a Negro policeman. And there was Joe Grant Masaoka, one of that set of Nisei brothers who collected an average of over five medals per man for bravery. There was another Nisei who'd served with the Marines on Guadalcanal. And there was E. W. Lester, who was former deputy police chief of Los Angeles.

What minority did he represent?

The policemen! That was the genius of Powers' approach. He made the parallel between stereotyped thinking about Negroes and Jews and Japanese—and the stereotyping of cops. He talked about the popular image of the policeman as an ignorant, brutal, flat-footed fellow who could be outwitted by any private detective or layman. And they got it! These Richmond policemen got the parallel between terms like "nigger" and "Jap" and "kike" and "flatfoot."

There were some ten of these sessions. The general subject would be stated—something like "The Nature of Prejudice" or "Facts About Minority Groups"—and then anything could happen. There were some pretty frank questions asked. One of the policemen wanted to know why so many of the internees up at Tule Lake had elected to renounce their American citizenship and accept deportation to Japan.

Well, that gave Joe Grant Masaoka a chance to tell the story of the evacuation from a viewpoint none of these policemen had ever considered. The loss of everything a whole generation of hard-working men and women had managed to acquire. The loss of dignity in being herded into camps. The separation of families, like the one that had to move on while the mother was on her deathbed. The fact was, Joe Grant Masaoka's mother was confined to that hell-hole up in the Owens Valley while her sons were fighting and dying for the country that had put her there.

Was there any way to evaluate the effect of the Richmond seminars?

I suppose the real test of it is what happened next. Or rather, what didn't. It looked as if things were ripe for just the sort of outbreak the city manager had been afraid of. But it didn't come. Apparently we had produced, with our encounter group, enough enlightened peace officers to step in and cool it.

Was the course given again?

No, and that was a great disappointment to me. Oh, I'm sure there have been courses in race relations for police officers—many of them. But I've never heard of one that used this approach—the encounter. We were ahead of our time, I guess.

Do you think the approach would be useful if applied to today's ghetto hot spots?

Our police today are a good deal more sophisticated than they were twenty years ago. They know more. Or ought to. But sometimes you wonder. . . .

One thing I'm convinced of is that you don't change people much by lecturing them on abstractions. I can't make myself read that stuff any more. Puts me to sleep. It's when you get down to specifics—that's what Powers was able to do: to start people on opposite sides talking to each other about concrete, practical problems; asking embarrassing questions and getting frank answers. Maybe if this sort of program were an ongoing thing between police departments and minority communities, there might not be so many hot spots in need of cooling.

Robert Kenny is presently a superior court judge in Los Angeles. He still actively champions civil rights. It was his opinion, upheld by the California State Supreme Court, that recently overthrew the loyalty oath for county employees—calling forth a storm of criticism from the political right that matched the vehemence of the anti-Japanese sentiments of 1945.

Janet Stevenson is writing a biography of Judge Kenny, tentatively titled Show Me One Man. *Her biography of Archibald Grimké, a fin-de-siècle Negro leader, will appear later this year.* Woman Abroad, *her account of a South Pacific sailing trip, has just been published by Crown. Miss Stevenson lives in Oregon.*

Citizen 13660, BY MINE OKUBO, COLUMBIA UNIVERSITY PRESS, 1946

Entertainment was presented periodically on makeshift stages in the mess halls or in the open air.

Americanization classes were held nightly for the Issei, the first-generation Japanese-Americans.

Miss Okubo's farewell to Topaz was dry-eyed; her mind "shifted from the past to the future."

The Longest Wait

CONTINUED FROM PAGE 15

much of it sown with mines. Now the shingle bank is gone, bulldozed away in the week after D-Day to make way for the thousands of tons of supplies that were to come. There are patches in the sand still heavy with metal, shell fragments mixed with rusted rivets from ships sunk in the bay, all smoothed now by the action of the sea and oxidized a bright and symbolic red. Occasionally a mine is still discovered and placed nonchalantly on display by a dispenser of *vins-liqueurs* near the beach. The French have built little summer villas at the foot of the bluffs beyond the mine fields, not seeming to mind the ugly blockhouse ruins that still yawn toward the beach.

At first, that morning, it seemed impossible. There were blobs in the water like sacks glistening wet, dead men drowned or shot, bobbing gently in the making tide. There was the flat, shrieking *zip* of 88 mm. shells coming in too fast to dodge, and a tearing, cracking detonation when they hit and opened armor and flesh like paper. There was a lot of smoke, gray and acrid, but the color men noticed was red. "There was blood all over the sand, on the rocks," Leo Heroux said. He was an assault engineer at the tail end of the first wave. The waves lapping up the beach were being kicked into spray by machine guns playing on them but still men were lying in inches of water pretending, though they knew it did not, that it gave them protection. All along the beach the landing craft hesitated, plunged forward and dropped their ramps, and instantaneously the openings were tangles of dead men.

Private Philip Guarassi of Brooklyn, New York, had made the trip with infantry of the 1st Division. His ordnance company went in minutes after H-Hour. "There was no gaiety among us," he recalled. "The craft slid a little on the sand and the ramp was quickly let down. We immediately removed ourselves and waded waist deep in water to the shore. Soldiers were falling all around us. All types of equipment was being blown up before we could use it. It began to look more and more like a gigantic junkyard." Guarassi found the officer in charge of his combat team crouching behind a rock and asked him what his plans might be. "Beats the hell out of me," said the officer. Guarassi "immediately notified him that I was getting my dead ass out of there."

Most of the initial assault waves had got as far as the shingle. Lieutenant James Drew lay next to his sergeant, waiting for a chance to get his beach party into operation. A few yards to their right some Rangers were firing grapnels onto the top of the cliffs of the Pointe de la Percée, trying to secure scaling ladders. The Germans kept cutting the ropes and lobbing grenades down. After several failures Drew's sergeant called over to the Rangers, not without a touch of impatience, "Why the hell don't you get up the cliff?" A sergeant of the Rangers turned around. "Why the hell don't you?" he asked reasonably. Slowly men with the cool courage of Guarassi began to inch forward and take a few comrades with them. Others were rallied by their officers. Colonel George A. Taylor, in command of the 16th Infantry, stood up and suggested, as Private Jean R. Bernard of Lawrence, Massachusetts, heard it behind the shingle bank, "Hell, we're dying here on this beach. Let's move *inland* and die." At that moment the battle was as good as won.

By the official estimate, the day's fighting cost 1,465 American lives for sure. Another 1,928 men were missing. The bodies of some of those who died that day still lie not far from the beach, most of them under white crosses marked "Known But To God." The American military cemetery at St.-Laurent-sur-Mer in Calvados lies atop the bluffs within view of the beach and nowadays is a picnic spot much favored by the French. It is green and beautiful and immaculate, and about it broods the terrible, useless decorum of death. But it is not the only or the most touching memorial.

All over England mature men and women remember how when they were children the big relaxed strangers tossed oranges at them, or gave them ice cream for the first time, or came to tea and called everything by the wrong name. Old people remember their vicarious fears for boys they had grown fond of, catching at premonitions, real or imagined, when a name is mentioned. "He was killed," a man says. "Yes," his wife adds, "we thought he might be. He *looked* like it." Mothers of teen-age families remember without rancor how as lissome girls they clung closer in dark parks or on the banks of placid streams and whispered, knowing already the answer, "Will you *really* take me to the States?" What was there and what is left are after all parts of a dream. But the dream has not yet faded. It is peopled with perilous, rangy young men who brought with them from the New World the innocent belief that all things were possible, and proved it before noon one spring morning across the Channel. The great gift of those Americans, as the British see it, was not their blood or their bravery, but their innocence.

Mr. Lord is a British writer-producer currently working in New York City for NBC-TV News. He wrote and produced a documentary called Four Days to Omaha, *which was televised by NBC in 1968 and which will be repeated this year. In World War II he was an infantry platoon commander with a British division and fought in Normandy.*

FIRST TO FLY the ATLANTIC

ship or shore and give bearings to the navigator. There were special instruments as well to keep the group on course. Commander Richard E. Byrd designed a sextant in which a bubble in a tube created an artificial horizon, making observations possible above clouds. He also invented a drift meter which used a flare or smoke bomb dropped on the sea to calculate the wind's force and direction. Special charts were drawn which radically cut the time of computation from observations; the shortcut was indispensable to plotting a course while whistling through the wind at a mile and a third a minute.

The Navy also chose the safest available route. The flight's first leg would be to Newfoundland via Nova Scotia. That is the shortest path to Europe, though on a flat map it deceives the eye. Cold, fogbound Newfoundland was the westernmost usable point of departure from North America. All the prospective Atlantic fliers began from there, like jumpers edging up to the very lip of a chasm, seeking the ultimate inch of advantage before leaping. The NC boats would not, however, fly the 1,700 nautical miles from Newfoundland to Ireland, the most direct line. Rather, they would swing southeastward in a 1,200 mile flight to Ponta Delgada, on São Miguel Island in the Azores, refuel, and then make for Lisbon, 800 miles farther on. They would, in that way, have a shorter nonstop distance to cover and prospects of better weather. And along the entire route destroyers would be stationed fifty miles apart. Theoretically at least, in perfectly clear weather the high-flying aviators could cross the ocean without ever losing sight of a ship. The thick hedge of precaution around the undertaking moved two British fliers to grumble to reporters that the American plan to "eliminate any risk and do away with any need of navigation" would guarantee the failure of the flights to prove anything "theoretically or practically."

The Englishmen were missing the point. The naval planners, with their marshalled resources of scientific organization, teamwork, and money, were laying the foundations for the aviation of the future. The flight they designed with their slide rules foreshadowed an age when pilots would be technicians—enormously skilled and brave, but technicians nonetheless—flying by the rulebook, using the pooled experience of years to guarantee success time after time. In 1919 hardly anyone could see that, because flight was still most vividly symbolized by lone adventurers in frail "kites." As it fell out, there *was* adventure, for sophistication in equipment had not yet caught up with sophistication in planning. Eighteen young naval officers would in fact fight wind, storm, fog, and the cruel sea itself, and some of them would lose.

Through the winter months, Towers picked his crews. His job was simplified somewhat by a February storm that seriously damaged the *NC-1* as she lay in the water. The *NC-2*, cannibalized for repair parts, would be left out of the flight. Towers had a free hand to go after experts, provided they had not seen overseas service during the war. He was therefore able to get some of "the senior and best aviators in the Navy," one man recalled—those who had been kept at home to train and plan for others, and some of whom had consulted with the builders of the *NC-1* as it took shape.

Towers himself would lead the expedition from the *NC-3*. Patrick N. L. Bellinger, commanding the *NC-1*, had learned to fly just after Towers and was also a skilled hand in gunnery and submarines. Lieutenant Commander Albert C. Read, in charge of the *NC-4*, was a thirty-two-year-old Connecticut Yankee, admitted to Annapolis at sixteen, an honor graduate, and a flier of four years' experience. Lieutenant James Breese, Read's engineer officer, was a reservist who had helped to perfect the Liberty engine. Ensign Herbert Rodd, radio officer on the *NC-4*, was a co-developer of the radio compass—at twenty-five he was only fifteen years older than practical radio communication itself. The mechanics were also hand-picked, like boatswain Lloyd Moore of the *NC-3*, known in the small world of naval flying as a man with an ear for engines.

By the first week of May they were ready, surviving the inevitable omens and crises that attend high enterprises at birth. On Friday, May 2, there was a reminder that death and injury would always be making a spectral bid for passage. Chief Special Machinist E. H. Howard of the *NC-4*, tinkering with his engines for the thousandth time, became absent-minded and lost his hand to a propeller blade. Less than seventy-two hours later, gasoline being pumped into the tanks of the *NC-1* and *NC-4* was accidentally ignited. Parts of both planes' wings were badly burned. Round-the-clock work by repair crews managed to get all three craft airworthy by Wednesday morning, May 7.

Meanwhile, preparations both solemn and trivial went imperturbably on. The tanker *Hisko* and the minelayer *Aroostook*, carrying fuel, spare parts, and repair facilities, dropped anchor in the bay of Trepassey, Newfoundland, to the wonderment of its nine hundred fisherfolk. Forty little New York schoolgirls, taken out to Rockaway by teachers (and, presumably,

Navy press officers), presented Commander Towers with a little red, white, and blue ribbon and their wishes for success. Weather reports crackled into Rockaway (they barred a take-off on the seventh), destroyers jockeyed into line all across the Atlantic, and a thoughtful Navy captain prepared to give carefully hoarded four-leaf clovers to each member of the expedition.

Thursday morning, just before ten, the crews pulled flying suits over their uniforms and donned helmets containing intercom earphones which would allow them to converse above the pandemonium of forty-eight cylinders exploding overhead. Reporters crowded around for the ritual departure statements, shouted over the engine clatter: "It will be good sport, though in no way a sporting venture," said Towers soberly. "It is a scientific experiment." Read, too, was cautious: "Whether we get there or not, we are going to get some fun out of it." Bellinger was cheery and chinup. "With the help of God and in spite of the devil," he said, "we'll get there." Then Towers, glad to stop posing, snapped "Let's go," and they scrambled into their places. The hulls were completely enclosed, but from the single navigator cockpits at each bow and the paired openings amidships and astern for the pilots and engineers, the aviators' heads protruded, looking from a distance like beads on a wooden shoe. The three ships taxied out, sun flashing off the doped fabric of their wings. Then the wind carried the roar of gunned engines back to the shore crowded with onlookers. Each ship moved forward, slowly at first, leaving a plumed wake, then going faster and faster, the plume levelling out, becoming a feather and then a thin pencil-streak of white on the blue water, until finally a crack of light appeared between hull and sea, and the great 28,000-pound machine rose, lightened, into the air in the breath-taking miracle of flight.

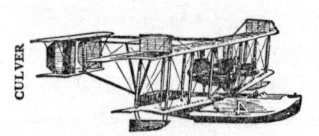

The *NC-1* and *NC-3* flew northeastward and covered the 540 miles to Nova Scotia easily, gliding down to a suppertime landing and a welcome by the American consul in Halifax. But the *NC-4* seemed unable to shake off the bad luck of the Monday night fire. Shortly after take-off, one center engine cut out; then, as the ship mushed along at reduced speed, a second engine hiccuped a connecting rod into the air and stopped dead. The *NC-4* fluttered down in a forced landing, mute because the long-range transmitter's antenna was a weighted wire which could be unreeled only in the air. After futile repair efforts, Read ordered pilots Elmer Stone and Walter Hinton to start the two good engines and begin taxiing. Through the night the crippled craft puttered along a course laid out by the commander as he pored over his charts in the dim light of the cockpit. At 5:30 A.M. on Friday the ninth, the *NC-4* arrived, as a surface vessel, at Chatham on Cape Cod. If discouragement burdened Albert Read's soul, his was not the face to disclose it. It was small and composed, with a "square jaw, straight, firm mouth, wide forehead, serious eyes, and generous ears," according to one newspaper. Navy regulations were Read's testament, but he was not a dress-parade sailor. Reporters covering the preparations at Rockaway had not known him by sight until one day when the absence of senior officers put him in command of the base. Going to his office, the press found "a rather slight man wearing a gray sweater and a pair of uniform trousers." He had been working on the *NC-4* and had not bothered to change. The newsmen noticed that "he did not appear to be in a hurry, but everybody around him hustled efficiently." His wife said he did not start anything he could not finish.

On May 10, 1919, however, he appeared to have little chance to complete his assignment. It would be nearly a week before he got replacement engines, and headquarters might tell the *NC-1* and *NC-3* to go on without him. Those two planes flew up to Trepassey Bay on the eleventh, landed neatly in choppy water, and waited for clear skies and orders. While there they were visited by two teams of British fliers from St. John's, which was about twenty-five miles from Trepassey; they came out of curiosity, courtesy, and jealousy. Harry Hawker and Kenneth Mackenzie-Grieve were the pilot and navigator respectively of a Sopwith single-engined biplane named the *Atlantic*, in which they hoped to win the *Daily Mail* award. Frederic P. Raynham and Charles F. W. Morgan were to make the same attempt in the *Raymor*, also a one-engine craft. Two other entrants were en route by sea with their crews—a two-engined Vickers bomber and a gigantic four-engined Handley-Page.

Hawker, Raynham, their navigators and servicing personnel were frankly disheartened by the arrival of the Americans, as each had hoped to be first away from the mark. They had been on the bleak, windy island for a month and more, and seen their advantage erased by almost unbroken foul weather. The take-off fields they had chosen (and painfully cleared of rocks and stumps) were narrow and uneven, like most of the country around their base at St. John's. After spending the better part of five weeks sitting in the Cochrane Hotel playing cards, drinking beer, talking aerial shop, and staring glumly at the gray windows, they now came to watch the NC's, serenely independent of landing fields, prepare to go.

102

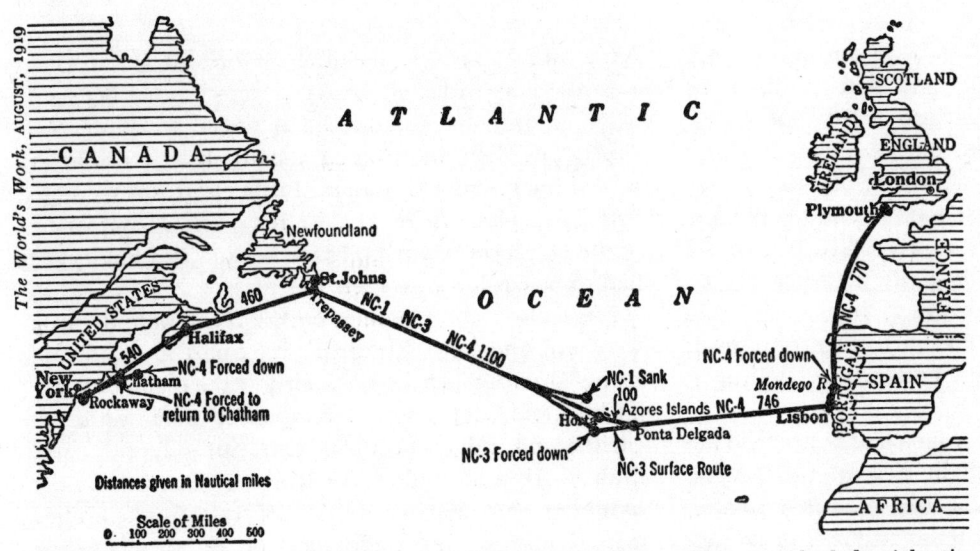

This map shows the various starts and stops of the NC boats as they assaulted the Atlantic.

However, it was not all that simple even for flying boats. Frost and storm clung to the hillsides; there were icebergs, and winds gusting to fifty miles an hour and more snatched greedily at the weather balloons aloft. The same winds were the death of a blimp, the *C-5*, which the Navy sent up from Montauk, Long Island, on the fourteenth. It flew 1,100 miles to St. John's in twenty-five hours, a record in itself and perhaps the prelude to a separate transatlantic attempt which the Navy's aviation section was keeping in reserve. But on the very afternoon of the *C-5*'s arrival, a violent gale ripped her from her moorings and sent her plunging out to sea. Fortunately, she was unmanned.

The frets and delays of Towers and Bellinger, however, were Read's opportunity. On the fourteenth he flew to Halifax. The next afternoon found the *NC-4* driving, bouncing, slewing through choppy air at ninety-five miles an hour, her crewmen painfully aware that the other planes had by now received instructions to proceed without them if necessary. At sunset in they came, banking low over the narrow harbor, and were relieved to see the long wings of the sister ships sheltered near the *Aroostook*. The two had actually attempted take-off earlier, but some miscalculation of their gross weight had overloaded them, and all the pilots' frantic gunning of engines had only sent them churning up and down the bay like clumsy speedboats.

On Friday afternoon, the sixteenth, all three planes were ready. Once more, curious crowds of onlookers gathered—fishermen and Navy personnel at the rails of their ships, townspeople at the water's edge. It was 6 P.M. in New York, an hour later in Newfoundland, and 10 P.M. by the aviators' clocks set to Greenwich Mean Time when the three boats taxied out. That the *NC-4* was operating was partly due to the stubbornness and courage of Lieutenant Breese, the engineer. One engine had refused to start. Breese, diagnosing the trouble as battery weakness, had hastily secured a more powerful standby battery. With neither time nor wiring available for a proper temporary connection, Breese joined the battery to the balky ignition apparatus with a pen-knife, its blades opened to form a U and the handle in his hand. When they pressed the starter the engine indeed fired—and Breese gamely gritted his teeth as he received a severe electrical burn. At any rate, they turned and once more strained forward into the wind, engines howling. Under the burden of 1,600 gallons of gasoline and oil, each rose sluggishly, the *NC-1* barely skimming the water as it cleared the harbor. They watched the shadowed waters only a few hundred feet below, and even in the deepening twilight they could spot icebergs. Soon they reached the first destroyer, then the next.

Night came on full, but reassuring signals pierced the darkness: the sudden, high, golden chrysanthemum of star shells, the silver rods of searchlights, the green-and-red fireflies of the planes' own running lights. So they kept in touch with each other and mankind in the black immensity, each hour moving as much as ninety miles closer to Ponta Delgada, São Miguel, the Azores, Europe.

But morning found them in trouble. Fog closed in; they lost contact and flew on through opaque solitude, each plane trusting to its navigator to keep it on course. The *NC-1* and *NC-3* soon believed themselves lost. Their radio-compass equipment was not picking up signals, and they rushed on in a wet, milky infinity which yielded no sight of sun or sea. Towers and Bellinger independently reached the same solution to the problem. If they were off their planned track, they could miss the islands altogether. Then they would fly on until their tanks were sucked dry and they had to land, without power, perhaps two or three hundred miles from the chain of ships, helpless to do anything but wait in the face of storms and possible injuries. Better to use their capacity for water landings, and sit down until the weather cleared enough for observations and a position fix.

Sometime Saturday morning, each plane dropped through the murk toward what appeared to be a gently heaving ocean. But waves iron out deceptively when viewed from a height, and stiff winds were actually churning the surface into thirty-foot crests. The *NC-3* smashed hard into one of them. No one was hurt, but the shock buckled the struts supporting her center engines. From that moment she could no longer fly. The *NC-1* touched down safely, but could not take off again in the state of the weather. Great waves began to smash at her wings, snap their ribs, soak and loosen their fabric, and turn them into dead weights on the bobbing hull. Towers and Bellinger had stepped into a trap.

Ironically, neither plane was far off the target. The *NC-1* was about an hour's flight west of the Azores island of Flores, while Towers was somewhat to the south. Both crews huddled in the rocking, groaning boats, listened to radio messages which they could not answer, and fought to keep their derelict craft upright.

Read, meanwhile, was having a flight of almost boring uneventfulness. He, too, was fog-muffled, but he caught sight of Destroyer 17 through a rift, thus confirming his position. Sometime later, however, it became clear that he had missed several other destroyers. Then he saw land—the steep, terraced hills of the island of Fayal. He made a quick decision: he was close to the sheltered and adequate harbor of Fayal, already designated an alternate landing site, with an American ship, the *Columbia*, waiting. Fully aware of the governing strategy of the flight—"the safest and sanest way"—Read took no chances on pushing on to Ponta Delgada. At about 1:20 G.M.T., some fifteen hours after lift-off, pilots Stone and Hinton set the *NC-4* gently down in a bay that they took for the *Columbia*'s anchorage. They found it empty, realized their mistake, then flew around a headland and saw the harbor and the *Columbia*. Sirens wailed in rising ecstasy, sailors in dress white lined both sides of the gangway, and salutes boomed as the rumpled aviators were brought alongside in small boats. It was a time for celebration, but the *NC-4* had so far flown only sixty per cent of the way. It was still eight hundred nautical miles to Lisbon. Yet from the time of Columbus the Azores had been regarded as Europe's front yard. The *NC-4* had risen from North American waters and was now safely in a port Portuguese beyond dispute. The headlines that stretched the width of Sunday's front pages treated the flight as a victory already complete.

It was a costly victory. Two thirds of the expedition was shipwrecked, after all, and while Read's crew was cleaning up aboard the *Columbia*, the men of the *NC-1* and *NC-3* were battling for life. At 6 P.M. that Saturday, the wings of the *NC-1* were spotted between wave crests by a lookout on a Greek freighter, the *Ionis*. The fliers were taken aboard; later a destroyer joined the rescue party and a futile effort was made to tow the airplane to Fayal. The remorseless hammering of the ocean continued to break her up, and finally she had to be cut loose and left to sink.

Meanwhile, the five men on the *NC-3* were drifting westward and were doing all they could to avoid capsizing. Drenched, chilled, wincing at the drum of spray on hull and wings, the crew munched stale, wet sandwiches and salty chocolate bars, and drank water drained from the radiators while they listened for the snapping and tearing sounds of catastrophe. They drifted through the night, and on Sunday morning saw land to the north, the Azores island of Pico. They could not taxi toward it without the risk of swamping, and Towers elected instead to continue the drift, which he estimated would bring them to São Miguel in another day. But drifting was a risky course also, since every hour increased the sea's inexorable chewing and crunching of the plane. A float under the right wingtip broke away, forcing the men to take turns crawling out in wind and wave to the opposite tip to swing the damaged one up out of the water, seesaw fashion. Part of the tail came off. The wing surfaces were slowly shredded by the fliers themselves as they cut through the tough cloth to drain heavy pools of water.

The *NC-3*'s soaked and tired men were not the only transatlantic fliers in the sea on Sunday the eighteenth. The news of the *NC-4*'s arrival in the Azores on Saturday, radioed to Newfoundland, stirred the British to action. They still believed they were in a race, and if they got into the air at once they might make it to Ireland before the Americans finished their two-stage flights. In mid-afternoon, Hawker and Mackenzie-Grieve bumped over their uneven runway and took wing. They flew through the night and covered more than half the distance to Europe, but a faulty radiator allowed their engine to overheat badly. Finally it failed over the eastern Atlantic. Hawker, long forewarned, was able to ditch the plane in a main shipping lane and clamber with his navigator into a small boat attached to the fuselage. After a short time a Danish freighter rescued them, but as it had no radio they were presumed lost until they reached a British port a week later.

Two hours after Hawker's take-off, Raynham and Morgan tried to lift their fuel-heavy plane from the ground. There is a point in such a flight when engine and overburdened wings strain to the limit, and the plane is neither securely footed on land nor yet a

104

bird, but a gawky, hopping, vulnerable creature rejected by land and air alike. At that critical moment a gust slammed the *Raymor* brutally to the ground, shattering its undercarriage and instrument panel. Raynham was shaken up, and Morgan's eye severely injured by glass fragments. So in less than thirty-six hours, between Friday evening and Sunday morning, five planes had attempted the Atlantic passage: one had crashed on take-off, and three, so far as the world knew, had disappeared into the sea.

But by Sunday evening the news was out that the *NC-1* crew had been saved. And on Monday, while the world still mourned Hawker and Mackenzie-Grieve, the sea gave up more of its supposed victims. Just outside the harbor of Ponta Delgada, the U.S.S. *Harding* came upon a bedraggled, broken-backed, droop-winged caricature of a one-time flying boat making for port on two slowly ticking engines. Proudly, Towers and his men answered the destroyer's hail and disdained an offer to be taken aboard. They had drifted and taxied 205 miles in some fifty-two hours, and they meant to finish in proper naval style, under their own power. Launches were lowered and took positions, at Towers' shouted orders, under the wings. Then, teetering first one way and then another, like a groggy drunkard being held up by small boys, the *NC-3* finished its crossing.

The next day, the *NC-4* flew in from Fayal. By naval protocol, a fleet commander who loses his ship transfers his flag to another, and Read fully expected to hand over his plane to Towers. But on orders from Washington, naval tradition yielded to public relations. An elated America was making Read a hero, and the Navy would blacken its own eye if, on a technicality, it deprived a hero of the chance to score the winning touchdown, inherit the fortune, and marry the beautiful girl. Towers was to go home by ship; Read would fly the rest of the way. Towers, who deserved better, swallowed the bitter dose, and Read, who fully understood, suffered in mute embarrassment during a period of nearly a week when bad weather kept the two men in each other's company in Ponta Delgada.

At last, on the morning of May 27, the *NC-4* flew eastward once more—almost one hundred years to the day, as the *New York Times* noted, after the American ship *Savannah* had begun the first steam-powered Atlantic passage. The *Savannah* waddled across in twenty-nine days, using paddle wheels to help her sails on only a few of them. The *NC-4* had flown some fifteen *hours* to reach the Azores, and took a mere nine and a half more to finish the journey that had been two years in preparation.

At Lisbon, twilight was deepening when the *NC-4* came down through a purple sky to land on a harbor streaked with the silver reflections of ships' lights. Almost before the hull swished into the water, a launch from the cruiser *Rochester* was on the way to pick up the six grinning crewmen. They came up the gangplank as the ship's band played "The Star-Spangled Banner," and the Tagus River resounded with the boom of saluting guns and the ringing of Lisbon's steeple bells. Thomas H. Birch, American minister to Portugal, stepped forward from a lineup of uniformed and dress-coated Portuguese officials to shake the fliers' hands. Portugal's minister of marine pinned on each flying suit the Grand Cross of the Order of the Tower and Sword. There was cheering and champagne; essentially, the flight was over and the Atlantic conquered, though on the thirtieth the plane left for Plymouth, England, so it could end its trip at the site of the Pilgrims' departure from England in 1620. Perversely, the *NC-4* developed its first mechanical flaw—radiator trouble—since Cape Cod, and had to lie overnight at Ferrol, Spain. But on the first day of June, it was all done.

The accomplishment was superb. Though two planes were downed no lives went with them, and the fault was partly in the judgment of their captains, who had landed in bad weather to take old-fashioned sea-level bearings. Read and his crew, on the other hand, had simply fulfilled their contract with engineering. They had faithfully used the equipment as planned, and it had functioned admirably. Reporters noted a certain calmness, almost indifference, among the *NC-4*'s crew. "We hardly realized that we were doing anything extraordinary," said radio officer Rodd, while Read himself declared the trip "uneventful." Except for the fog, "everything went off as we planned." The stance was not merely the expected modesty for the newspapers; it was realistic. The fliers had simply recognized the proper relationship between man, equipment, and technique. They had been so unspectacular, in fact, that their achievement fell into near obscurity. Fifty years later many Americans are still under the impression that Charles A. Lindbergh's New York-to-Paris hop was the first transatlantic flight. But that honor belongs to the United States Navy and the *NC-4*.

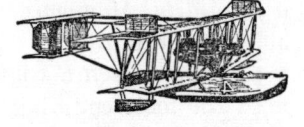

Bernard A. Weisberger, a former professor of history at the University of Rochester, is the author of many books, the latest being The New Industrial Society *(John Wiley & Sons). This account of the NC-4 is part of a new work in progress tentatively entitled* 1919, *which will be published by Little, Brown. Dr. Weisberger gratefully acknowledges the valuable co-operation of Dr. Richard K. Smith of the Smithsonian Institution in preparing this article.*

"The scene of slaughter was ... picturesque"

CONTINUED FROM PAGE 71

in article form in the *Overland Monthly,* a San Francisco magazine. Writing in a simple, direct, relaxed style ("Indeed," he wrote concerning the polygamous habits of whales, "much of the Turkish nature is observed"), Scammon began attracting scholarly as well as popular attention. Professor Spencer F. Baird of the Smithsonian Institution singled out Scammon's studies in one of the institution's annual reports to Congress. "Too much cannot be said in praise of gentlemen like Captain Scammon," Baird announced. The National Academy of Sciences in Philadelphia put its official imprimatur on his reputation by electing the whaler-turned-mammalogist a member. On a visit to San Francisco, one of America's foremost scientists, Louis Agassiz, inspected the drawings that Scammon was preparing for his book. "It is the first time I have seen the whale properly exhibited on paper," declared Agassiz.

The costs involved in the lithographic reproduction of the scientific drawings made it difficult to find a publisher, but Scammon finally convinced John Carmany of the *Overland Monthly* to underwrite the printing expenses. In 1874 his magnum opus appeared, bearing the mammoth title *The Marine Mammals of the Northwestern Coast of North America; Together with an Account of the American Whale-Fishery.*

This 317-page volume, replete with more than seventy handsome illustrations, was offered at a subscription price of ten dollars. There were few takers. "All attempts to sell your book have failed me," Carmany informed Scammon three years later. But the book's financial failure in no way obscured the favorable reception it received from the scientific community; indeed, *Marine Mammals* is today a valuable and honorable item in university rare-book collections as well as a popular reference volume for mammalogists. Perhaps the most enduring assessment of his work appeared in Scammon's obituary in 1911, when *Science* magazine declared that his book was "the most important contribution to the life history of marine mammals ever published and will remain a worthy monument to his memory."

What has continued to change, however, is the condition of the gray whale itself. In his pioneer treatise, Scammon expressed gloomy concern about its survival: "Ere long, may it not be that the California gray will be known only as an extinct species of Pacific cetaceans?" After two short revivals of lagoon whaling, Captain Scammon's prophecy very nearly came true. Originally, it has been estimated, the grays numbered some 30,000; but by 1930, according to one San Diego naturalist, there were "no more than a few dozen." Fortunately, in 1937 the International Convention on the Regulation of Whaling instituted voluntary conservation quotas on whale kills. Recognizing the precarious condition of the grays, the convention accorded the species a special status: henceforth, it was forbidden "to take or kill gray whales except when the meat and products of such whales are to be used exclusively for local consumption by the aborigines."

Today Scammon Lagoon again teems with gray whales—as many as 2,000 of them—during breeding season. The only hunters who pursue them now are scientists armed with buoy hydrophones and electronic harpoons. But even though the lagoon is considered a unique marine laboratory in which to study the world's largest creatures, the researchers frequently find themselves frustrated by the same aggressive whale tactics that temporarily confounded Captain Scammon.

One such episode occurred in 1956, when Dr. Paul Dudley White, the famous Boston heart specialist, set out to record the heartbeat of a gray whale. White and his colleagues made elaborate preparations to implant sensitive electrodes under a whale's skin to transmit the heartbeat by radio back to an electrocardiograph aboard the expedition's flagship. But before a single "harpoon" could be fired, the party's boat inadvertently made the same mistake that Scammon's men had made a century before: it got between a mother and her calf. Flukes flashed, and the craft, listing dangerously with

---

Mr. Marx, the author of The Frail Ocean *(Coward McCann, 1967), is a California writer who specializes in conservation of the ocean frontier. He became interested in the gray whale one day in December, 1964, when he sighted whale plumes in the ocean off Malibu and learned they were grays on the way to their warm-water breeding grounds. He spent some time aboard a Scripps Institute of Oceanography vessel in Scammon Lagoon, and subsequently consulted the collection of Captain Scammon's papers in the Bancroft Library at the University of California at Berkeley. These and Scammon's* Marine Mammals *were his major sources for this article. Among useful and popular recent books on whales and whaling are Ivan T. Sanderson's* Follow the Whale *(Little, Brown, 1956) and E. J. Slijper's* Whales *(Basic Books, 1962). Younger readers will enjoy* The Story of Yankee Whaling *in the American Heritage Junior Library series.*

a foot-wide hole in her bottom, barely made it back to base. After the boat had been repaired, another attempt to plant the electrodes was made, but the struck whale, with a mighty lunge, snapped the connecting wire on one dart and swam away with the harpoon gun that had fired the second. The expedition was a failure. It seems that the whales are more of a threat to the scientists than the scientists are to the whales.

The same cannot be said of industry. Exportadora de Sal, a salt refinery licensed by the Mexican government, operates a factory at Scammon Lagoon. Approximately one hundred million gallons of sea water a day are pumped from the lagoon into ponds on the adjacent Vizcaíno Desert. After the water has been evaporated by the wind and sun, the salt residue is collected, washed, and then shipped by barge to Cedros, where it is loaded onto ocean-going freighters.

Recently a controversy has raged over the possible effects that increased barge traffic in and out of the lagoon might have on the breeding habits of the grays. Exportadora's salt-harvesting operations are expected to expand considerably, requiring more and more barge trips to Cedros. Since the bustle of shipping a century ago caused the gray to desert its breeding grounds in San Diego Bay, some scientists are deeply concerned lest the same thing happen in Scammon Lagoon. Others contend that the desalinization operations and industrial pollution might further jeopardize the future of the species. The salt company's position, naturally, is that the grays have not been affected at all; to substantiate its argument, it points out that the herd in Scammon Lagoon has doubled in size during the decade Exportadora has been in operation.

The final decision is, of course, up to the Mexican government, which has assigned a special team of fishing experts to study the gray's breeding habits and to determine how they are affected by shipping activity. No decision will be made until this team completes its investigation. It would, however, be ironic if Captain Scammon's prophecy were fulfilled not because of man's demand for whale oil but because of his need for a cheap industrial chemical and seasoning for his food.

The President's Progress   CONTINUED FROM PAGE 77

Antifederalist journalist Philip Freneau was bowing to Washington from a vessel "dressed and decorated in the most superb manner" but featuring on its deck "Dr. King from South Africa with a collection of natural curiosities." Washington's startled look was answered by the cold stares of "a male and female ourang outang," a species, so the reporter noted, "remarkable for its striking similitude to the human species."

Washington (who was in the end to be given more pain by Freneau than by perhaps any other man) did not have time to meditate on what this strange sight portended, for his barge was now approaching the tip of Manhattan Island. He could see (as another observer noted) from the fort in the harbor to the place of landing and on into the city, "although near half a mile," little else on board every vessel, along the shore, and jamming the streets but "Heads standing as thick as Ears of Corn before the Harvest."

Handling their twenty-six oars flawlessly, the pilots brought the barge into a perfect landing on Murray's Wharf at the foot of Wall Street. Here carpeted steps, flanked with railings upholstered in crimson, descended to the level of the deck. Washington mounted to be met by Governor Clinton and a pack of other dignitaries. Clinton's words of welcome were made almost inaudible by ear-splitting huzzas.

The carpeting led to a carriage, but Washington announced that he would walk to the house which the new government had hurriedly procured for him on Cherry Street. It took him a half hour to traverse the half mile, since all the efforts of city officers and soldiers could not hold back the crowds that wished, screaming or tearful, to touch the tall gentleman in his cocked hat, blue suit, and buff breeches. "The General," one spectator wrote, "was obliged to wipe his eyes several times before he got to Queen's Street."

As soon as he was indoors, Washington had to receive, despite his fatigue, a flood of dignitaries and former Revolutionary officers. There was no time to change his clothes before he was rushed off to a banquet given by Clinton. And then, although the evening was "very wet," he had to move through the streets and admire the illuminations in the windows. There were still vast crowds and many cheers.

The journal Washington kept of his trip to New York has disappeared, but his biographer, John Marshall, the future Chief Justice of the Supreme Court, copied from it a comment on the finale of the journey that is, in its clumsy phrasing, revealing of Washington's exhaustion as well as of his emotions:

The display of boats which attended and joined us on this occasion, some with vocal and some with instrumental music on board; the decorations of the ships; the roar of cannon and the loud acclamations of the people, which rent the skies as I passed along the wharves, filled my mind with sensations as painful (considering the reverse of this scene, which may be the case after all my labors to do good) as they were pleasing.

Although Washington arrived in New York on April 23, 1789, he was not inaugurated as President until April 30. The intervening week was a stormy one in Congress and in the drawing rooms and taverns where men discussed politics. The issues that so agitated their minds seem to modern eyes at first glance trivial, since they concerned etiquette and nomenclature. Washington would appear before Congress to take his oath. How should he be received so as to preserve a proper balance between the dignitaries of the Presidency and the legislature? John Adams was in anguish concerning where he, as presiding officer of the Senate, should meet Washington, and where each of them should sit.

An even more grievous issue was how the President should be addressed on formal occasions. A committee of the House of Representatives wished him to be called merely, as in the Constitution, "the President of the United States." The Senate rebuffed the committee's report. Although, as presiding officer, Adams was not supposed to get into the debates, he could not restrain himself. "What will the common people of foreign countries—what will the sailors and soldiers say" when asked to speak of " 'George Washington, President of the United States?' They will despise him. This is all nonsense to the philosopher; but so is all government whatever." Adams plumped for "His Most Benign Highness," while a Senate committee voted for "His Highness the President of the United States of America and Protector of the Rights of the Same."

Washington, who saw little but foolishness in John Adams' point of view, was upset at this squabble which so soon endangered unity. The Comte de Moustier, the French minister, reported to his government that it was the fear of offending Washington that kept the Federalists from establishing titles, and Madison remembered Washington's annoyance at the efforts "to bedizen him with a superb but spurious title." It was, indeed, Washington's friend Madison who led the continued resistance in the House that finally forced the Senate to topple the whole dream of aristocratic nomenclature by agreeing that the Chief Executive should be called simply "the President of the United States."

Washington's most immediate political problem was to make a final determination on his inaugural address. He decided (if he had not previously done so) to scrap the sixty-four-page speech on which he had spent so much labor. Instead, he perfected an address so short that, when read at the inaugural ceremony, it occupied less than twenty minutes.

To the constitutional provision that he recommend measures he judged "necessary and expedient," Washington responded by outlining only the most general principles. The legislature should avoid "local prejudices and attachments," "separate views," "party animosities." It should "watch over this great assemblage of communities and interests" with a "comprehensive and equal eye" and lay the foundations of policy "in the pure and immutable principles of private morality." He went on to state what he had often himself exemplified in his role as Commander in Chief: "There exists in the economy and course of nature, an indissoluble union between virtue and happiness, between duty and advantage, between the genuine maxims of an honest and magnanimous policy, and the solid rewards of public prosperity and felicity."

His text went briefly into the matter of amending the Constitution: Congress would, he was sure, avoid any changes that would weaken the government or which "ought to await the future lessons of experience." However, he endorsed the Bill of Rights, although not specifically by name, when he urged Congress to expedite amendments reflecting "a reverence for the characteristic rights of freemen, and a regard for the public harmony."

For the rest, the speech Washington polished during his first week in New York was concerned with matters personal and religious. He wrote that he had accepted the call to the Presidency with reluctance. In insisting on his own inadequacy, he surely went beyond what he really felt when he added to his statement that he was "unpracticed in the duties of civil administration," that he was conscious of "inheriting inferior endowments from nature." Having from the start of his services to the nation renounced "every pecuniary compensation," he wished to be exempted from whatever salary was established for the Presidency. He should merely be reimbursed for "such actual expenditures as the public good may be thought to require."

The most remarkable aspect of what Washington wrote is the depth of its religious tone. In the past he had often expressed gratitude for the assistance of Providence to the American cause and had expressed hope that the boon would be continued. But never before had he devoted so much—more than a third—of a complicated pronouncement to religious considerations. That he was not just striking a popular attitude, as a politician might, is revealed by the absence of the usual Christian terms: he did not mention Christ or even use the word "God." Following the phraseology of the philosophical Deism he professed, he referred to "the Invisible Hand which conducts the affairs of men," and to "the benign Parent of the Human Race."

In the speech he was preparing, Washington appealed for a celestial guidance which he undoubtedly felt the need of now more than ever before in his public career. As Commander in Chief, he had consulted and obeyed an earthly superior, the Continental Congress, to a point which his critics considered extreme. As President of the Constitutional Convention he had been, if the presiding officer, one of a team. But now, although Congress flanked him on one side and an as yet unestablished judiciary would flank him on the other, in the powerful duties that had been assigned to him he stood alone, with no superior to turn to but the heavens. No wonder he looked upward imploringly to "that Almighty Being . . . who presides in the Councils of Nations, and whose providential aids can supply every human defect."

Fortunately the ceremonial aspects of Washington's inauguration required of him few decisions, since they had, after long debate, been established by Congress.

The morning of April 30 came in fair. He was roused at dawn by thirteen cannon shots. After that, there were church bells and the moving about (with much staring) of crowds in front of his house; but, hour after hour, there was nothing to pull Washington from the meditations and memories that undoubtedly flowed through his mind.

With the approach of noon came the need for action. Washington donned the suit made from the brown Connecticut cloth he had purchased to encourage American manufactures and had brightened by adding silver buttons decorated with spread eagles. He pulled on white silk stockings, stepped into shoes with silver buckles, and made sure that his dress sword with its steel scabbard was ready.

Finally there were steps in his hallway. The delegation from Congress had arrived. Washington buckled on his sword, grasped his hat, went into the parlor, bowed, shook hands—and then he was sitting alone in a ponderous state coach that Congress had procured for the occasion. Manned by lackies he did not know, the unfamiliar coach moved slowly behind strange horses through a phantasmagoria of cheering faces. Bowing to the left and then to the right, Washington now and then looked behind him, for he could sometimes glimpse through the back window his own horses pulling the now somewhat battered coach from Mount Vernon in which he knew were his two old friends, his aides David Humphreys and Tobias Lear.

Bands appeared and shrank into the distance, militia companies wheeled and fired. Surely, as he rode in solitude amidst all the jubilation, Washington's mind must have dwelt on contrasts. How, when the British and Hessians had invaded Manhattan, the militia and even the continentals had fled like ghosts, deaf to his shouts, avoiding his sword, until at last he turned in despair to defy the enemy as a solitary horseman, and would (had not his aides intervened) have been captured or killed. And then, so much sorrow and bloodshed later, with the city repossessed, how he had ridden through these very streets to see broken houses sag around him and to listen to the thin cheers of a few emaciated citizens.

Now the city blossomed and the well-fed citizens

A detail from an engraving of Washington's inauguration at Federal Hall in New York City on April 30, 1789. This is based on a drawing by Peter Lacour which is the only contemporary illustration of the event. The site of Federal Hall, on Wall Street, is now occupied by the Subtreasury.

lived in peace. The eyes of the whole world, the hopes of all posterity were fixed, so to speak, on this occasion which, if its promise were properly improved, would demonstrate the ability of men to govern themselves.

The carriage stopped. Washington alighted and walked through ranks of militiamen into Federal Hall. Followed by dignitaries, he mounted a flight of stairs, passed through a door that was thrown open at his approach, and entered the Senate chamber. He bowed to the senators, to the envoys of foreign powers, and to the members of the House of Representatives. He saw ahead three windows, curtained in crimson damask, that opened onto a balcony. In front of the central window were a crimson canopy, a dais, three chairs, and John Adams looking nervous and constrained.

Adams stepped down, bowed to Washington, conducted him to the central chair, and then took his own seat on the right. Speaker of the House Frederick A. C. Muhlenberg slipped into the seat on the left. There was a moment of complete silence, and then Adams rose. He made as if to speak but was unable to do so. Finally, he said, "Sir, the Senate and House of Representatives are ready to attend you to take the oath required by the Constitution. It will be administered by the chancellor of the state of New York."

"I am ready."

Adams led the way through the central window onto a small portico that jutted out over the street at the second-story level. Washington saw in front of him an armchair and a small table draped in red and bearing a large Bible on a red cushion. Beyond the low railing —down the long, receding vistas of the streets, filling every window, on every rooftop—there reappeared the endless movement of cheering faces. Washington bowed and bowed again, with his hand on his heart, and then sat down on the chair. By now the portico was jammed with dignitaries.

Washington rose once more and approached the railing so as to be visible to as many of the onlookers as possible. A complete silence fell on the crowd. Chancellor Robert R. Livingston faced Washington, and between the two tall men Samuel A. Otis, Secretary of the Senate, a small man, held up the Bible on its crimson cushion. Washington put his right hand on the book. "Do you solemnly swear," asked Livingston, "that you will faithfully execute the office of President of the United States and will, to the best of your ability, preserve, protect, and defend the Constitution of the United States?"

"I solemnly swear," said Washington, and repeated the oath. He bowed to kiss the Bible.

Livingston turned to the crowd. "It is done." Then he shouted, "Long live George Washington, President of the United States!"

Taken up by the crowd, the cry rose thunderously. Echoing among the buildings, it reached Washington's ear as an almost incoherent roar. From the harbor came the booming of cannon, the Spanish frigate again making the most noise. A faint, almost drowned-out tinkling was the massed voices of all the church bells. Washington bowed and bowed and then, when the sounds gave no indication of ceasing, he walked indoors and sat down in his chair.

It took some time before the dignitaries could get back into their seats and sink into quiet. Then Washington stood up with his speech in his hand. The audience also rose. His aspect, wrote a senator, was "grave, almost to sadness." His simple words of modesty and faith, his few broad recommendations were delivered in so low a voice—"deep, a little tremulous" —that all had to lean forward to hear. "This great man," wrote another senator, "was agitated and embarrassed more than ever he was by the leveled cannon or pointed musket. He trembled, and several times could scarce make out to read."

As he proceeded, Washington moved his manuscript from his left hand to his right and put several fingers of his left hand into his breeches pocket. Soon he pulled out his left hand, again shifted the manuscript, and put his right hand into his pocket. Then he extracted his right hand and made with it what one witness considered "an ungainly impression."

The famous orator Fisher Ames watched entranced at the effect of this simple delivery that so denied the

Saint Paul's Chapel on Broadway, where the new President attended a service immediately after his inauguration. A superb example of eighteenth-century architecture, it is now the only pre-Revolutionary public building in Manhattan.

importance of the elocutionist's art: "It seemed to me," Ames wrote later, "an allegory in which virtue was personified, and addressing those whom she would make her votaries. Her power over the heart was never greater." The whole audience, even the man most passionately jealous of Washington—Vice President Adams—gave way to tears.

When Washington finished and sat down, he looked old and tired. "Time," Ames noted, "has made havoc upon his face." But his day's duties were far from done. After much shaking of hands, Washington walked between walls of saluting militiamen to Saint Paul's Chapel, where the Right Reverend Samuel Provoost, the Episcopal bishop of New York, strung out at length his petitions to the Almighty. However, there was no sermon, and Washington was allowed to have his dinner quietly at home. Then he was out again in his carriage to attend a pair of receptions and to see the illuminations and the fireworks. His horses moved more and more slowly as ever thicker crowds engulfed them. Finally he had to abandon his carriage and walk.

After the church service, while Washington was wooing rest in preparation for the evening's festivities, the Senate had reconvened in the chamber where he had so recently moved all present to tears. A squabble instantly erupted, made the more heated, probably, by reaction to the previous emotion.

The object of the session was to prepare a reply to Washington's speech: the angry issue, whether it should be referred to as his "most gracious speech." That this was the wording traditionally used by Parliament in replying to addresses of the British king stirred up so many objections that the debate had to be continued the next day. Then it was decided to strike out the phrase lest the people consider the words "the first step of the ladder in the ascent to royalty."

The successful campaign against that sinister adjective "gracious" had been led by the hypochondriacal, radical, and suspicious senator from western Pennsylvania, William Maclay. Some historians have considered Maclay, although his character was very different from Jefferson's, a prophetic figure who took what was to be the Jeffersonian stand long before Jefferson himself had dreamed of leading an opposition.

In addition, because of a documentary freak, Maclay plays a major role in historical literature. Determined to protect its proceedings from the vulgar eye, the conservative Senate kept no detailed journal, thus inadvertently throwing the ball to its most radical member. Maclay filled the gap by jotting down from day to day a voluminous diary. Not only do his pages supply the only indications of what took place at many sessions, but, being in a perpetual rage of disapproval or indignation, he wrote in a spirited style that begs for quotation. The result has been to distort in an anti-Washington manner the record of the first year of the new government.

Maclay's reactions to the Virginian combined awe, suspicion, and resentment. Before the inauguration, he wrote in his diary: "This day... General Washington, the greatest man in the world, paid me a visit." Yet during the debate over titles, Maclay could not doubt that Washington had sparked the aristocratic agitation because of a lust to be addressed as "Your Majesty."

The President had prepared an acknowledgment of the Senate's reply. Maclay noted that, when his turn came, he took the paper "out of his coat-pocket. He had his spectacles in his jacket pocket, having his hat in his left hand and the paper in his right. He had too many objects for his hands. He shifted his hat between his forearm and the left side of his breast. But taking the spectacles from the case embarrassed him. He got rid of this small distress by laying the spectacle-case on the chimney piece. . . . Having adjusted his spectacles, which was not very easy, considering the engagements on his hands, he read the reply with tolerable exactness and without much emotion." Maclay commented that Washington should have received the Senate with his spectacles on, "which would have saved the making of some uncouth motions."

Maclay's gleeful mockery might well seem, as the first President of the United States grasped the wheel of state to almost universal cheering, a sour note so miniscule as not to be worth recording. Yet had Washington been conscious of what was happening in Maclay's mind, he would have been alarmed. The enthusiasm that had accompanied his inauguration had not calmed the anxiety engendered during his triumphal progress from Mount Vernon to New York. "I fear," he wrote an old Virginian associate, "if the issue of public measures should not corrispond with their [the public's] sanguine expectations, they will turn the extravagent (and I may say undue) praises which they are heaping upon me at this moment, into equally extravagent (though I will fondly hope unmerited) censures. So much is expected, so many untoward circumstances may intervene, in such a new and critical situation, that I feel an insuperable diffidence in my own abilities. I feel . . . how much I shall stand in need of the countenance and aid of every friend of myself, of every friend to the Revolution, and of every lover of good Government. I thank you, my dear Sir, for your affectionate expressions on this point."

This is the third installment in a series taken from the forthcoming last volume of Mr. Flexner's three-volume study of Washington.

HELP-WANTED AD FOR JUNE GRADUATES

WANTED, BOY—High-school graduate to work in general merchandise store in small interior town and learn to be a shoemaker. One who can help milk the cow and play in the band preferred. Must be youth of clean habits; cigarette smokers, sheiks and loafers need not apply. Boy who understands Diesel gas-engine and Fordson tractor will be given preference. Users of intoxicating liquors and profane language will not be considered. Boy who gets this job must not be too proud and aristocratic to mingle with the livestock and chickens and help out in the kitchen now and then. Tenor singer who is a good strike-out baseball pitcher will find this an ideal situation. Must be early riser and not afraid of work. You will work in a very healthful climate with beautiful surroundings, fine fishing, woodlands abound in wild game and flowers. Horse to ride Sunday afternoons. Good chance to learn a trade and the principles of business and see the country. Must be a good salesman. Apply in your own handwriting, sending late photographs with three recommendations. $12 a month to start for live wire, with chance to buy interest in the business. Employer can furnish board and room at $9.50 if you will mow the lawn in your spare time. Address "Newton," care Orange Daily Leader.

—*Advertisement in the Orange, Texas,* Daily Leader, *1925*